THE ROPES TO SKIP
AND
THE ROPES TO KNOW

GRID SERIES IN MANAGEMENT

Consulting Editor
STEVEN KERR, University of Southern California

Clover & Balsley, *Business Research Methods,* Second Edition
Deitzer, Shilliff & Jucius, *Contemporary Management Concepts*
Deitzer & Shilliff, *Contemporary Management Incidents*
Kerr, ed., *Organizational Behavior*
Lewis, *Organizational Communications,* Second Edition
Lewis & Williams, *Readings in Organizational Communications*
Lundgren, Engel & Cecil, *Supervision*
Moore, *The Management of Organizations*
Murdick, Eckhouse, Moor & Zimmerer, *Business Policy: A Framework for Analysis,* Third Edition
Ritti & Funkhouser, *The Ropes to Skip and The Ropes to Know: Studies in Organizational Behavior,* Second Edition
Rogers, *Corporate Strategy and Planning*

OTHER BOOKS IN THE GRID SERIES IN MANAGEMENT

Klatt & Urban, *Kubsim: A Simulation in Collective Bargaining*
Murdick & Cooper, *Business Research: Concepts and Guides*
Nykodym & Simonetti, *Business and Organizational Communication: An Experiential Skill Building Approach*
Roman, *Science, Technology and Innovation: A Systems Approach*
Sandver & Blaine, *Teachneg: A Collective Bargaining Simulation in Public Education*
Tersine, Altimus & Davidson, *Problems and Models in Operations Management,* Second Edition

THE ROPES TO SKIP
AND
THE ROPES TO KNOW

Studies In Organizational Behavior

Second Edition

R. Richard Ritti
The Pennsylvania State University

G. Ray Funkhouser
Rutgers University

1 2 3 4 ⊠ 5 4 3 2

Library of Congress Cataloging in Publication Data

Ritti, R. Richard.
    The ropes to skip and the ropes to know.

    (Grid series in management)
    Bibliography: p.
    Includes index.
    1. Organizational behavior.   I. Funkhouser, G. Ray
II. Title.   III. Series.
HD58.7.7.R57   1982   650.1   81-6714
ISBN 0-88244-242-2 (pbk.)   AACR2

FOREWORD TO THE SECOND EDITION

"IF IT AIN'T BROKE, DON'T FIX IT"

In the years since *The Ropes* was born I have been gratified by its success. In fact, every now and then someone is moved to write me a piece of fan mail recounting how the episodes in *The Ropes* mirror their own corporate experiences. Most also express regret that they had not read *The Ropes* earlier in their careers. Naturally, these things make me feel good.

I've also received lots of suggestions about possible additions to or changes in the text. Many of these seem to me to be good ideas but for one thing: making those changes would require some significant alteration of the basic character of this book. And so in revising *The Ropes* for this second edition I have chosen to heed the dictum of Bert Lance, the Peanut Country philosopher: "If it ain't broke, don't fix it."

Still, those of you familiar with the first edition will recognize substantial changes that incorporate a number of the suggestions you have made. A thorough-going tune-up, shall we say. You will find one entirely new part, some new characters, some new episodes, some deletions, and some revisions. Nonetheless I've taken care to preserve the old faces and places.

But something else has gone on since the first edition was printed. Your comments and your suggestions concerning one issue in particular have led me to reflect considerably on the purpose and philosophy of *The Ropes*. So if you've got a moment, I'd like to share some of these thoughts with you.

The issue is ethics. And it's an important issue. The question is this: "Professor Ritti, do you really intend to *advocate* the kind of 'unethical' behavior you describe in these pages?" At first I would reply "Of course not." But it's been such a persistent question that it deserves a better answer than that. And here it is.

You know, I don't believe that anybody in *The Ropes* really does anything unethical. Sure, they're playing to win, playing "hard ball" as it's said. So I think there's something else; maybe a flavor of cynicism, I guess I'd call it. For if you believe, as does Candide's Dr. Pangloss, that "all's for the best in this best of all possible companies," why, then you're going to be disappointed. You're not going to see much altruism in the behavior of your company colleagues.

But is *The Ropes* instructing you to behave that way? Frankly, I don't think that it could even if that were its intention—though that's not the point. Admittedly there are a few tongue-in-cheek remarks to that effect strewn about *The Ropes'* landscape. But the primary purpose is just to get you to recognize some of the moves of some typical corporate characters so that you will come to recognize and understand the nature of organizational behavior. For, when you get right down to it, *The Ropes* has just one goal: to convince you that what goes on in organizations is far more complex than the dispassionate application of technical solutions to decide on best alternatives for the achievement of clearly stated goals. Read that again, if you will. It is the reason in being for this text.

Following this logic you will recognize several persistent themes here. The first is that people react to situations in which they find themselves in such ways as to insure outcomes that are in their own best interests, and that these outcomes are usually more immediate and apparent than the best interests of the organization. The second is— though not explicitly—that often these short-run best interests of the individual are in conflict with the long-run best interests of the organization.

Now, I haven't really thought much about this before, but it's true. *The Ropes* is a subconscious reflection of the character of organizational events that I've witnessed over the years: the vast majority of corporate management careers are lived out in terms of short-run consequences, often with the long-run being left to take care of itself, or being of little significance in rapidly moving events. Thus *The Ropes* is rooted in a feature of corporate life that I've observed and simply assumed to be typical. I hadn't really thought of it consciously in reliving these episodes.

To my surprise, then, a series of recent writings has singled out just this feature of the American corporate enterprise as being responsible, at least in part, for our international fall from grace. Two factors are mentioned—both of which are reflected in our scenarios.

The first of these is the ascendancy of the corporate staff type, people with little interest in, or knowledge of, the productive sectors of the company—manufacturing, design, and the like. These are the staff experts, the "can't do" guys, people who have discovered that higher profit margins result from short-term strategies such as mergers, tax deductible losses and other legal and financial shenanigans that have little or nothing to do with product excellence. Take note: in the hundred biggest U.S. corporations, the percentage of chief executive officers with financial and legal backgrounds is up 50 percent from its level 30 years ago.[1]

The second factor is the obsession of our corporate leaders with the short-term outcome, the game strategy we will call "deferred responsibility" in Part 4. This short-term mentality has permeated every facet of the corporate environment and is responsible in large measure for what you will observe in the pages of this book.

So what I'm saying, I guess, is that I think now that you can use this text for something that was never intended, in addition to that which was. Those among you interested in organization development can use *The Ropes* to ask the question, What might be done to set the American industrial enterprise aright? And that should be enough to keep you busy for a semester at least.

To conclude, some credit where it's due. Had it not been for Ray Funkhouser the task of writing would never have been undertaken. Ray provided encouragement and help in writing material that is, after all, considerably different from that in your average text. Incidentally, the title of this text was Ray's suggestion. Otherwise, I would like to acknowledge an intellectual debt of gratitude to both Bill Whyte and Fred Goldner, each of whom has greatly influenced my ideas about the issues presented herein. I am also indebted to the Graduate Women in Management at Penn State for their ideas about the special problems women must overcome in corporate organizations. I owe a debt of gratitude (which in some cases I will be able to pay) to people in The Company and The Agency who provided the insights and the models for the characters in this book, and to Norma Eckenroth and Mary Anna Rauch, our indefatigable "lower participants."

Finally, I would like to thank the people who reviewed the second edition manuscript: Susan Schaffer, George Washington University; Phil Mounts, University of Wisconsin, Oshkosh, Wisconsin; I. Thomas Sheppard, University of Texas, El Paso, Texas; William Fagan, Oregon Institute of Technology, Klamath Falls, Oregon; Kathryn Lewis-Oritt, California State University, Chico, California; and Steven Kerr, University of Southern California, Los Angeles, California.

R. Richard Ritti
The Pennsylvania State University
June, 1981

1. William J. Abernathy and Robert H. Hayes, "Management Minus Intervention," *New York Times,* August 20, 1980, D2.

USING "THE ROPES": A WORD TO THE INSTRUCTOR

Occasionally a reviewer will begin a comment, "it strains my credibility ... " There usually follows an excerpt from one of Stanley's adventures that Ray and I have faithfully reported almost verbatim. The truth is, that no one would invent something so obviously bizarre. And believe me, stranger things than you and I can imagine have been attempted by some very bright people. In retrospect it is easy for us to wonder how these people could have seized on such a course of action. But hindsight is better than foresight, and most of these actions were motivated by a deeply felt desire to make things work.

Each of the chapters that follow is a striking occasion that demonstrates vividly some fundamental fact of organizational life. Obviously, many of these things don't happen every day, or week. This is an important fact in knowing how to use *The Ropes*. Since much of the action depicts people reacting to situations, the point of discussion should *not* be whether what was done is well or ill advised, or whether it is profound or silly. Rather, the issue is one of *why's;* why do people behave as they do in these kinds of situations? I want to especially emphasize this situational aspect.

In one sense, those "far out" examples show how pervasive is the underlying problem. Take, for example, the measurement of performance in professional jobs. For a variety of reasons every manager would dearly love to have some clear-cut, objective and unarguable system of performance measurement. But for another variety of reasons that will never be. So when you, as teacher, discuss the several cases that deal with measurement as an issue, the fact that something "incredible" was done is *not the point at all*. No, the point is to try to develop in the student an understanding of the organizational reasons why we continually strive to develop such systems of measurement and what the consequences of these systems can be.

Now then, how might you proceed to use *The Ropes?* First, the experiences of different instructors shows that there is no "one best way." What works depends on both the experience of the teacher and the class, as well as the particular educational aims of the teacher. Still, several methods seem to work well. My own preference is to assign *The Ropes* in entirety at the beginning of the term and have students complete the assignment within the first five or six periods. Students should be required to prepare questions for class discussion, and the teacher can then use these questions to introduce the general issues in organizational behavior. (The subject index included in this edition should help you to place each case within that O.B. framework). At this point the teacher then either can lecture on the standard O.B. topics or work from a standard text for the rest of the term, using *The Ropes* as a casebook from topic to topic. Variations on this are to (a) devote the final two weeks to case analyses of stories in *The Ropes* giving the students the opportunity to employ the O.B. concepts he or she has learned, or (b) base a final exam or paper on a case analysis of stories from *The Ropes*, each in application of concepts learned during the course.

Beyond this I think it is important for the teacher to recognize that many of these stories present situations that have no simple solution. The problems encountered are products of a very complex set of organizational forces beyond the control of the individual problem-solving manager. Students naturally are unhappy with this and will want some statement about what might be done to correct the problem. Part of their reality training must be to come to grips with the fact that in many cases such a solution is possible only in terms of some much more comprehensive, organization-wide change.

CONTENTS

Foreword v
Word To Instructor ix
Prologue xvii

PART I   ENTER THE MEN'S HUT

Chapter
1   Rite Of Passage 5
2   "Hi, Call Me ____" 9
3   The Power Of Positive Thinking 12
4   Ted's Boy 15
5   Cleanliness Is Next To 18
6   Your Job, My Reputation 21
7   Society of Equals 24
8   The Men's Hut 27
9   The Ropes To Know (I) 31

PART II   DE GUSTIBUS NON DISPUTANDUM EST

10   Look Of A Winner 39
11   Friday Go To Meetin' 43
12   The Sincerest Form Of Flattery 46
13   By Your Works Shall Ye Be Known 49
14   Better The Devil You Know 53
15   Spacemen 57
16   Like It Is 61
17   The Ropes To Know (II) 65

PART III   BUT SOME ARE MORE EQUAL THAN OTHERS

18   "Hi Sweetie . . ." 73
19   Cat In The Hat 76
20   Bite Of The Apple 79
21   You Can't Be Too Careful 82
22   My Brother's Keeper 86
23   Scarlet Letter 90
24   The Ropes To Know (III) 94

PART IV   AN INFORMAL THEORY OF GAMES

25   Hold That Line 104
26   Extra Effort 108
27   Ghosting For Gain 111
28   Watch Dogs 115
29   Back To The Drawing Board 120
30   Sunrise Service 124
31   The Ropes To Know (IV) 127

PART V   MORE GAMES

32   Cowboy 134
33   Praise/Criticism 137
34   Hellfire and Brimstone 141
35   Don't Ask 144
36   Spend It, Burn It 147
37   Made To Measure 150
38   Prophet Without Honor 154
39   Sic Transit 158
40   The Ropes To Know (V) 163

PART VI   SKATE FAST OVER THIN ICE

41   Stitch In Time 170
42   Success Story 174
43   The Rating Game 177
44   The Pearl 181
45   Most Valuable Player 185
46   Just In Case 188
47   Top Secret 192
48   Management By Objectives 195
49   As I Recall 198
50   The Ropes To Know (VI) 202

PART VII   THE POWER OF LOWER PARTICIPANTS

51   Coffee Break 210
52   Haste Makes Waste 212
53   Figures Don't Lie 217
54   Fair Day's Work 222
55   Player Piano 224
56   Point of No Return 227
57   The Ropes To Know (VII) 230

PART VIII   COOLING OUT THE MARK

58   More Bang For The Buck 240
59   Incredible 245
60   The Life Of Staff 248
61   The Threefold Way: 254
     Education
     New York
     Distinguished Scientist
62   The Ropes To Know (VIII) 262

Conclusion 267
Epilogue 277
Selected Readings 281
Subject Index 287

CAREER ADVICE CIRCA 1880

As office boy I made such a mark
That they gave me the post of a junior clerk
I served the writs with a smile so bland,
And I copied all the letters in a big round hand—

In serving writs I made such a name
That an articled clerk I soon became;
I wore clean collars and a brand new suit
For the pass examination at the Institute,

Of legal knowledge I acquired such a grip
That they took me into the partnership.
And that Junior partnership, I ween,
Was the only ship that I had ever seen.

I grew so rich that I was sent
By a pocket borough into Parliament
I always voted at my party's call,
And I never thought of thinking for myself at all

I thought so little, they rewarded me
By making me the Ruler of the Queen's Navee.

Sir William S. Gilbert
H.M.S. Pinafore

CAREER ADVICE CIRCA 1930

"You cannot erase a spoiled first impression anymore than you can recover lost maidenhood."

"An actor, like an infant, must learn everything from the beginning, to look, to walk, to talk, and soon . . . . We all know how to do these things in ordinary life. But unfortunately, the vast majority of us do them badly."

"An actor lives, weeps and laughs on the stage, and all the while he is watching his own tears and smiles. It is this double function, this balance between life and acting that makes his art."

"An actor should be a good guesser."

"An actor should catch things on the fly."

"An actor must have presence of mind [and in the case of uncertainty, decide]."

"Truth on the stage is whatever we can believe in with sincerity, whether in ourselves or in our colleagues."

"Truth cannot be separated from belief, nor belief from truth."

"To play truly means to be right, logical, coherent, to think, strive, feel, and act in unison with your role."

"Talent without work is nothing more than raw unfinished material."

"Never begin with results. They will appear in time as the logical outcome of what has gone before."

Constantin Stanislavski
An Actor Prepares
Creating a Role

PROLOGUE

The announcement reads, "Franklyn Named to New Corporate Post." Young men—and some not so young—gather around The Company bulletin board to read the details.

> The office of the President announced today that Ben W. Franklyn has been named to the newly established office of Corporate Director for Safety Programs. Mr. Franklyn moves from his post as plant manager at Portsmouth.
> M. M. Marsh commented personally on this appointment. "Over the years I have seen a growing and essential need for us to develop a comprehensive, hard-hitting approach to safety. In appointing Ben Franklyn to the new post of Corporate Director for Safety Programs, I am giving my personal support to this important effort. Mr. Franklyn's long years of association with every phase of our manufacturing effort make him admirably qualified to drive this important program ahead."
> Replacing Mr. Franklyn at Portsmouth will be Edward Wilson Shelby IV. Shelby will hold the position of Acting Plant Manager with specific responsibility for the development of our new Expandrium program. Ted Shelby has been staff assistant to the President, responsible for financial control systems.

The gathering digests this announcement with an assortment of mumbles, grunts of approval, some envy, and some questions.

"But what does *he* know about safety?" asks one young man of his companion. "It doesn't seem right to me. With all that responsibility— Corporate Director—you'd think they'd have picked a man with real professional experience. Just doesn't make sense to me."

Over to the side a greying but still youngish man is shaking his head. The greeting tag stuck to his lapel reads, Hi . . . call me *Stan*.

"Poor Ben," he is thinking, "wonder what he did this time?"

"What do *you* think, Stan?" The young man addresses him in keeping with the tag. "Isn't that a lot of responsibility for somebody without any *real* background?" (Emphasize real.)

"I take it you're new with us, Jimmie?" (Hi . . . call me *Jimmie*.) "Well, don't worry about it. Mr. Marsh and our top executives know what they're doing. Do you think they'd be where they are if they didn't?"

Stanley is giving Jimmie a ritual answer, of course. For, in fact, Stanley could tell Jimmie exactly what is happening, but that is not the way the game is played in The Company. And what Stanley would tell Jimmie is this.

First of all, read that announcement again, carefully. Notice the "named to" instead of "promoted to." Also, it is a "newly established" office. That's significant, too. Why *now?* Surely we haven't just discovered the need.

Now read down a little bit. Ted Shelby is "Acting Plant Manager." You would have thought the communications boys would have massaged that one a little more. Of course, it *is* possible that The Company needed a Safety Director so badly that they couldn't wait to find a permanent replacement—but, well, you get a feel for these things. Also, the "specific responsibility for, etc, etc . . . . For that line read, "The new Expandrium program is SNAFU."

Shelby obviously is Marsh's hatchet man. The financial control boys always are, and Shelby comes right out of Marsh's office. He doesn't know a damn thing about manufacturing and never will—because he's one of the "new breed."

And don't let the Corporate Director business fool you either. Corporate Directors (of given varieties) come and go, but plant managers are crucial, though the ring of the title is not as exotic.

So what Stanley might have told Jimmie is simply this.

"Look, Ben Franklyn has served The Company faithfully and well since he started as a machinists apprentice at the age of sixteen. He's tough and capable but the business has passed him by. It looks to me like Ben got into some kind of hassle with the big boys over this new Expandrium line, and when Ben gets it in his head that he's right, he's not about to back off.

"This time Marsh has finally had enough. Ben's about three or four years from retirement, so Marsh is going to ease him out of the way with a face-saving corporate directorship where he can't do any damage. Ben doesn't know a damn thing about anything but manufacturing so you can't just turn him loose in the china shop.

"But the rest of those poor bastards at Portsmouth are in for real trouble. Marsh wants that Expandrium line on time, and Shelby is out there to wield the axe. In other words, heads will roll. And that's where the acting manager part comes in. You can't go in there and rough up the troops, then expect them to love you. So when the dirty work is done Shelby will be lifted and a permanent manager named to secure the peace."

There you have Stanley's exegesis of a corporate announcement. And we would have to say that he is right on target. Stanley's ability to read the corporate tea leaves is the product of hard-won experience, the experience we are going to relate to you here. For what you are reading is a textbook, a serious text, though it may not appear to be, nor read exactly the way you might expect a text to read. Yet, it is no less than a text on organizational life. More specifically, it deals with organizations that constitute America's greatest institution—business. It is an instruction manual for the novice, for the junior executive, and for the man in the September of his career. For each there is a different function. The novice learns what to expect, how to interpret the ritual events of his new undertaking. The junior executive finds confirmation of his early observations, plus valuable lessons about future activities which he only now has started to anticipate. And for those in the golden years of their careers, we provide either a comforting affirmation of rightness of thought, or perhaps an unhappy revelation on a fall from grace.

But for all this, what we have here is a book primarily for the beginner whose career is yet to unfold. With the lessons of these pages, you will quickly understand what is taking place, will be able to translate the apparent into the real much as does the dream analyst for his patient. That this is a painless and rather pleasant way to get to "know the ropes" is simply added merit.

This is not a novel, nor a frivolous treatment of serious events. Every exemplary story that we present is real, contains an important lesson, a genuine exhortation or caution about the ropes to know and the ropes to skip. For easy reference, the text is divided into eight major parts, each of which is tailored to a given career stage or point of development. Part I—"Enter the Men's Hut"—is for the raw novice. Confronted by strange and possibly incomprehensible surroundings, the novice needs an analytical description of what is taking place. In much the same way as an anthropologist would describe the various functions of ritual, ceremony, and law in a strange tribe, or as the travel guide tells the new visitor the do's and don'ts of the local culture, so does part I provide the newcomer with some insights into the folkways of his new culture.

Part VII, just as obviously, is *not* for the newcomer, but rather for the person whose organizational associates are primarily subordinates. For now you must come to understand the "Power of Lower Participants." Reading this section will be particularly beneficial at the executive stage in your career. Finally, Part VIII—"Cooling Out the Mark"—is for the September of your career. Though secure in occupation and station, still you must guard against those who would seek to usurp your influence. Especially important is it that you recognize the confidence game played in the upper echelons of the organization, gambits for removing people from positions of influence, opportunities which seem highly desirable at the outset but result in later losses.

As for the remaining parts, II is an exposition of something we all know but generally refuse to take seriously: that ninety-nine percent of the judgments we make are based on woefully incomplete information, and that our perception of a new experience is completely colored by previous experience. Appearances truly are more important than reality. We examine in Part II some of the appearances people use to create the desired impressions of themselves—their presentations of self. That these presentations are sometimes accidental or ill-advised in no way affects the importance of the message. "De Gustibus non Disputandum est" is only for those who don't understand the principles of advantageous self-presentation.

Part III follows directly on the impression management theme, but it portrays the problems experienced by women and minorities in dispelling unfavorable impressions—impressions rooted in cultural expectations and stereotypes. The unhappy message is: all in The Company are equal, still, "Some Are More Equal Than Others." The task for you is to understand why, and what you might do about it.

Returning to a cheerier theme, Part IV is about game theory. Having established a beach head in the organization you now can earnestly pay attention to building your position. You will learn that the strategies used by older hands, strategies seemingly built up as accretions of experience, actually have an underpinning of but very few, though powerful, principles. By using principles of rudimentary game theory you will know when or not to write that memo. You will be able to guarantee a positive expected value for your career. You will come to recognize when you should graciously defer a new position to a competitor, for you will have come to recognize the characteristics of a situation with a negative expected value.

But not all organizational games can be subject to formal theoretical analysis. There are, after all, "Just Plain Games," and so we treat these in Part V. Again we develop a few principles to guide our reader. Most of these have to do with career traps, with negative outcomes deriving from what seem to be positive strategies. "Cowboy," by way of example, illustrates that too much success, in too well defined an activity, can bring ultimate grief both to participant and organization.

Having avoided these pitfalls, however, careers quicken their pace in higher organizational strata. Having shed the pack and assumed management responsibilities, you must learn that rapid movement is essential to continued success. In the phrase of Part VI, you must learn to "Skate Fast Over Thin Ice." You must learn to define yourself as an energizer, a shaker, a mover, for your greatest potential lies in this path. The developer and builder is a satisfactory role for some, but this is a slower path to success, fraught with circumstantial hazards and the continual danger that someone else will take credit for your achievements. The inventor who launches the enterprise can never lose credit for that fact. The builder, though, must ever face the possibility of being regarded as the one who lacked the talent to bring a splendid dream into reality.

Our Characters

Inasmuch as this book is a series of allegorical stories and cautionary tales, the cast of characters does not, strictly speaking, constitute a true reflection of real life. Our characters are relatively few, and each is not truly an individual but a representation of a type of person. Occasionally this may cause you a feeling of disjointedness, as when the mail boy in one sequence is a millhand in the next. But the organizational characteristics of the positions are similar in many ways, as are those of their occupants. So why invent a new character? Put another way, there may be inconsistencies in positions but not in social roles.

Mr. Marsh is the universal executive, top man in The Company (an allegorical corporation).

Bonnie is our secretary, at once innocent and all-knowing, understanding though not truly conscious of the power of her position.

Our main character is *Stanley,* the universal subordinate. He is not a janitor, of course; in fact, in our opening chapter he has only recently graduated from college and is just launching his career. Here we chronicle Stanley's agonies and triumphs as he learns the ropes. Later we will find him at various stages in his development as a corporate employee, never a failure, never outstandingly superior. For Stanley is Everyman, both sinew and fat in the corporate body. You ask, "Stanley who? Doesn't he have a last name?" Answer—no. Stanleys and Bonnies just don't have last names in The Company. Nor does Mr. Marsh have a given name. Nonsense, you say? Well, try this experiment. Pretend you are looking for your mail boy (who, by the way, may be older than yourself). Find out what his last name is, and ask one of your friends, "Say, have you seen Mr. Szekely?" Your friend will look at you blankly, "Who? No one by that name here. Where does he work?"

"Mail room," you will say.

He says, "No such one, only Jimmie."

"Yeah," you say, "Jimmie, Jimmie Szekely."

"Well, why didn't you say so?" etc., etc.

Now, try the equivalent thing asking about Mr. Marsh.

"Mason been through lately?"

This last exercise will also prove informative and undoubtedly more interesting. Things in The Company are ordered and orderly. We keep track of who's who in small, but meaningful ways. And so it is that Mrs. Matson is Mr. Marsh's secretary, and Bonnie is the secretary for Department D.

Lesley is, so to speak, Stanley's twin in The Company. A recent addition to *The Ropes'* family, Lesley's main problem in the corporate world is to convince the Shelby's and the Franklyn's that she's really serious about her career.

Another newcomer to The Company's management ranks is *Claude Gilliam*, a graduate of the Polytechnic Institute and one of The

Company's first "Equal Opportunity" professional employees. Like Lesley, Claude has certain barriers to overcome as he moves up The Company's career ladder.

The Executives and corporate staff of The Company are in New York, an allegorical city. People in The Company refer to corporate headquarters simply as "New York." And here we find *Edward W. Shelby IV*, our universal staff-manager. His intermediate position is indicated by the fact that he has both first and last names. Ted Shelby is there to advise and devise. As far as he is concerned, the key to a successful business is to apply the most modern techniques of management. He cannot believe that anyone without an MBA (including, some suspect, even Mr. Marsh) could possibly know anything about running a company.

Out in the Plant (wherever it might happen to be) we find *Ben Franklyn,* the universal line manager, bull o' the woods, Ted's antithesis in the dialectic of corporate existence. Ben's job is to get things done.

Ben has come up through the ranks and has been with The Company forever. As far as he is concerned, the only important activity in a business is getting the product out the door. He cannot believe that anybody who has not been a foreman could possibly know anything about running a company—except Mr. Marsh, and the "Old Man" (Marsh Senior who gave Ben his first promotion to foreman).

Kerry Drake is Ben's counterpart in the professional ranks of middle management, running things in design, finance, or production. Kerry's given name actually is Junius. As a boy he was called Skip, but that didn't seem appropriate in The Company. And then someone noticed his resemblance in a handsome, prematurely grey way to the comic strip character of the same name and so he became Kerry to all. He's been down and up in The Company. Kerry will be a success, but he lacks the single-minded drive, self-interest, and strategic sense to make it to the top. His fundamental qualities are honesty, openness, and loyalty to The Company.

Now you will also find that many of these stories have a narrator, for the authors are simply the chroniclers of events in The Company. But our narrator (for personal reasons) has asked not to be named and we have respected this wish, though we have maintained the form in which the stories were told.

Finally, we have our universal consultant, *Dr. Faust,* chairman of The Department at The University. Faust is called in whenever there is some sort of problem, and times are good enough that nobody is watching budgets very closely. Occasionally he will present a seminar or a training session. His major function is to sanctify with the aura of outside expertise that which has already been decided upon by the management of The Company. But make no mistake, Faust knows whereof he speaks. In fact, now and again he finds himself wishing he had the time to set down in writing some of his more "instructive" experiences.

PART I

ENTER
THE MEN'S HUT

Introduction to Part I

In those societies termed "primitive" (those lacking amenities such as super-highways, inside flush toilets, and TV dinners), there is most usually a social institution known as the men's hut. It is a place of taboo, a repository of arcane and secret lore and, incidentally, a place where a man can be free from the women, children, and dogs of the tribe.

While the explanation for all this might be simply "male chauvinism," some different explanations have been advanced. The "male bond of friendship," so 'tis told, is the manifestation of an atavistic impulse resulting from no less than the principle of natural selection. Men in groups had a better chance of survival in hunting cultures than did men alone, or than men and women in groups where obviously the mind might wander occasionally to other than the business at hand. This being so, individuals with greater intrinsic drive and capacity for the male bond of friendship had a greater probability of survival than did their less fortunate fellows. The conclusion then flows directly from something termed genetic epistemology (lately known as Sociobiology). To wit, as creatures of instinct, men continue to band together mindlessly on various pretexts, though the need, and hence the reason, no longer exists.

And what becomes of the men's hut in a literate and sophisticated society? Well, there are the Moose, the Elks, the Eagles, and indeed a whole assorted bestiary of men's fraternal organizations. Also the Masons and the Knights of Columbus. Observe the Harvard, Princeton, and Yale Clubs (though admittedly their purpose is being weakened in a misguided rush of egalitarianism). There are, of course, the Railroad Club and the Men's Faculty Club.

These are surely excellent examples, yet the world of business and industry remains the foremost exemplar of the men's hut.[1] And though it may be that the male is simply responding to a lemming-like urge to congregate, still it is interesting to examine the symbols and functions of this institution in a modern setting.

Now, no organization functions as it is commonly understood to function by subordinates. The reason, no doubt, is that it couldn't, and pretense is necessary to maintain the allegiance of the faithful—the recruits, lower echelons, the public. For the principles of rectitude, fair play, and equality that support the faith of the mass membership are quite antithetical to the sound conduct of the affairs of the organization. Senior inhabitants of the men's hut know this well. And so one wonders, for example, if school superintendents believe in learning, or colonels in patriotism, or bishops in God in the same way as do the faithful. We suspect that the allegiance of these leaders is rather to the school system, the army, or the church—which is at least a very different thing. Put another way, their allegiance is to a semisecret core of personal relationships, operational practices, and public rituals that constitute the temporal body of the organization.

Socialization is the name given to the process whereby new members of the organization learn these things. The process is informal, by word of mouth and by action rather than by declaration. It is stepwise; different things are learned at different levels. A thirty-second degree Mason knows more of the secrets of his organization than does the novice. And just as certainly he is more committed to the organization and consequently more trustworthy of having these secrets. Just so it is in the average organization.

But back to the men's hut. The first problem faced by the new member is that of gaining entry into the men's hut—of gaining access to the basic organizational secrets. A key episode here is the rite of passage. This is more or less an affirmation to the individual of the fact that he has been accepted into the men's hut. And, as in the tribe, simply attaining puberty is not sufficient. There must be an accompanying trial and appropriate ritual to mark the event. The so-called primitives had the good sense to make these trials meaningful and direct. Upon attaining puberty you killed a lion and were circumcised. After a little dancing and what not, you were admitted as a junior member and learned some secrets.

Other practices of these primitive men also made good sense. They recognized that self-decoration, magic, and ritual dancing constitute important and difficult work to be reserved for adults. Different styles are appropriate for different statuses. Relationships between inferior and superior should be highly formal and constrained. Yet, there should also be areas of privilege, much like the ship's galley, where opinions and facts can be spoken without invocation of the usual codes of honor.

All this, of course, still exists today in the form of official Company gatherings and retreats, especially the retreats where high-ranking members of the organization can divest themselves of their feathers, as it were, and mingle with the ordinary folk.

The hut is a symbol of, and a medium for maintaining, the status quo and the good of the order. Secret knowledge about the organization and its members is necessary, as Erving Goffman points out "to give objective intellectual content to subjectively felt social distance."[2] For, as subsequent examples will show, the jealously guarded secrets and intimate participation in restricted circles often turn out to be either trivial or disappointing or both. The real prize is the attainment of membership rather than the knowledge that objectifies that membership. And the fact that the worth of knowledge tends to be exaggerated once gained is supported by sociological theory and experiment, as well as by every man's intuition. What follows, then, is a set of stories, each demonstrating a point in the process of introducing the organizational adolescent into the men's hut.

1

RITE OF PASSAGE

Several factors conspired to discomfort Stanley's first few days with The Company. For one thing, starting off in Ben Franklyn's section meant that his office was stuck back in the furthest reaches of the plant (a single building, sprawling over several blocks). For another thing, his parking lot was also near the furthest reaches of the plant, which would have been convenient, except that Security Regulations stated all employees must leave by the front door. Finally, Stanley had arrived in November, the start of the rainy season (which had arrived with Stanley's first day on the job).

Stanley's plight was thus: arrive in the morning, park, walk all the way around the building in the rain, go in the front door, and walk all the way back through the plant to his office, which was about fifty feet from where his car was parked. At the end of the day, walk all the way to the front of the plant, walk all the way around the building (raining harder, usually) to his car, which was about fifty feet from his office.

After his third or fourth good soaking, Stanley noticed a door at the back of the building, right between his office and his car. It was a loading gate, attended by a Security Guard who was to make sure that all employees left by the front door, at least the ones who tried to leave by his station.

Yet one day Stanley could have sworn that he saw one of his fellow workers coming in through that back door. So that night, just before quitting time he stood by to confirm his suspicions. Sure enough! Lots of people were going out that gate, and the guard was happy to let them do it.

Well, that's all right, thought Stanley as he hurried back to his office to get his briefcase. He strode to the door, happy in the thought of the rain he was avoiding.

"Your name, please?" demanded the guard. Stanley recited his name. "Sorry, sir, you can't use this door." So saying, the guard stepped aside, nodding good-day as the guy from the office next to the candy machine went out through the door.

"But why not?" asked Stanley. "These other people are using it."

"Yeah, they're on the list."

"List?"

"Mr. Franklyn's list," said the guard. "He's got this list of people it's okay for to go through here."

"Oh, okay," said Stanley. "No problem. I'll get on the list and be back tomorrow."

So Stanley took his long walk, consoled by the thought that it was the last time. Only it wasn't. Stanley knew enough not to go directly to Ben Franklyn, but went instead to Bonnie, to first find out about the list. He had reasoned correctly that Bonnie, being a secretary, would know everything about the office that was worth knowing. She informed him: "Oh yes, Mr. Franklyn's list. Listen, nobody's supposed to use that door, not really, but Mr. Franklyn works it out with the guards so that some of his people, he has this list of them, can go through there."

"Well, how do I get on the list?" Stanley was becoming irritated. Having picked up a sore throat and sniffles, he was anxious to avoid pneumonia or influenza or whatever serious ailment might attend a four block walk (two coming and two going) in the rain every day.

"I'm afraid you don't, Stanley," said Bonnie. "When it's all right for people to go through that door, well . . . Mr. Franklyn just tells them, that's all. When it's okay, he'll tell you."

Thoughts that could never be uttered in front of Bonnie about Franklyn and the door and the list and Security Regulations race through Stanley's head. But he *thinks* them very loudly and for a very long time, because he is really miffed. It is the most childish, the most bureaucratic, the most inconvenient, the most unfair, the most sense-less situation he has ever encountered in his life, and who the hell does Franklyn think he is, and if there was ever a dumb regulation, and The Company, and, etc., etc., etc.

But for the next several months he takes the long walk twice a day (four times, if he goes out to lunch), and during those months he learns more about Ben Franklyn. Franklyn, a self-made man, has worked his way up through the ranks, and in a number of ways he is old-fashioned. His office is up a stairway in the loft of the mill, and from strategically placed windows he can look down over his area much as a feudal lord surveying his fief. Actually, he is a good guy to work for, but in that part of the plant the world is divided in two—his boys and other people. His boys use that back door, other people don't.

Then one morning Bonnie came over and said, "Stanley, Mr.Franklyn wants to see you. I think it's time for your semiannual review."

This is just fine with Stanley. He is sure that he has been doing his work well, he's been getting along with everybody, and it was only last week that he homered in the winning run in the softball game with the traffic department. He strides up the metal stairway to Franklyn's office, only a little apprehensive. He thinks he deserves a raise, but he knows that Ben thinks of The Company's money as his own and doesn't like to part with it too easily.

"Come in and sit down, Stanley," said Ben Franklyn. "Bonnie passed the word along? Good. You know, Stanley, every time we hire one of you high-priced college boys . . ." like all self-made men, Franklyn is at least ten years behind the times ". . . I wonder if they're really worth it. But you're okay, you do good work and you get along. And quite a centerfielder, too, I hear. So I'm giving you a raise; you'll be making $1,250 from now on."

Stanley is extremely grateful; Ben Franklyn has a way of making people grateful even for things not only due, but overdue. They talk a little more, and then Stanley gets up to go.

"One more thing, Stanley," said Ben Franklyn. "I've put your name on the list. Just tell the guard who you are." Stanley hesitated a moment and thought . . . list? The list? Sure, the loading gate list and the guard. He'd almost forgotten. And it was just like Ben to assume that everyone knew about the list and the guard, though no one ever talked about it.

"Yes, sir," said Stanley, beaming. He bounced down the stairs back to his office, and in spite of himself spent the rest of the day looking forward to going home through the back door. At quitting time he strode to the door, gave his name in a confident tone and was standing in the parking lot in a second. The rainy season was over, and the sun shown warmly down on Stanley as he walked the twenty-five feet to his car. All the way home he thought what a good day it had been.

Now, Stanley isn't the kind of person who likes to play The Company's game, and he's likely to tell anyone where to get off if they play "Mickey Mouse" with him, so to this day he still can't figure out why he didn't tell Franklyn to take the loading gate and shove it, that it was none of his damn business who went where. Because, really, it wasn't.

But Stanley still remembers that his feelings that day had been quite the opposite—not irritated, or even indifferent, but genuinely pleased and grateful. That day he was part of the mill management. That day he knew he was one of Ben Franklyn's boys.

When you worked for Ben Franklyn, you did more than work; you became part of his family. By contrast, when you worked for Ted Shelby you became part of his "team," were "welcomed aboard," and were entered onto the payroll through the data terminal.

But family or team, you were incorporated into the group through certain events which marked the fact—nor did these events happen right away, because it takes a little time for true acceptance to happen. Everybody, for a while, is a provisional member of the men's hut.

Different men have different styles, and Franklyn—bull o' the woods—had grown up in the traditional kind of organization, based not so much on paperwork as on personal relationships and loyalty. He will never trust "the new approach" and instead finds ways of extending his own authority into areas not covered by the formal rules. By his control of favors and sanctions he maintains the personal loyalty of His Boys and broadens the range of his influence.

Franklyn, in his way of handling his territory, is not too different from the medieval church. It granted indulgences to parishioners, who, in accepting the benefit, implicitly recognized the right of the church to bestow it. Thus they bound themselves even more completely into the system.

2

HI, CALL ME

Every summer The Company has a Company Picnic. It is similar to a picnic, a time when a family and friends drive out into the country to spend a pleasant day, but there is an important difference. The Company Picnic is not for the purpose of having a pleasant day in the country, and is always held in a big park in the middle of town. If anyone has a pleasant day that is just fine, but incidental to the purpose of the event.

The Company Picnic is a genuine ceremonial rite. It is a day for setting aside the usual roles and relationships among Employees. Executives shed their corporate uniforms and spend the day on display for the faithful. Ben Franklyn proves to be surprisingly human, and Edward W. Shelby IV has memorized the first names of the entire top management. Perhaps he will come across some opportunities provided by the camaraderie of The Picnic. And Stanley, Lesley, and Bonnie are expected to talk quite casually and openly to anyone, about anything.

For this is a day for renewing belief in The Company and reaffirming the values it stands for. The Company as family is the theme of the day, with this sentiment embodied in the sticky-back tag that every attendee is given when his name is checked off the sign-up lists. The tag says: "Hi, Call Me _____," and everyone from Mr. Marsh to Jimmie Szekely writes in his *first* name and sticks the tag on the front of his flowered sport-shirt or her cotton blouse. When the tag is securely attached, everyone collects a hot dog and a paper cup of beer and dutifully mingles.

I noticed Stanley mingling over on the horseshoe courts, playing a game with a man considerably older than himself. Stanley had been with The Company for about a year by now. Like most newcomers he started at one of the outlying locations, but recently he had been transferred to "new responsibility," and is now working out of Company Headquarters in New York. (New York, of course, occupies a place in Company legend analogous to Camelot—those in outlying areas are simply told by their superiors, by way of justification, that "the people in New York want this," or more simply, that "New York wants this").

I hadn't seen Stanley for quite a while, but I did run into him several days ago, just in time to tell him that since he was in town for The Company Picnic, he really ought to go. Stanley obviously had gained considerable self-confidence and a sense of importance from his "new responsibilities"; in fact, he had a tendency to overdo it.

As I approached the horseshoe courts, it was clear that he was overdoing it today. Although not an extrovert by nature, Stanley had been near the beer tap all day and was always willing to give it another try. After all, isn't it the outgoing guy that gets ahead?

". . . yes, I was transferred to New York about two months ago," Stanley was saying. And the emphasis he placed on *New York* revealed how impressed he was with this. Stanley still retained his "plant mentality." Clankety-thud. His last toss knocked away his opponent's leaner, replacing it on the stake. From closer up, the older man was a rather distinguished looking, silver-haired fellow.

I don't think Stanley took notice of this. "I was out at Pawtucket before that, but now I'm working out of the home office here, got a project going in Portland." Clank. Another ringer for Stanley. He is playing a good game of horseshoes.

"Portland, eh?" said his opponent. "Then you're with the sales force?"

"The *sales* force?" said Stanley. "Oh, hell, no! Listen, don't you know about the expandrium processing line we're installing in Portland, Maine? I've got full responsibility for getting it on stream."

"I guess I hadn't heard about that one . . . " his opponent paused and looked at Stanley's name tag, ". . . Stanley."

"You'd think," said Stanley, as he tossed another ringer, "that in The Company people would have a better idea of what's going on. One thing I've learned, and I'll pass it along for what it's worth, if you don't know what's going on, you'll never get anywhere in this outfit."

"I won't argue with you there," said the older man.

Stanley tossed another ringer. "That's the game!" he said. "You know, horseshoes isn't as hard as it looks."

"Takes some practice." And looking at Stanley's name tag again, "Thank you for the game, Stanley."

"Don't mention it, see you around," said Stanley.

"It's nice to see you being so democratic here today, Stanley," I said.

"Well, I don't see any harm in talking with workers," said Stanley.

"They probably don't get much of a chance to talk to management people man-to-man."

"You don't know who that *was*?" I asked him. Come to think of it, if Stanley had known, he might have acted a little differently.

"I looked at his name tag once, but I don't remember what the name was," said Stanley, "Why? Who was it?"

"That, Stanley, just happened to be *Mr. Marsh!*"

Clankety clankety thud. Stanley dropped two handfuls of iron horseshoes on his feet, but I doubt if he noticed. His face went white. "M-m-m-mr. M-m-m-m . . ." he stammered and stared blankly off in the distance at the distinguished gentleman he'd just trounced in his first game of horseshoes, who was now conversing with another group of young people.

Did Stanley blow it here? Is his bright career nipped immediately in the bud? Will the edict come rolling down from on high: "Send him to Petaluma."

No, of course not.

There are several reasons why no ill will befall Stanley, no matter what he might say to Mr. Marsh in this situation. In the first place, this is a ritual—a time when the great men leave the men's hut and mingle with the tribesmen. Mr. Marsh must show personal interest in each and every person he encounters. He assumes that all know him and that he is performing a duty similar to that of a prince of the church going among the faithful—that is, to be touched and rejoiced in. His common clothes are only part of the ritual, for his presence remains, and in spite of what his tag says, he is still Mr. Marsh.

Stanley's anguish is really unnecessary and is the result of a basic error that he is making. He grossly overestimates his own presence. He sees the world, and particularly The Company, from a very egocentric viewpoint. Whatever interest Mr. Marsh might have shown in anything that Stanley said or did was nothing more than rote role behavior, which Stanley mistakenly interpreted as genuine interest.

The other reason why nothing will happen to Stanley is a consequence of the fact that there is but one Mr. Marsh, and the thousands of Stanleys know who he is, or will soon find out. But Mr. Marsh doesn't know who *any* of the thousands of Stanley are. In truth there is virtually no way that Stanley could either make it or blow it on this sort of occasion, for the picnic is a solidarity ritual, a gathering of the clan, a reaffirmation of belief. What anybody actually says or does in this context makes little difference to anybody else.

Some day perhaps Stanley will move up high enough in The Company that his behavior on these occasions will indeed become significant. But it will not be so much for the way he deals with the Mr. Marshes of that day as for the way and the style he uses in meeting the faithful. Even then the judgment will be based on how well he carries out the ritual of The Company.

3

THE POWER OF
POSITIVE THINKING

"*Where* the hell *is* he?" Ben Franklyn's bellow reverberated through the building. Stanley's first impulse was to answer back. "Over here, sir," but he luckily caught himself. He knew it was he to whom Ben was referring, and he knew that everybody else a hundred yards in each direction knew it too. But for the life of him, he couldn't figure out what he'd done.

A minute or two later Ben Franklyn came into Stanley's office, where Stanley had been sitting all the time (Ben could have found him without all the bellowing, but Ben liked to bellow, given any plausible excuse).

"Stanley," said Ben with a sarcastic melody in his voice, "what the hell have you been doing in Building B?"

"Nothing, since the crew finished installing those overhead pipes," said Stanley. "Why? What's the problem?"

"Let's take a little walk over to Building B, and I'll show you." Stanley tagged along after Ben, still bewildered. There was certainly nothing wrong with the overhead pipes, so what could it be?

Ben pointed up at the overhead pipes and sputtered, "What *is* that stuff?"

"You've never seen Insuban?" said Stanley. "Insulating material. The specs called for those pipes to be insulated, so I ordered the best stuff I could find. Gee, I thought everybody knew about Insuban. They even told us about it in school."

Ben is just about purple. "Insuban?" he fumed. "*Expandrium!*
Expandrium! That's what *we* make!"

"For insulation?"

"Damn right, for insulation and a lot of other things you've never
thought of. And we use it too. Jesus, Stanley, if *we* don't use it, then who
the hell else will?"

"Well, we can't take it down now," said Stanley. "There's a lot of
money up there around those pipes. What can I do about it?"

"You can get hold of some spray cans of Expandrium paint and have
somebody go up there and cover up that stuff. Now! Right away! Before
somebody sees it!"

". . . so I had it taken care of," Stanley is telling me, several weeks
later, "but can you imagine Franklyn getting so excited about something like that? Who the hell is ever going to see what's up on those
pipes? Who the hell cares? And who ever heard of insulating anything
with Expandrium anyhow? Man, I'm an engineer, not a salesman!
That's not the kind of thing I'm supposed to worry about!" Stanley, in
retelling the story is excited all over again, raising his arms in mock
supplication.

"Well, Stanley . . ." But, before I can say anything, Ted Shelby has
come around the corner, apparently in a hurry to find somebody.

"Oh, great," says Shelby, "listen, I'm glad you guys are here. Mr.
Marsh just showed up with The President of Another Company, and he
wants to take him through our new Building B. Can you guys come
along, in case they have any questions?"

So it is that Mr. Marsh, The President, Edward W. Shelby IV, Stanley,
and I take a tour of Building B. Mr. Marsh likes to promote The
Company as a dynamic outfit, likes to show visitors (especially visitors
from Another Company) the new buildings. And so to provide an even
better view of Building B he has us all climb into the cab of an overhead
crane, and soon we are winging along through Building B, fifteen feet
above the floor.

"Well, I'll be . . . !" The President suddenly blurts out, pointing at the
overhead pipes, which are now staring us right in the eye, "I didn't know
you could use Expandrium for *insulation!*"

Stanley seizes the moment, "Mr. President, he says, "when a guy's own
outfit makes the best product, he'd be an idiot not to use it! We use it for
insulation, and a lot of other things that most people would never
think of."

Mr. Marsh positively beamed for the rest of the tour. Perhaps it was
even intentional, because Mr. Marsh doesn't make mistakes, but just
before he and Ted Shelby were out of earshot Stanley and I overheard
him say, "Good show, Ted, I wish that more of our people would
understand, like young what's-his-name there does, that everyone of us
is a salesman for The Company."

So it is that Steel People take their beer from cans (but not aluminum cans), just as Glass People favor disposable bottles, and, incidentally, conservationists prefer returnables. Automobile People drive their own products rather than their competitors', and clothing store clerks wear the same garments they sell. Are all these people selling their souls?

Not really. You don't have to BELIEVE in the product any more than you believe in driving to work in the morning. You just do it. And you do it for the same reason that the ecologically minded trouble themselves to carry their empties back and forth from the grocery store: to save yourself some embarrassing explanations.

4

TED'S BOY

Here I am, says Stanley to himself, nowhere already. I've been with The Company for over a year and a half and, I mean, I'm not doing badly (don't get me wrong), but I'm not really getting anywhere.

And I can't see that there's anything wrong with what I've been doing. Well, there isn't—that's no kidding. Degree from a good school, hired in at a better than average starting salary, got a raise at six months and another one just a couple of weeks ago, been getting the work done, get along with everybody. But nothing's happening.

If something doesn't happen pretty soon, I suppose I might as well just hang it up around here. Because if you don't have a foot into top management by the time you're thirty, you probably never will. Look, there's hardly a guy up there that wasn't at least a plant manager by the time he was thirty, everybody knows that. That means that I've got about six years to get up there from here. No way at the rate I'm going. I'd be lucky if I made it to plant manager in ten years.

You know, I think what's wrong is that I've been waiting around; you don't just float up to the top. You try that and every hustler uses you for a stepping stone.

You've got to find a guy to move ahead of. And, it's that Shelby guy—Edward W. Shelby IV. He's about my age, see, and he's been around, oh, maybe a year or two longer than I have. And he's ahead of me—by quite a bit, I'll admit. I don't know why I didn't notice him before. Well, I know he is around, but I didn't really notice him until Ben suggested that I talk to him about the Project because Shelby's doing that kind of work. In fact, Ben said that he's the expert around here on it. But I must have talked to Shelby for two hours, and when I was finished I didn't know any more than I did when I went in. Shelby just *isn't that good*. I know as much about it as he does, and he's the "expert" around here.

So I started watching him—"followed him home to see what he eats," like the ad guys say. He's got that big office, all to himself, and he shares a secretary with only two other guys, and I'm pretty sure he's making a couple hundred bucks a month more than I am. How does he do it?

To be honest, he's not *in*competent, but you can't say that he's very likeable, he's a little too standoffish for that. And, while you can see that he doesn't miss any opportunities, he doesn't really try to hustle either.

So I think I know how to leapfrog him. There's bound to be an opening up ahead in a couple of months, and if it doesn't open too soon (if it just holds off for about two, maybe three months), I think I can make a good enough showing on this project that I can slip around him. And if I can, that's going to look real good—maybe even good enough that the next move up will come a little faster. So what I've got to do is bring this project in with colors flying, and make sure that the right people see who did it.

It does seem a little merciless, but you can bet that Ted Shelby would do the same thing to me. That's the kind of thing you have to do; they don't mind. They expect you to do it. Mr. Marsh didn't get where he is by being a doormat, you can bank on that.

I do need to know a little more about Shelby, though, if I'm going to pull this off. He seems to have something going for him, but I don't know what. What I've got to do is ask around, get to know the score, what's he doing that looks so good?

And there's the guy to ask—Ben Franklyn. He's been bull-o'-the-woods around here for so long, what he wouldn't know about the place wouldn't be worth knowing. Well, I might as well get started on this, ask him a few roundabout questions (you've got to be subtle) and see if I can't get a line on Shelby.

"Hi, Mr. Franklyn."

"Hello, Stanley; how's it going?"

"Just great, project's moving fine. Just in talking to Shelby."

"Who?"

"Shelby, in the office by the front windows. Edward W. Shelby IV."

"Oh, you mean Ted's boy."

"Ted's boy?"

"Ted Shelby III. Set up the first Expandrium line at Paducah."

"You mean Shelby's dad is plant manager at Paducah?"

"Not any more. That was years ago, just before they made him general manager of the Pacific region. Sort of a big change from Kentucky, I guess, but people figured that the way he set up the Expandrium division in the South, he could probably handle about anything that came his way. Haven't you heard about Ted Shelby? Well, you're new here. He's on the Board now; maybe he's some sort of vice-president, but I don't know for sure. Look him up in an Annual Report if you're interested. He and Marsh, well, hell, it's practically their company, if you want to know the truth. Those two guys damn near did the whole thing themselves. Best of friends, too. When little Ed was born, it was at his baptism, I understand, Marsh looked at him and said to Ted, "I can tell this young man has a great future with The Company."

Stanley did the right thing here. He wanted to move ahead in the Men's Hut, so he found out who was ahead of him. And when he found out, he gave up for the time being, which was also the right thing— because you don't waste your time on the chief's son, you pick somebody who can be beaten.

At this stage in his life, Stanley is impatient; in this respect he is a typical, ambitious young man. But contrary to myth, most of those people "up there" were *not* plant managers by age thirty. A few, but not all by any means. It all takes time, and sometimes you move faster than others. One year is no time at all in this context, and five years isn't much. Sometimes you can leapfrog and sometimes you can't. But five years is not nearly as long a time at thirty-five at it is at twenty-five.

And Stanley has learned one other thing from this incident. You're never sure why some people are where they are. A wide range of abilities determines your advancement. A good style and technical ability are both important, and these are usually visible abilities. But other, less visible abilities, such as the ability to pick the right parents, can be important, too.

5

CLEANLINESS IS
NEXT TO . . . ?

Stanley met Lesley for the first time when each had been with The Company only a matter of months. Stanley had just become Ben Franklyn's engineer at the Pawtucket Rolling Mill. Lesley, a trainee in technical sales, was aiming for a position as a manufacturer's representative. A manufacturer's representative? The Company made its own Expandrium fabricating machinery because that was a specialized business. So to make sure that these machines were installed correctly and functioning well they had a group of their own technical sales people—manufacturer's representatives—to whom fell the task of making sure that such was the case.

Les and Stan had spoken to each other a few times previously as each went about the day's tasks. Today Stanley decided to make her acquaintance. Les was sitting at the far table of the mill cafeteria poring over her manufacturer's manual in her slightly nearsighted squint.

"Um, mind if I sit down? I'm Stan."

"Lesley. Hi."

"You're new here, aren't you. Just in the past few days?" Stanley pressed on, "What department do you work in?"

"Oh, I'm not really *here*, I'm out of the New York sales office. I'm a technical sales trainee," said Les, still a little impressed by her good fortune in landing the job.

"Uh, then, what . . ."

"What am I doing here in the mill?"

"Yeah."

"You know, actually, I'm not too sure myself. I guess what I'm supposed to be doing is . . ." Les went on to describe her job. It seems that whenever a piece of Expandrium processing equipment went "down" for a day or so her job was to give it a thorough inspection: check for worn parts or stress fractures—almost anything that might be out of whack. This was done exactly as outlined in the official step-by-step maintenance procedure set forth in the manual she had been given—"the bible" as it was called by the New York staff. When the maintenance check was completed to her satisfaction she supervised start-up, checked samples of product and generally made sure that everything was okay.

"Only thing I *can't* figure out, really, is why *I'm* supposed to be doing this. The guys you've got right here in the mill have been doing this stuff a lot longer than me, and I just know there have to be some shortcuts in this business. Why even now I can see that there are only a few spots where there's ever going to be any . . . . Would you *mind* moving that cup?! Oh, look! . . ." Lesley had been so caught up in describing her job that she had only just noticed Stanley's coffee cup sitting on the open page of her "bible." And there right in the middle of the page, larger than life, was a wet, brown ring. As she scrubbed at the offending trace with a napkin Stanley tried to apologize, but only made matters worse.

"Honestly, Les, I don't see why you're so upset. It's just an old manual."

"A *new* manual," came the tart reply.

"New, old, so what? You can still read it, can't you? Look I really *am* sorry. I just don't see . . . ."

If Stanley had paid a bit more attention to the manual he might have seen why Lesley was so agitated. For one thing, he would have seen that the manual was encased in a neat plastic cover that Lesley had fashioned herself. And look at her. The coveralls were smeared with grease to be sure, but she herself was the essence of neatness and organization; blond hair pulled back into a bun—all business.

"Oh, I guess you're right, Stan, maybe I am getting upset about nothing. But I think this manual's pretty important to them. You know, they replaced the first one after just one month. And—and I still don't understand this, but I got kind of a long 'dutch uncle' talk about how maybe I hadn't been paying enough attention to the manual. But how could they know? As a matter of fact . . . ."

"Sure, I *do* see," Stanley broke in, "*that's* the problem. I think I know the answer, Les. Listen, you're so worried about keeping that thing in its pristine state—but that's just the problem."

"Sure," Lesley was unconvinced.

"Now wait, you'll see. When I was in the service I spent some time in the motor pool. Now I know it's different, but it's the same thing, I think. My first assignment was to the routine maintenance section. Every six months or whatever we were supposed to put each vehicle through a complete maintenance check. Just like you, by the numbers, as they say. Everything exactly like it says, step-by-step. And just like you I found out that there's never anything wrong with most of the parts. Pretty soon you find out most of the places where the trouble's likely to be. So the first day on the job one of the older guys, a sergeant, stops me and says, 'Don't worry about that, kid, we'll never finish if you do all that stuff.' I started to object and he says, 'Shut up and just do what I tell you.' But what if the CO finds out, I say. 'Don't worry, he won't,' he says. And with that he takes my brand new maintenance manual, open to my procedure, throws it in the grease on the floor and tromps on it with his GI boot.

"Hey wait, I say, what are you doing to my manual? If you've a gripe, take it out on yours. Then he says, 'I already have. Listen kid, after you've been around here awhile you'll smarten up. How do you think they check to see if you've done it all by the book, anyway? Think about it. They know that we don't do every different job often enough to have it all down pat, so we have to check the manual as we go. And if you do that, well, certain pages get dirty, greasy, dog-eared and everything. There's a lot of wear and tear when you, er—follow the book like you're supposed to. And pretty soon you're going to find out that every month they issue a new manual—a *nice clean* new manual. Get the idea?'"

So that's how Lesley finally figured out what the problem was. The Company figures that it is important to have some measure of performance for all its people. And Lesley's no exception. But The Company isn't about to assign someone to look over her shoulder every minute to make sure that she's following the detailed maintenance procedure. No, they have a better way. They look at the telltale tracks on the "bible." Coffee ring here, good; she's been studying that particularly tough section. Grease? Okay. Edges of these pages worn? Yes. And so in taking great pains to keep her "bible" in its "pristine" state, as Stanley called it, Lesley actually had been providing evidence that suggested she hadn't been doing her job.

And what was that job? Not maintenance, no, of course not. Her real job was to learn exactly where and how problems were likely to arise in every special piece of Expandrium processing equipment manufactured by The Company. She had to be familiar in physical detail with each part to recognize instantly its appearance and the common symptoms of trouble. But, you say, if that's the case then why didn't The Company just tell her that? Now that is a tough question to answer in just so many words. Look at it this way. It's basically a question of motivation. It's just possible that you may learn some things better by thinking that people are depending upon you to do something else. The lesson: things in The Company aren't always what they seem, and often they work better that way.

6

YOUR JOB,
MY REPUTATION

"Now look," says Stanley, his eyes flashing, "I'm fully aware that Mr. Marsh wants it that way! But that's not what we all agreed on when this project was launched, and Mr. Marsh can't change his mind now. We'll do it like we said, or not at all!"

Stanley is having a heated argument with his mentor, Dr. Faust of The University. Faust, chairman of The Department, had been approached by The Company to recommend somebody to head up The Project, and he had named Stanley. Stanley had seen some of the correspondence involved in his selection and had found it flattering in the extreme. Faust had even told a meeting of top management that they were lucky indeed to have a young man of Stanley's calibre. Stanley had even begun to believe it.

Stanley's first task had been to write up a project description. "This is basic, not applied, research," he had emphasized several times. Once begun, it was strictly hands off. It was to be understood from the outset that no outcomes were to be expected for at least five years, if even then. Progress reports would be issued twice a year, but on no account was anyone to ask the project group to justify its existence every couple of months. The reasons why this must be so filled several pages.

Stanley submitted his project description, and after the usual "whys" and "what ifs" and "have you talked to so-and-so," eventually it was accepted all tied up with blue ribbons and promises. The budget, a generous one, was approved after a suitable number of recycles and the project was on its way. Stanley was to direct it; Professor Faust to be retained as consultant.

Now, only eight months into The Project, Stanley and his mentor have fallen into bitter disagreement.

"Absolutely not!" says Stanley, on the verge of pounding his fist on the table. "I will not do it! This is *exactly* what we were trying to avoid in the first place. I made that perfectly clear in the project description. There isn't any product yet, and there won't be for years, and everybody agreed to The Project on that basis. Taking this new direction will . . . why, it's selling out!"

"Well," Professor Faust replies testily, "I'm afraid you don't have much choice. New York is asking some very pointed questions. We're going to have to come up with something, show them something!"

"No, I don't agree," says Stanley. "Tell them to read the project description; Mr. Marsh okayed it himself."

Faust is beginning to get excited. "Stanley," he says, "I don't think you understand. It isn't up to *you*. I say we've got to show them something. The New York people are taking a very hard look at this work."

"All right, let them," says Stanley, staring Faust in the eye. "If it comes to it, I'll lay my *job* on the line!"

Faust explodes. "*What? Your job?* Maybe it's your job, but it's *my reputation!*" He grabs his briefcase and storms out of the office, leaving a bewildered Stanley.

Good grief, thinks Stanley, could Faust possibly have meant what he just said? But he must have, because he isn't a person to kid around in this sort of situation. What an egocentric perspective to have. Here I am willing to lay it all on the line and all he worries about is his connection with this project. As if it's any skin off his nose—with all the consulting he does, he'd never miss this one. After all, I'm the guy who's responsible. Consultant . . . !

This is a good story to tell over drinks, and during the next few months Stanley gets a lot of mileage out of it. Yet the time will come when Stanley will realize that he has missed the point entirely.

Stanley does not understand his relationship with Professor Faust. Faust recommended Stanley for the job because Stanley was available at the time, not because he fit perfectly the description given to the executive committee by Faust. Right there, Faust's reputation works for Stanley. If Faust, the consultant, says that Stanley is the right man for the job, then, by God, he is! Faust recognizes that no job ever requires more than about twenty-five percent of what it pleases management to believe, so there's not much risk of failure even with Stanley at the helm.

Faust, when asked, must find someone for the job, someone with whom he has a plausible connection—preferably a graduate of The

Department such as Stanley. Stanley's mistake, a familiar one for him at this stage in his career, lies in accepting as truth statements that are made to fulfill necessary ritual requirements. And from his understandable egocentric perspective (he, not Faust, is the guilty one here) he fails again to see that there are thousands of Stanleys and thousands of Projects in this world, but few Professor Fausts. In truth, Faust's reputation *is* more important (yes, even to Stanley) than Stanley's current job. Since Stanley is where he is as a direct result of Faust's stated judgment, it is in the best interests of both to demonstrate the correctness of that judgment. Certainly Stanley wants to look good in his new position. But more to the point, he is obligated to make Dr. Faust look good as well.

7

SOCIETY OF EQUALS

Ted Shelby doesn't make very many mistakes, but . . . .

"Hey, Stanley," said Ted Shelby, leaning in through the door, "you got a minute? I've just restructured my office. Come on and take a look. I've been implementing some great new concepts!"

Stanley is always interested in Ted Shelby's new ideas. For if there is anyone Stanley wants to do as well as, it is Edward W. Shelby IV. Stanley follows Ted back to his office and stops, nonplussed.

Restructured is right! Gone are Ted's size B (Junior Exec.) walnut veneer desk and furniture, his four filing cabinets, and his telephone table. In fact, the room is practically empty save for a large stark-white cafeteria table (circular) and the half dozen padded vinyl, swivel chairs that surround it.

"Isn't it a beauty! As far as I know, I'm the first executive in the plant to actually innovate this. The shape is the crucial factor here—no front or rear, no status problems, we can all sit there and communicate more effectively."

We? Communicate? Effectively? Well, it seems that Ted has been attending a series of Executive Development Seminars given by Dr. Faust. The main theme of the seminars was—you guessed it—"participative management." Edward W. Shelby IV has always liked to think of himself as a truly democratic person. And when you are Ted Shelby's son, you can afford to do things like that.

"You see, Stanley," says Ted, managing his best sincere/intense attitude, "the main thing wrong with current mainstream management practice is that the principal communication channel is down-the-line-oriented. We on the top send our messages down to you guys, but we neglect the feedback potential. But just because we have more status and responsibility doesn't mean that we are necessarily (Stanley duly noted the word, necessarily) better than the people below us. So, as I see the situation, what is needed is a two-way communication network: down-the-line *and* up-the-line. You guys have a lot of good ideas, I'm sure, and there is no reason why you shouldn't input them directly to top management. But for years nobody thought of that! Here we all sit, behind our desks, giving the impression that we know it all, when we could be managing seventy-two percent more effectively (Ted must have taken notes, thinks Stanley) if we just cut out that artificial barrier."

"That's what the cafeteria table is for?" Stanley says.

"Yes!" says Ted. "We management people don't have all the answers, and I don't know why I never realized it before that seminar. Why . . . let's take an extreme example . . . those guys who run those machines out there, I'll bet that any one of them knows a thing or two that I've never thought of. So I've transformed my office into a full-feedback communication net. Anyone and everyone will be able to sit right here in my office, together, on equal ground. Me, Ben Franklyn, you, Lesley, Kerry Drake, Bonnie, those guys on the line, possibly (here Ted's eyes glaze slightly) Mr. Marsh. The management process will receive direct input from all participants."

"That certainly is an innovation around here," says Stanley. "When can we start?"

"I'll be circulating a memo shortly," says Shelby.

A few days later Stanley passed by Ted Shelby's office and was surprised that Ted's desk, filing cabinets, and telephone table were back where they used to be, that the white cafeteria table had vanished. He backpedaled to the door and asked, "Say, Ted, what happened to the table?"

"Er . . . Kerry Drake suggested that the cafeteria needed it." Without turning to Stanley, Ted mumbled something about overcrowding. Stanley couldn't tell whether Ted meant crowds in the cafeteria or his office, but didn't think it made much difference. Stanley, still curious about the un-restructuring, went to Bonnie for enlightenment. "What" he asked, "happened to Shelby's round table?"

"That table we were supposed to sit around and input things?" she said. Apparently Ted Shelby had spread his late enlightenment even to her. "All I know is, about two days after he had it put in, Mr. Drake came walking through here. He looked in that office, and then he sort of stopped and went back, and he looked in there for a long time. Then he came over to me, and you know how his face sort of gets red when he's *really* mad? Well, this time he was so mad that his face was absolutely white, and when he talked to me I don't think he actually opened his mouth, and I could barely hear him he was talking so low, and he said, 'Have *that* removed. Now. Have *Mr.* Shelby's furniture put back in his office. Have *Mr.* Shelby see me.'"

Picture the aboriginal men's hut. Then imagine one of the tribal leaders leading a group of young boys through the sacrosanct interior and saying, "See? What did I tell you? There's nothing but this old hut, and there's a bunch of old masks that we wear, and there's some feathers, and some fake spears that the priests carry, and here's the chief's throne. See, just a chair with some zebra skins wrapped around it. And see, we weren't struck dead by lightning for coming in here, and believe it or not, you won't even have bad luck from now on. Really, there's nothing special at all about the men's hut. You youngsters probably know almost everything we know."

Now that simply wouldn't happen. No member would think of doing it, and even if he did, none of the kids would dare venture in there. Everybody knows: It's the men's hut.

Occasionally Dr. Faust or Ted Shelby might have a lapse of memory, but Kerry or Ben Franklyn will be quick to set them straight. A company office bespeaks privilege and achievement, is an important symbol of authority in the hierarchy of The Company. Equality is nice, but there are contexts in which it can be carried too far. Officers do not fraternize with the enlisted men. Disagreeable orders issued by Lieutenant Szekely are more likely to be followed without question than are requests from good old Jimmie.

8

THE MEN'S HUT

I suppose I should not have dropped by on a Saturday morning, but I was curious to find out how it had gone. That meeting with the Task Force had been a continuing source of anxiety for Stanley for the last five or six weeks.

"And how did your Task Force meeting go?" The Task Force, I should explain was the final "contribution" of a vice-president who, on the verge of retirement, wanted to leave a lasting monument to his name to The Company. He put together a Task Force, mostly comprised of people at the plant manager level—or above—whose purpose was to "insure The Company's continued leadership in product excellence."

"I don't know," said Stanley, "sort of a let down, I guess. I came away from there feeling that somehow I just hadn't scored. And you know how I'd been waiting for this."

"Waiting" was quite an understatement. About a year ago Stanley had first started trying to persuade Ted Shelby to let him present his own report to the Task Force. Ted at that time had pointed out that only recently had he himself been able to attend any meetings of the Task Force, and Stanley knew that he was telling the truth. Prior to that, Stanley had spent afternoons in loading up Ted with all he knew, after which Ted would spend the following mornings briefing Ben Franklyn so that Franklyn could report it. This struck Stanley as terribly roundabout, since in this particular case he was the person most familiar with what was going on.

But Ted, as usual, had a perfectly logical explanation for it. "Those people on the Task Force," he reasoned, "are important men, very busy. They don't have time to listen personally to every project report. By the time it gets to them, it has to be down to the bare essentials—crisp and hard-hitting. You know what I mean. If everyone working on a project went to those meetings, things would get out of hand." But Stanley remembered, Ted distinctly had told him that he would eventually meet with this important group.

Now, a year later, Stanley had just had his crack at the Task Force. For weeks he'd worked on his presentation, complete with rehearsals—five dry runs on his series of flip charts. Ted had cautioned him that he would be up in front of the sharpest people in The Company, that they don't hesitate to ask pointed, even embarrassing questions. Stanley would have to anticipate the questions, know all the answers, have his talk down cold. Above all he should not drag out his presentation. Those guys have no sympathy for wasted time.

"Well, what happened?"

"I'm not sure that anything *happened*." Stanley looked downcast. "Here's how it went: first of all, you know how they hold those Task Force meetings—out away from everything—no distractions at all. This one was at an offseason ski resort in the Poconos. So I arrive about eleven in the morning, and the place is still pretty well deserted. They've got this suite of rooms on the second floor, so up I go. The room they use for the meetings is really messy, and a couple of guys I recognize—plant managers—are having coffee at a table. In comes the Paducah Plant Manager.

"He looks a little sick. Something he ate, maybe. One of the guys at the table gives him the elbow and says "Hey, Kenny! What'd Bill take you for last night anyway? He's some player, huh? I figure that's another pair of galoshes on your expense account after that one!" The plant manager, Kenny they call him, goes over and cracks something about this cocktail waitress. I didn't hear much, but he's really laying it on this other guy.

"Well, what the hell, it's the third day of the meeting, and my report is about the last thing on the agenda. Why *shouldn't* they play some poker? They've been working hard. They've got to blow off some steam. I'm scheduled to make my pitch that afternoon, then the meeting is going to break up. If they're going to relax a bit, I suppose this is the time for it. They've probably gotten most of the important work done already.

"The meeting starts a little late; they can't find a couple of Task Force members. But finally I start my talk. The plant manager from Paducah does nothing but drink tomato juice and look sick. About every fifteen minutes somebody says, "Let's break for a minute or two," and then they disappear for a half hour. One guy keeps going out to the telephone, turns out that he runs his plant single-handed and the place falls apart in his absence.

"But I keep plugging away and finally finish my report, flip charts and all. By now two guys are almost asleep and Kenny from Paducah is into his second pitcher of tomato juice. This is because Bill, who I don't think looks much better than the rest of them, has been taking half of it. So I ask for questions. Okay, the guy from Portland doesn't understand one of my charts. I explain it to him, and when I finish, it turns out I've confused another guy, who thought he understood it the first time around, but isn't sure now.

"Then this guy from Plant Operations staff asks why I haven't taken account of the five-year forecasts New York sent around earlier this year. But my whole point is what those forecasts mean for what the Task Force is doing! This guy hasn't listened to the first thing I've said—not that he's the only one. Keep cool, Stan, I say to myself. So I try my best to go back diplomatically and rehash what I'd said earlier. And now the plant operations guy breaks in and says, 'Son, you'd better do your homework. Those forecasts say a lot about what we're doing here. If you can't talk about *them,* why, why'd you bother to come up here in the first place?' And then Ted pipes up, 'I'm afraid Bill's got a point, Stanley!' Jesus! Ted knows what I'm doing all along, and he knows damn well that I've answered Bill's question, and a few more besides. And here he is putting me on the spot.

"Then, just as I'm about to try again to make my point clear, there's another coffee break and everybody runs off to the bathroom or the phone or the bar. Half an hour later most of them come back and talk about the cocktail waitress again for a while. You know, I finally got a look at her, and in the daylight. I don't know what the fuss was about. Then the meeting adjourned; or, at least, they sent me home.

"So what I want to know is: with guys like that running The Company, how come we're still in business?'"

How come? Well, at least one reason is that the men running The Company are no different from the men who run organizations throughout the nation. Stanley's observation is that the members of the Task Force are not extraordinary men. But neither are they ordinary men, for after all, it takes talent and acumen to reach top management. It is just that Stanley's expectations of them are overinflated.

The difficulty is that Stanley has gained admission to the Men's Hut too soon, in the wrong context and before he has had sufficient preparation. Had Stanley been with The Company longer he would have seen some things more clearly, would have had a more realistic idea of how things actually work. And, most important, he would have had a greater investment in the system—an investment that would help him see things in a different light. For this is the crux of Stanley's problem. Admission to the Men's Hut ordinarily comes only after a long period of waiting, a period during which the initiate gradually builds an investment in things as they are. By the time he is admitted he has paid his dues, as it were, and is committed to the system and its perpetuation. Consequently he finds that the other, older members of the Men's Hut are people not much different from himself. Obviously, they are there on the basis of merit, just as himself.

And so the customary procedure of subordinates briefing superiors, who in turn brief their own superiors, who only then carry the message to executive councils is not so foolish as it seems in the eyes of youth. "The Management" of The Company is symbolic as much as it is real. The social order of an organization depends at least in some degree on the imputation of special and extraordinary abilities to those in charge. This myth provides an unassailable answer to the question continually asked by Stanleys throughout The Company, "Why should we do it this way?"

Now, the Task Force is in large part another ritual of the Men's Hut. Their project is important, but things in The Company are so arranged that nothing and no one is really indispensible. The work involved could be done by fewer, more junior people, and the people who are working on it certainly had better things to do with their time. But again, the Task Force is symbolic. It requires the prestige of top men, and for the participants it is partly duty, partly a reward. It is right that Stanley should have taken his own part in it seriously—for that is his proper place in such things. Yet had he been in the system longer, he would have had a truer appreciation of the meaning of the event. To put it another way, don't be overanxious to take your place in the Men's Hut. Each thing in its season.

9

THE ROPES TO KNOW (I)

So Stanley has been taken through the first stages of his career in The Company and had a glimpse, at least, of the Men's Hut. Several significant occasions have arisen, and we have learned a thing or two about our actors. Let's look back for a moment and inquire into the meaning of these events.

Stanley has done some things that seem silly, but he has also caught the moment once or twice. His basic difficulty is that he has just begun his socialization into the microcosm of society that is The Company. No, he doesn't recognize ritual occasions for what they are, and he can't tell myth from reality.

As a boy Stanley would wonder at the awesome process of American democracy that somehow managed to find the best, the *very* best man in the country for the presidency—a necessary feat considering that it is the top office of the country. Political reality and the mass media have since disabused him of that particular myth, but Stanley is still capable of having the same feeling for Mr. Marsh. And in The Company there aren't allegedly knowledgeable Democrats or Republicans to tell you what "Marsh is really doing," or that he's the one directly responsible for the fact that we've fallen way behind in this or that race. No, the only ones who can know that are the other top people, and there's no way Stanley will ever talk to them—except at The Company Picnic.

To put it another way, Stanley has learned to translate the rhetoric of politicians—even the President of the USA—into its real meaning, but in his first years with The Company he is unable to do the same thing with the noble statements of Mr. Marsh and his fellow top managers. Neither can he comprehend Company ritual, the acting out of things as they should be/are.

But, you say, if The Company doesn't mean it, if it's not true, why does it go on? And if it's the buncombe you say it is, then why do the employees of The Company put up with it? The answer is quite simple. First of all, some don't, and they are probably the worse off for it. But the real answer lies in the great capacity of the human species for the construction of private reality. Or, as the social psychologists instruct us, the relief of "cognitive dissonance."[3] The Employees want The Company to be something it isn't and can't be. And in their own way they know this, but the acting out helps. Yes, Mr. Marsh does know all his people. "How are you today . . . ah . . . Bonnie?" The picnic is The Company as extended family.

And, "Sometimes I get the feeling that no one here really cares about me as a person—I mean, does any one in management really know what I'm doing?" Don't worry, Stanley, His eye is on the sparrow. We know, we know all our people. Company as community.

And, "There are times when I feel like I'm just a cog in this giant machine, grinding away at my little part, with nothing to say about the things that really matter." "Oh, the Suggestion Box? But does . . . ? Mr. Marsh does? Mr. Marsh personally answers some of those!" Company as democracy.

The dissonance, cognitively speaking, has two basic sources: the first of these is reflected in the reasoning that runs—"If I'm a better than average person, then surely The Company must be a better than average company or I wouldn't be working here, would I?" The second line of reasoning is related: "I'm not running things in this better than average company, and it seems to me that what we're doing isn't very smart, but Mr. Marsh must know what he's doing, he wouldn't be where he is if he didn't, so it must be okay."

Victor Thompson, pointing to the desire of subordinates to justify deference to superiors provides this analysis.

> Incumbents of high office are held in awe because they are in touch with the mysteries and magic of such office . . . Since one knows less and less about the activities of superordinates the farther away in the hierarchy they are, the greater is the awe in which he holds them . . . The hierarchy is a highly restricted system of communication, with much information coming in to each position; but the amount sent out to subordinates . . . for strategic and other reasons is always limited. There results an increasing vagueness as to the activities at each level as one mounts the

hierarchy, and this vagueness supports the prestige ranking which we call the status system.[4]

This, of course, is the point in *The Men's Hut*.

Thus the big men are there, not because they are older and have been with The Company longer, but because they are wiser, with a well-publicized record of past accomplishments. Their trappings and general demeanor complement and bear witness to the rightness of position of Company people. And this, of course, will be the topic for analysis in the next part of this book. But for now it is sufficient to recognize that the ritual and myth, the quasi-religious mystery of The Company, all serve to bind-in employees and organization. The procedures of the Men's Hut help in this regard. Initiates are not privy to all secrets. But as loyalty and proper behavior become increasingly assured through accrual of privilege and status, the mysteries are revealed. And, certainly, human experience has shown that being sole possessor of something silly and trivial is, of itself, neither silly nor trivial.

A final word for those of you who might suspect that the past paragraphs are not entirely earnest. Unquestionably it had become fashionable on the outside to laugh at The Company and its ways. Even Stanley found it hard to believe that, until recently, Company salesmen used to start the day with an institutional song. In fact, some years ago everyone in The Company did so. Hokey? You bet. But cynical, no, and likely born of the same kind of impulse that has lots of people unabashedly singing antiwar or ecology tunes in this and recent decades.

ENDNOTES

1. With regard to industry, and even the Yale Club, the winds of change are blowing, of course. Grudgingly, but steadily, males are conceding the place of females in the "men's hut."
2. Erving Goffman, *The Presentation of Self in Everyday Life.* (Garden City, N.Y.: Doubleday, 1959), p. 142.
3. Social psychologists use this term to describe the existence within an individual of conflicting views concerning some issue. The theory holds that individuals will change one or the other of these views to relieve such cognitive dissonance.
4. Victor Thompson, *Modern Organization* (New York: Knopf, 1961), p.70.

PART II

DE GUSTIBUS NON
DISPUTANDUM EST

Introduction to Part II

Epigrams sum the essence of human experience—a shorthand by which ancient and modern cultures succinctly express their collective wisdom. "De gustibus non disputandum est," "chacun à son goût," and "There's no accounting for taste" say precisely the same thing in three different tongues, and are uttered when their respective speakers are baffled by the speech, dress, or actions of others whom they expect to speak, dress, and behave differently from what we observe.

The principle being invoked is actually the *opposite* of that implied by the saying. In fact, there *is* a great deal of accounting for taste, and as social animals people are continually doing it. "Birds of a feather flock together" is more collective wisdom, and makes the point directly. And yet "you can't judge a book by its cover"—another expression used in ironic reference to an exception to common practice. Books are judged by their covers (usually accurately), but *this* time mistakenly.

Oh, this is all very interesting, but the point escapes you? Well, the point is this: people like predictability and dislike uncertainty. They want to know in advance what to expect and how to guide their own behavior. And they want to accomplish this with minimum effort. Consequently, generalizations are developed about others to help predict their behavior and as a guide to responding to them appropriately. These generalizations are based on a limited number of observable indicators, such as dress, speech, and manners, from which a much larger behavioral repertoire is then inferred.

That's a bit hard to digest? Then try some analogies from the physical world and the psychology of perception to illustrate perceptual filling in and distortion. A primary rule is that what you perceive—what registers on your consciousness—is not what you see or feel in the objective sense. You add to it, you patch it up, and you distort it to make it consistent with other perceptions or to accord with experience.

For example, you look far across a field and see a cow. It looks like a cow at a distance. Everything fits together. Your two-year-old daughter, however, unless she is being raised in a rural area, is quite likely to say, "Doggy." Why? Because she has not yet developed perceptual "size constancy" a process whereby we unconsciously adjust size perceptions to fit other perceptions. Color contrast and the relationship of object to field is another example. Suffice it to say that the French Impressionist painters understood why yellow looks green when surrounded by the proper combination of other colors. Finally, try this experiment on yourself. Rig up a series of five cylinders, say, cans of different sizes but like shapes, and load them so that their weights are identical. Now judge their weights subjectively, picking them up by an identical handle attached to the top of each. If you're like most everyone else, you will swear the big one is the lightest and the small one the heaviest. Why? Because unconsciously you expect the big one to weigh more and when it doesn't your perception is "less than it ought to" compared to "more than it ought to" for the small one. A context effect.

Yes, yes, don't be impatient. I'll get to the point, which is social perception. A well-known experiment in social psychology involves briefly showing a picture to participants in the experiment. In this picture a poorly dressed white man with a straight razor in one hand is making a threatening gesture at a well-dressed black man. After getting a quick look at the picture, the participants (all white) are asked to recall what they saw. What happens? Roughly half recall seeing the razor in the hand of a poorly dressed black threatening a well-dressed white.

The principle is simple. Brief exposure to the depicted social situation leaves the participant uncertain as to what he saw. Therefore, when asked to report the facts, he calls on accumulated facts, prejudices, and stereotypes to fill in and consequently arrive at a coherent (though erroneous) account of what was seen.

Now you're getting it? Yes. The fact is that in organizational life judgments about others have to be made that are woefully uninformed. We get to know few people well, expecially in large organizations with planned geographical mobility. Consequently, the facts do not always have a chance to "speak for themselves," and other bases of judgment are sought. More often than not the basis is in what Erving Goffman has termed the "presentation of self." And here is where speech, dress, and manner come in, and why symbols and symbolic activities are so important. The need for presentation of self in organizational life also explains why people attach so much importance to symbols of high status—the rug on the floor, the window, the corner office.

Thus, "impression management" becomes important in shaping relations among superiors and subordinates. Superiors project the image of the generalist, knowing the stuff of many specialties, but *only* enough to make the necessary decisions. The superior must display an appropriate sense of urgency. His manner must be crisp and hard hitting. Why, you ask? Because few know, and fewer still are able to judge, the work that has actually been done. Hence, the impression may be more important than the work activity itself. For their part, subordinates must project the image of restrained dependability; a willingness to learn and a recognition that simply doing the work is not nearly as important as providing the initial structure, making the decisions.

Of course, the kind of impression management talked about here is not limited to The Company. People everywhere dress, speak, and act in ways that they believe convey important facts about themselves. Thoroughly middle-class "Marxist" professors show up at conventions in blue denim shirts and jeans (solidarity with the workers). And you don't have to ask to find out who is, and who is not liberated. Various personal service workers affect the white smock—even optometrists, though the functional requirement of sterility is lacking.

But back to The Company. In the early days, when the systems clan was just getting established, the use of the letter K for thousand was a symbol of membership. (Most had a background in electronics, and that's how their myriad resistors are labelled.) Outsiders from personnel and elsewhere picked up the usage to show they belonged, to show they they understood the special problems of a systems organization.

But enough. The chapters that follow will illustrate the motives and consequences of impression management—the dramaturgy of The Company. Symbols, actions, dress, and speech provide cues for our actors, and their script is a common basis of socialization within The Company. Your task, reader, will be to bear in mind the principles just set forth as we now illustrate the presentation of self within The Company.

10

LOOK OF A WINNER

Looking up from my typewriter I see that it has begun to snow. A bitter nor'easter is swirling in over the harbor, kicking up puffs of foam. A good day to be indoors, I think.

But there are some of us not so lucky as to have the choice—Stanley, for one. So it was on a day just like this one, some years ago now, that he had one of his earliest instructive experiences. Stanley had been with The Company for just several months. New experiences were cascading over him, many of them difficult to evaluate. On such occasions he would seek out his former mentor, Dr. Faust—consultant to The Company—and ask for interpretation. Faust, for his part, seemed to enjoy the role.

"It all started out innocently enough, I suppose," reflected Stanley. "I was in New York for a week to go to this 'systems procedures' seminar for all new plant people. One day it was really cold, windy, just miserable weather. The warmest thing I had was this old Army overcoat and headgear, but I figured, What the hell, who cares what you look like for one day? So I walk into the Headquarters building where this seminar is being given, and the first thing I know this older guy gives me this fishy look. Then he says, 'Can I help you. Who do you want to see?' So I say, 'It's okay, I work here.' While we're waiting for the elevator you can see him kind of working up to something, and finally he says, '*You* work for The Company?'

"I tell him I do, and then after a while he says, 'Don't you think it's a little risky to dress that way?'

"Now I'm starting to get the picture. But even if I didn't, as we ride up the elevator he gives it to me in detail. 'People in The Company don't dress that way,' he says, 'and if you ever want to get anywhere son, you'd better think it over and change your ways.'"

"Interesting," said Faust, puffing as always on his pipe, "I suppose he was one of the old timers." "I don't know," replied Stanley, "but wait, I'm not finished yet. I go up to the seminar room and take off my coat. Now I've got on this wool checked shirt, you know the kind. No room for a jacket under the overcoat, and just a shirt and tie isn't warm enough, so I've got this shirt on.

"Things go okay until we break up into work groups. Everybody introduces himself and someone says to me, 'Where do you work, Stan?' So I say, 'The Company, just like you.' The guy says, 'Come on, you're kidding me. *You* work for The Company?'

"Now he's a young guy, but he sounds just like the older guy. So he starts laughing, I mean uncontrollably. Then he says, 'Hey, this guy works for The Company, he really does, can you believe it?'

"Well, this breaks them all up. They all sit there, sort of pointing their fingers at me and saying, '*He* works for *The Company!*'

"I won't drag it out any longer, but what I want to know is what the hell do *they* care? How come they get so excited about something like that?"

Faust paused to ensure that Stanley was indeed through. Then, repeating the obvious he said, "Yes, they *do* care . . . But don't misunderstand, they weren't mocking you. They simply were amazed.

"Why should they be amazed?" Faust continued, giving words to the thought that had formed in Stanley's mind. "They were amazed because they have never seen anything quite like that before."

Faust puffed his pipe in silence for a moment to give proper emphasis to his next metaphor; then he went on.

"They were amazed in the same sense as the savage who has just seen the violation of an ancient taboo without visitation of the promised retribution by the gods. It is amazing and a little frightening, and suggests also that the one committing the violation may just be a bit special. Beyond this I can't really *explain* anything more to you except by way of example."

Stanley prepared himself for one of Faust's Socratic exercises. "Now consider this situation and tell me what you think is going on," said Faust. "Think carefully about it, and tell me why you retain or discard the possible explanations."

Faust went on to describe a meeting involving a dozen or so lower and middle management people at The Plant. They were working out a long-range manufacturing automation strategy that had great consequence for the entire Company. All were suitably attired (coats and ties) save one. This one had on an old, faintly grease-stained flannel shirt, with sleeves rolled up to elbows, consequently exhibiting a muscular pair of forearms.

"Well?"

Stanley thought. "I guess you want me to account for the guy in the flannel shirt," he replied.

"Precisely," Faust puffed slowly.

"It wasn't just that he didn't have time to change, because then you wouldn't have asked me to explain it."

Faust nodded in acknowledgment.

"And I guess since they're all management people he'd have to know better."

Another nod.

"Does he dress this way all the time?"

"Almost invariably, except when he travels to New York."

"Then he's trying to prove something?"

"That is essentially the question I have posed for you, not the answer," Faust intoned.

"Okay, okay. Then he's advertising that he's something special. But what? Yeah. It's that he's not *just another* middle management guy. He's something else, and more."

Faust gave no visible encouragement but Stanley felt he was getting somewhere.

"Yeah, the grease . . . the arms. Here's a guy that not only knows management, but knows The Company right where it lives, the manufacturing floor. Gets along with the men, too. I'll bet." Stanley could hardly contain himself as new inferences raced through his head.

"Go on."

"He's so good that he doesn't have to give a damn about wearing a stuffy old shirt and tie, except when he goes to New York . . . and that's good, too, because that way he gets to show that he can suit up when he wants to." Stanley actually felt himself developing a deep admiration for this phantom of his imagination. "Now I'll bet . . . ."

"Enough, enough." Faust held up his hands. "You now feel that you know this fellow don't you? And I've told you almost nothing about him. You, yourself, have supplied the details through logic and deduction. And so, of course, do all the others. This is the point I wished you to see."

Faust continued, "You must understand that none of us knows another very well, and especially in organizations such as The Company. We continually call on our store of knowledge about the world, and our sense of what is, and what is not, reasonable in order to interpret what is going on about us.

"We seem to have a need for consistency that compels us to come up with reasons for what appears at first to be unreasonable. So each will create for himself a phantom endowed with qualities and capabilities to fit the image received.

"That is part of the answer to why your friends got so excited about your appearance. Each believes that The Company is a superior company and fittingly hires superior people—and, by George, they ought to *look* that way."

"I understand," said Stanley. "But let's get back to your example. If what you say is true, then why doesn't *everybody* manufacture an image for himself?"

"They do," said Faust enigmatically.

"Now, wait a minute, you said . . . ."

"No, *you* wait a minute." Dr. Faust punctuated his command with a thrust of his pipe stem at Stanley. "And think before you talk. I said that everyone presents an image to others that is to some extent calculated and shaped. In large measure these presentations of self are consistent and raise few questions. Managers look like managers, workers like workers, and so on. I presented an extreme case—ah—for heuristic purposes."

"No, what I meant was, since there seems to be some advantage in it, why doesn't everybody pretend to be something he isn't?"

"When did I say anything about pretense?"

"Sure you . . . ," Stanley caught himself. "I mean, isn't this guy pretending to be something he isn't?"

"Did I say that?" The tone of Faust's query conveyed the answer. "What I pointed out, quite simply, was only that *you*, not I nor he, had supplied the details as to his status in The Company, his ability, his social relations with the mill hands, and the like. In fact, I doubt if any pretense is involved, as I understand the word. Obviously, this man is acting out something he *wants* to be. And I doubt that this could be done convincingly through sheer calculation. Even the complete charlatan at one level of his consciousness must believe that, indeed, he *is* a doctor or psychologist or whatnot." Faust was no longer speaking directly to Stanley.

"After all, in an existential sense, which of us knows what he *really* is. Which is more real, what we pretend we are, what we think we are, what we are afraid we are, what others think we are? . . ."

Faust suddenly remembered Stanley and returned from the cosmic realm to the situation at hand.

"No, I don't think this is consciously calculated behavior, quite the opposite. I am quite sure that this fellow would not be able to articulate what he was doing. His pattern, his display has more or less evolved because it 'feels right,' and because he likes the things that happen to him in this mode. He likes the questions people ask, the inferences that they draw. What they make of him is what he wants to be. And who are we to deny that this is what he really *is*?"

11

FRIDAY GO TO MEETIN'

Ted strode by briskly wearing his best urgent/serious look.

"This is the big one," he was telling a compatriot, "we're down to the crunch, systemswise. New York is going to be asking some pretty pointed questions soon, so we've got to get our ducks lined up."

As Ted moved on, Stanley thought, "What *now*? What's the big crisis *this* week?" By all appearances Ted's career is strung together from a never-ending series of crucial events, much as beads on a loop of string. He moves from one to the next, incidentally making the most of each by getting to know the right people on a first-name basis.

Ted is also the office Stakhanovite, a model for capitalist emulation. He is there when you get there, there when you leave, and there when you don't have to be. This has always puzzled Stanley, for to his way of looking at things, the office is an undesirable place to be, dreary and generally depressing. And there is nothing that Ted has to do on the average work day that couldn't be handled in, say, three or four hours of honest application. The fact is that Ted spends most of the day wandering around socializing.

Stanley's musings end temporarily as he arrives at Ben Franklyn's office. He has been assigned to pull together the facts for Ted, who will then edit and rearrange them ("massaging" the facts, Ted calls it). And Ben has some of the crucial facts.

"This is another one of those Things That Can't Wait, is it?" Ben growled. "Let me tell you something, son. I've been with The Company for twenty-six years now, and there's something for the life of me that I'll never understand. We *never* seem to have the time or money to do it right in the first place, but we *always* seem to have whatever it takes to bail us ou when we get in trouble. I don't understand why in hell we can't . . . ."

Ben, obviously primed to talk, is interrupted by the phone.

"Mr. Mason for you, Mr. Franklyn," Bonnie calls in. (Marshall Mason is Assistant Plant Manager for Plant Manufacturing Automation.) "There is? . . . Tonight you say . . . uh, today's Friday. No, I won't be able to make it. I promised my family I would take them to church tonight . . . . Yes, I do understand that . . . .No, I don't need to think it over . . . . Yes, I know, I *do* accept that." Ben is now holding the phone about three inches from his ear. "How about first thing Monday?. . .Oh c'mon, you know better than that . . . . Well, I can do this. If you're still in session, I can make it by eleven . . . . No? Not good enough?. . . No. No, you won't."

If Stanley could have heard both sides, here is what he would have learned. First, Mason (basically a staff-type like Ted Shelby) is preparing for the witchhunt brewing in New York (more staff-types of the Corporate variety). So he's called a meeting of all involved management the soonest he can. Because of other commitments this turns out to be 8 o'clock Friday evening. Franklyn (through his secretary) had already told Mason's secretary that he cannot make it.

No good. So Mason personally "gets on the horn" to put the squeeze on Ben—to "communicate his sense of urgency." But Ben isn't buying. To him this is just more staff nonsense whipped up by people who don't have any real work to do. They can't do anything over the weekend anyway, so why not wait until Monday A.M.?

Mason isn't used to this. After all, management is a seven-days-a-week, twenty-four-hours-a-day proposition. "We're always on call. That's what it takes to keep The Company a step ahead." So he tells Ben to think it over and call him back in a half hour. Presumably, with a little time to ponder it Ben will come to realize the enormity of his refusal and will come in with the right report. But actually Mason is upping the level of implied threat and providing a face-saving mechanism for capitulation (think it over and call me back). Ben counters with his own proposal to be there by eleven o'clock. Presumably Mason, therefore, will understand that Ben is not just avoiding his duty and will accept this proposal as sufficient. But again, in reality what is being done is that Ben is providing Mason with a face-saving way of backing off, a symbol of submission, "turning the neck." And now Mason isn't buying, so finally, "No, that's not good enough. We've got to have your input. See you tonight at eight." This last followed by Ben's refusal.

Well now, what is going on here? A battle of wills? Dereliction of duty? Possibly. But mostly what has been witnessed is symbolic rather than real. And Mason (who really isn't such a bad fellow) is probably more astonished than anything else. He's got himself into this situation because it never occurred to him that Ben would flatly and finally refuse. In his eighteen years with The Company, from staff trainee on up, he had *never* seen anyone in a responsible management position refuse to attend an important meeting for personal reasons.

Ted's reaction also is revealing. Stanley had left Ben's office with the information and is now with Ted getting an item by item rundown.

"But I don't have a good grasp of what this means for us manufacturingwise, Stanley. It's not clear how we're supposed to interface on this one . . . .Well, we don't have time to work it out now. I'll toss the ball to Ben tonight."

"Uh, if you mean Mr. Franklyn, well—uh, I've got an idea he isn't going to be at your meeting tonight."

"Where did you get a crazy idea like that? Of course he'll be there, he's got to be! We've all got to be right on top of this thing."

"Uh, it might be a good idea to call him, Ted."

Ted did and found out for himself.

"Can you beat that, he isn't going! And there's a lesson for *you*, Stan. Have you ever wondered why after twenty-six years Franklyn hasn't made it beyond mill superintendent?" (Of course, he hadn't. From where Stanley stood Ben's job looked impressive enough.) "He's got no sense of urgency, that's why. The people who make it to the top in this Company are the people who are always willing to give a little more than the next one: the Marshes, the Masons (. . .the Shelbys. Ted's look said it for him). These people care about The Company, and The Company takes care of them."

No, it is not possible to understand what goes on in The Company without an appreciation of the difference between the symbolic and the actual. Symbolic acts communicate a great deal. How does anyone know that Ted Shelby is a hotshot young manager? After all, few people ever get to see what he actually does. Well, there are *ways*.

"That young Shelby, a real comer. Right on the top of things, you can bet. Many a time I've thought I closed the building down, but Shelby's still there hammering away at it." And . . . .

"I'd feel better if we got on it right away, sir. Dollarwise we're not talking a whole lot, but I like to treat The Company's money as I would my own. How about this evening; we can grab a bite in the cafeteria and get right on it . . . if that's okay with *you*, Mr. Mason."

Dedication, zest for work, a sense of urgency—these are management qualities. But they are difficult qualities to display with actual work, for the simple reason that in most cases the actual work does not require them. That is why these attributes must be displayed symbolically by the management aspirant. Oddly though, as careers mature, the distinction between symbolic and actual may blur and fade. With added responsibilities, the evening and weekend sessions actually become necessary, if only symbolically.

12

THE SINCEREST FORM OF FLATTERY

In his early days with The Company Stanley moved around quite a lot. He had started at Pawtucket, gone on to New York, then to Portland, and finally to Portsmouth to be involved in building and modernizing some new facilities. Company policy held that the operating management of the new facilities should be in on the construction phase, and so it happened that Stanley first came to work for Kerry Drake.

Drake is an interesting character. Totally dedicated to The Company, sincere and blasphemous, a stickler for detail and totally intolerant of incompetence, Kerry is capable of being both very human and unreasonably inhumane to his subordinates. Yet Kerry had a kind of charisma based in his technical competence, his obvious sincerity, and his dedication to the job. The self-image he liked to project can be summed in two of his favorite slogans: "You have to fire a man a week to keep a healthy organization," and "I don't have time to separate the unfortunate from the incompetent." In point of fact, however, he seldom fired anyone (transferring them instead to a "more suitable opportunity"), and he put a great deal of effort toward winnowing the unfortunate from the incompetent.

Kerry also took care of his boys—and occasional girls. If you worked out with Kerry your next step would be a big step forward. People in management who knew Kerry knew that his people would have the right attitude and could do the job. Kerry was not one to suffer fools lightly.

And so it was that early on Stanley came under the sway of Kerry Drake as one of his assistants at the Portsmouth construction site. Kerry had a substantial management position with The Company, and Stanley was just a beginner, but the construction group was small enough that Stanley and Kerry worked closely together. Also, quite typically Kerry didn't give a damn if you were a V.P. or a sweeper. If you worked for him, you worked. Honest mistakes were okay (to some extent) but woe to the one who erred by oversight, sloppiness, or lack of application.

This was quite a heady situation for Stanley. His daydreams were visions of rapid progress to the upper echelons of Company management, and in these visions Stanley the Executive bears an uncanny resemblance to Kerry Drake. No, not in looks—but in manner, grit, determination, and unbounded intolerance of folly. Yes. That is the way it should be.

Occasions that one would expect to dampen this enthusiasm had quite the opposite effect. For example, in one such situation Stanley was Company spokesman in bid negotiations with a group of contractors. His responsibility was for presenting construction specifications to the assembled group and answering questions that arose. Typically, Kerry let his people do this while he observed how things were going.

"Finally, the successful bidder will have the responsibility for restoring all sites to grade, with backfill in accordance with specs as described in Section One. Questions, gentlemen?"

Quite pleased with his success thus far, Stanley awaited the next challenge.

"It says here on page twenty-one that under no circumstances will contractors be allowed to use substitutes for expandrium fittings. Under *no* circumstances? Will you guarantee availability?"

Stanley's answer was crisp and to the point. "Gentlemen, the specs are clear enough here. I don't believe anything is left to guesswork. And, I believe, the specs are quite clear on the issue of whose responsibility it is for the purchase of materials." (Quite right, the contractor.)

"Say, I have something maybe you could clear up for me," said another, pointing to a stack of blueprints on the table, "these gizmos here are blacked in on the drawing while these aren't. Otherwise they look the same to me. Does it mean anything? I don't think so but I want to be sure."

Stanley thought a moment before answering. Fact is, he'd never noticed that before. It looked as if the draftsman had colored some in just to give the idea, but didn't want to waste the time doing all of them. Sure, that was it. Stanley no sooner conveyed this intelligence to the assembled group of contractors than Kerry was on his feet gesturing wildly.

"No, that is *not* so! Gentlemen, this young man doesn't know what the hell he is talking about." And turning to Stanley after a brief explanation of what it did mean, "Keep your goddamned mouth shut when you don't know what the hell you are talking about. It's that kind of goddamned fool talk that can cost The Company money."

End of quote.

You, of course, need no elaboration as to Stanley's feelings at that point. But was this the end of Stanley's admiration for Kerry? Not at all! Kerry was absolutely right. No place for that kind of thing in The Company. And that was the way to handle it, too. No nonsense. A promptly administered kick in the ass would serve the memory well. The fact was that half consciously and half not, Stanley's behavior in all respects came more closely to resemble Kerry's.

Oddly, the results obtained were somewhat different. When Stanley sat down with the electricians and the "mechanical people" to knock heads together, well, somehow nothing happened. And after a few months Stanley himself noticed that no one paid particular attention to his edicts. Somehow injunctions from Stanley, such as "you people said next week, and next week it's going to be. And if you can't bring it off, well, we'll just have to get someone in here who can. We don't have time to separate the unfortunate from the incompetent!" just didn't bring results.

Months passed and mercifully, Stanley toned down. Actually, he became absorbed in the details of the work he was responsible for, and started to become quite good at it. Kerry was around less, traveling to various locations to pick up the "latest thinking," and consequently was less of an influence. And so the time was at hand for Stanley to understand what had happened.

"Little Kerry." Yes, over the previous year Stanley had been dubbed "little Kerry" by the entire crew—and not by way of admiration. You see, Kerry himself wasn't exactly loved by his counterparts and coworkers in other divisions of The Company. But he had the authority of office and, more to the point, he was just about always right in technical matters, so he had their respect. Furthermore, you didn't get one of Kerry's "treatments" unless he was sure that you were wrong. And you probably knew it too.

The upshot of all this is that Stanley's presentation of self had been entirely inappropriate and had, in fact, served as a focal point for the resentment engendered by Kerry. And "little Kerry" was a legitimate target. Stanley didn't have the rank or expertise (or, let's fact it, the grey hair) to pull off Kerry's act.

The lesson: Presentation of self is important, *but* the message must be plausible. Even the *best* method actor is to some extent limited by the materials with which he must work—that is, himself.

13

BY YOUR WORKS SHALL YE BE KNOWN

"Mr. Marsh's office will need this by Tuesday, Stanley. So you've got to get right on it. We've got to be sure The Company is doing its best to properly compensate our top contributors."

Ted's manner was fittingly important/urgent as he explained to Stanley what was needed on his special assignment.

"These people are the backbone of The Company's technical thrust," Ted explained. "Each one has been nominated as an outstanding technical contributor by his own top management. So naturally Mr. Marsh wants to make sure that they are being compensated ('paid,' Stanley translated to himself) appropriately."

Ted departed, leaving Stanley with a list of twenty-one outstanding contributors and the assignment to unearth the personnel data necessary to determine whether or not the people corresponding to the names on the list were being "appropriately compensated"—whatever that might mean.

It did not take Stanley very long to find out what those words *did* mean, and mostly by contrary example. For here was an outstanding contributor who was given only a C rating by his manager in his last performance review. (The Company's merit rating system ran A, B, C, D, and out, not unlike those used in the school systems through which Stanley had passed.) Another was rated B by his manager—not bad but not outstanding—with summary comments appended by his manager

49

indicating that the man needed to improve his technical skills to qualify for his next promotion. And then there were other cases, those who in fact were rated A but who, if they really *were* outstanding contributors, were underpaid by anyone's standards. Stanley pondered the situation for a while and came to a conclusion: "Something's wrong here."

Since the day that Stanley had been given his pass through the rear door in the mill loading dock, he felt quite free to consult Ben on puzzling bits of Company business—which this was. It took some delicacy to explain what was going on, for Ben Franklyn was a Company loyalist. He is not eager to accept evidence of error, especially when it comes to top management ("they wouldn't be where they are if they didn't know what was going on"). But yes, there did seem to be something wrong here.

"I don't understand this, son. You know, each one of these people was picked first by his own manager. That guy *had* to know what was going on. Then the nominations from each department go to the group manager, and he picks two or three from that list and sends them up to the plant manager. And the plant manager is supposed to pick the one or two best people from *that* list and send them on to New York. In that way we get one or two from every plant and so you wind up with these twenty-one people. But *my* guy isn't on this list."

"Well, uh—I can understand that," Stanley said brightly, "maybe he wasn't picked."

"No, no," growled Ben, "listen, I mean the guy on this list works for me all right, but he isn't the guy *I* picked."

"Why not?" Stanley most definitely has a genius for the unnecessary question. By now his usual bright red, Ben looked as though he doesn't even hear that one, but—

"For Christsakes how the hell should *I* know! If I had anything to say about it, *he* (Ben stabbed his finger accusingly at the list) sure as hell wouldn't be there."

At this juncture discretion seemed the better part of valor, and Stanley managed to escape Mr. Franklyn's office. Perhaps Bonnie might have some idea, since she knew just about everyone.

"What do you know about this guy, Bonnie, this A. Sayles Barker? Mr. Franklyn says he works here."

"Oh, Al," it was not a question, "everyone knows Al Barker. Honestly, he's the nicest guy. And he knows all the big words. He always helps us with our letters and things. And he's going to be something in The Company some day, too. You just *know* it by looking at him. And you know . . . ."

From what followed Stanley is able to construct part of the story. And through subsequent consultations with second and third level staff people (the "assistants to") he is able to piece together the rest. The process by which you become an outstanding contributor—at least for some—is this.

The first level managers, the ones on the firing line, have a pretty good sense of who their technical hotshots are. Oh, they don't always have an outstanding contributor, but they almost always nominate someone. After all, they want to give one of their own people at least a shot at it. These names are then sent up to the group manager (next level). He is a little farther from the action, but still pretty knowledgeable. Now he knocks off the obvious weak ones and sends maybe one, two, or three names to the division manager (next level), who isn't quite so knowledgeable. Same process there, and then on up to the Plant Manager who isn't knowledgeable at all. The Plant Manager then okays one, possibly two names, and these are sent to New York to appear on the final list.

Now, what Stanley found was that it is these last two stops, Division and Plant, where the process goes awry. The names that reach Division level are usually, though not always, those of quiet, competent, technical citizens known only to their own managers, and, through an occasional flash of brilliance, to other quiet, competent technicians. But at the upper levels, different criteria are brought to bear by managers, whose different responsibilities necessitate a different perspective. And so it is that the scenario runs about like this:

Barker's no dummy, make no mistake about that, but he isn't, and doesn't even *want* to be, a top technical man. Like anyone with sense, he wants to get into top management some day, and most likely will. He's good with words, makes a good appearance, and has poise. He knows how to make his point and isn't easily flustered.

Now these are ideal qualities for the person who will make the technical presentation—the omnipresent link of communication between the troops in the technical trenches and middle management. And who would you guess is worst at the Technical Presentation? Right. The technical man. He's not too good with words in the first place, but he's death with top management. After all, he doesn't give a damn about sales or dollars or market share or anything but the beautiful technical details—in *infinite* detail.

So Al Barker makes the presentations. He's got the style, enough of the facts, he's got the right answers, and he delivers well. Above all, he likes to do it, and he knows how to manage his presentation of self.

Now you're starting to see, are you? Sure. The Division Manager gets the list, looks it over and thinks, "Say, where's Al Barker?" Turns out Barker made a really top-notch (crisp and hard-hitting, in Ted's words) presentation yesterday.

"Well, that won't do. This fellow's got to be one of our real comers. Let's see, he's in Ben's outfit isn't he? Uh, I'll just cross off this Gregor

Mendel, whoever he is, and put in Barker. Yes sir, he's a real comer. Wonder how Ben missed him?"

And so with this process taking place again at the next level, and throughout The Company, the result is inevitable.

Why is it inevitable, you say? It is inevitable because of who is involved. These top and middle managers have been away from the technical firing line for a long time. They don't have the same perspective any more, if they ever did in the first place. In any event, their role now is to make decisions about alternative programs based on a broad set of criteria, one of which is technical excellence. They are busy people (at least to their way of thinking) and don't have the time or inclination to be buried under an avalanche of detail. They want the necessary facts, answers to a few key questions, and a balanced (again from the management perspective) presentation. So Al Barker strikes a resonant chord. He's "got his head screwed on right."

The problem, you see, is that it's one thing for Marsh's office to say, let's make up a list of our outstanding contributors and quite another to do it. As with any complex judgment, the facts simply do *not* speak for themselves. More to the point, it is even far from clear what facts, or *whose* facts, to use. And after the facts are selected according to one set of criteria, they are then judged on the basis of *different*, though equally valid, criteria.

What makes it at the outset seem deceptively simple is the existence of one or two individuals, those one-in-a-million, who have it all or who have produced something of unquestionable genius *and* at the right time. But the problem is that they *are* one-in-a-million. And so the ultimate judgment comes to rest with top management who, consciously or unconsciously, like to see a little "balance" in their technical people.

The net result? As usual, the quiet, competent technician gets passed over and the one with the management flair, the one with the look of a winner, comes out on top again.

14

BETTER THE
DEVIL YOU KNOW . . .

"How ya doin', Kerry? How's Bette and the kids?"

"Not too bad, I suppose. How's y'self? Still trying to break eighty?"

The initial meeting of the Portsmouth Plant manufacturing staff group was being convened in New York—a group selected from various company locations which was getting together for the first time. As *The Company Clarion* put it in a recent feature story:

> The manufacturing staff team put together for the Portsmouth effort represents the very best of The Company in this area. New York wanted the top people regardless of current responsibilities, so the new staff team represents many of our plants and facilities—a *Company* team . . . .

The story went on to describe the team members and their previous responsibilities, with special emphasis on the expertise and representativeness of the individuals selected.

The Company is a big company and a growing one—which means, of course, that it is also a successful one. Growth comes from expansion of existing plants and facilities and the construction of new ones. Growth also means the expansion of management opportunities for people within The Company, for, quite typically, the policy is to promote from within. Finally, growth means that every two to three years you will be moved on to a new management opportunity at least several hundred miles away.

Stanley knows all this. Consequently he is suprised to find that of the roughly dozen or so people here, (a) most of them know one another, and pretty well ("How's Bette and the kids"/"still trying to break eighty") and (b) don't *really* seem, in all instances, to represent the "best thinking of The Company in the area." This last observation is based on Stanley's estimate of his own abilities and his opinion of Ted.

As the meeting continues the initial impression is strengthened and other anomalies appear.

"I think you're right, Kerry," Ted was saying, "the way we handled it at Paducah is the right idea, with a little more sophistication systemswise."

"Leave the systems aspect to Sheila, will you, Ted? That was the one angle we had whipped in Pawtucket. We need *you* in training."

And so it goes.

Kerry, it turns out, is on his fifth or sixth assignment for The Corporate Director heading the team. He's worked for other people, but sure enough, every other year or so the now Corporate Director moves up; so does Kerry. And the same with Sheila, and now Ted.

For his part, Dr. Faust had Kerry in his Middle Management Advanced Study Course at The University for four months. And Stanley, of course, has been Faust's graduate assistant.

On the operating side things aren't much different. Ben Franklyn, the new plant manager, has worked with Robbie, his manufacturing manager, at four locations, and Bill, Robbie's Chief of Expandrium Operations, has been with Robbie off and on since he was recruited from Another University ten years ago.

Among the anomalies are the fact that Bill probably wouldn't know an Expandrium pellet if he had it for lunch (he had been plucked from maintenance engineering at Portland) and that Kerry really didn't seem to think all that much of Ted's ability.

Mulling over the situation and its apparent contradictions with both the story in *The Company Clarion* and the genuine importance accorded the project by executive management, Stanley cautiously approached Dr. Faust.

"Uh, it strikes me as kind of funny that most of these guys know each other so well. You know what I mean?" Faust's facial expression answered that he did not.

"I mean, if this group has been selected *individually* to get our best people from all the plants—uh—isn't it kind of funny how they all know each other so well . . . . And isn't it kind of funny that some of them—uh —well, they really don't seem to *know* very much about the new Expandrium process, either."

Faust puffed on his pipe noncommittally. "I think that you will find the group assembled here to be entirely adequate to do the job," Faust intoned finally.

"Swell," thought Stanley. And then, throwing caution (which God knows he has little enough of) to the wind, "C'mon, Doc, you know what I mean. I really think these guys picked each other as sort of a personal favor, not because they were the best for the job."

Faust thought a minute and then decided that no particular harm would be done by answering Stanley's query. As usual, Stanley seemed to have the facts but to have missed the point.

"Hmmm, yes, you are right. But no, you are wrong. You are right that all these people have worked for one another on numerous occasions previously, and that it is not by chance that they are here as a group today. In fact, *you* (pipe stem pointed accusingly) are not here by chance today.

"But you are wrong in thinking that because of this these people are not best for the job. True, some know very little of Expandrium processing, but they know a great deal about one another."

Stanley's facial expression posed the obvious question.

"Why is that so important? I will tell you. These people have to work together as a team on a new and risky venture. This means that occasionally one must, ah, subordinate one's own interests or ideas for the good of the project. Now I *absolutely* guarantee you that the group made up of the top Expandrium processing experts in The Company will be incapable of doing this. Some simply will not fit in, will not be able to get along personally with others. But more to the point, it will take months, possibly years before they develop sufficient knowledge of one another, and hence trust, to be able to work together effectively. And that is just too long."

Dr. Faust paused to relight his pipe, then continued.

"I think it would be impossible for you to overestimate the importance of past relationships in helping these people work together. Kerry has been with our corporate director in a number of situations. Kerry knows that he will be, ah, taken care of later no matter how things look *now*. And the director knows that Kerry understands this and is intelligent enough to be counted on to do the right thing at the right time. And so now it is the same with Kerry and Ted.

"And yes, I see that you have concluded that Kerry does not place a high estimate on Ted's technical capacity. Quite right. But that is not what Kerry is looking for from Ted."

Now it was Stanley's turn.

"I see your point, all right. But still, it seems to me that this is a little too cozy. I mean, wouldn't it be better to bring in *some* outside talent. Isn't this a little *incestuous*?" Stanley was proud of his turn of phrase.

Faust actually smiled. "Well, yes, I suppose it *is*. But one must consider the alternatives. Suppose one does bring in a stranger to a key position. First of all, one never knows whom one is going to get. There is quite definitely a tendency to unload problem people on this sort of

56

venture—especially *bright* problem people. One rationalizes that this sort of person will work out better in a new setting. Possibly yes, but mostly no, unfortunately. And one simply cannot tell much about a new person in a day or two, much less an interview situation.

"The second point is one that I have already made. Over the years these people have built a bond of reinforcement. Ted knows that Kerry will be able to move him ahead in the future. Ted, for his part, will do what is necessary—and Kerry knows this. And yes, Kerry also knows that there may be better men than Ted for the job—in a technical sense. But he also knows that Ted will never get him in trouble by doing something organizationally naive, stupid, or self-serving."

With this Faust got up abruptly and strode off.

"Better the Devil you know than the one you don't," thought Stanley.

Yes, that's the principle here. But typically, Stanley did not grasp the entire principle, for Faust quite necessarily had left some things unsaid. Such as one thing that Kerry had learned at Dr. Faust's Advanced Management Training Course was that Faust understood well the role of the consultant—to help management get the job done. Faust wasn't the kind to embarrass you with untimely facts. For his part, Dr. Faust discovered that Kerry was properly appreciative of an effective consultant. He knew that Kerry would see to it that his consultants received proper credit within management (and in consequence additional opportunities).

Faust also left unsaid anything of Stanley's relationship to the project.

And that was unfortunate, for Stanley is the type that has to learn the ropes himself. Faust had expected Stanley to understand the nature of their mutual obligation. But in his naivete, Stanley was going on the assumption that in fact he *was* the best man for the job, and Faust had been lucky to find him. Stanley took at face value Dr. Faust's laudatory introduction of himself to management (recounted in *Your Job, My Reputation*) and hence his failure to fulfill his part of the implicit bargain. All of which goes to illustrate our point, *Better the Devil You Know*. Trouble was, perhaps Faust didn't know Stanley well enough.

15

SPACEMEN

Stan settled back into the chair in his temporary office.

Comfortable enough, he thought. Since his initial assignment had been to help out Dr. Faust in the first stages of developing The Program, Stanley temporarily had been assigned space in Faust's office. And while Faust had spent a good deal of his time here during leave from The University, that leave was now over—hence, the available space.

However, within a day or so one of the people from Plant Administration (Stanley was later to learn that in plant common parlance, they were called "spacemen") happened by, looked around, paused, looked at Stanley, and at length, spoke.

"Doesn't Dr. Faust use this office?"

Answer, yes.

"Er, I mean, this isn't Dr. Faust's personal office any longer, is it?"

Answer, yes. No, it isn't.

"Well, then, that won't do." And he left.

"What won't do?" The obvious question was left unanswered—but not for long.

Next day the "Spaceman" returned.

"We're going to replace your furniture," he said flatly. "If you've got anything in the desk take it out and pile it over there. The men will be by in a couple of minutes."

"Uh, would you mind if I asked you what's going on?"

"Well, this isn't the right furniture for you, so we're changing it." At this point, two workmen entered, lifted the desk, turned it on its side, grunted out of the office down a narrow stairway, muttering and cursing *sotto voce*.

Not the right furniture?"

"No, this is for an assistant section manager."

More grunting, muttering, cursing, this time *up* the stairway. The workmen enter with a new desk, walk out with an unnameable (to Stanley) item. The new desk looks pretty much the same to Stanley. Well, it's a *little* smaller, and it's light green instead of pastel pink or mauve or whatever that color is, and its vinyl top looks like plastic instead of simulated woodgrain plastic.

"Well, that's it," said the Spaceman. "We don't have the right chair at the moment so we're going to let you keep this one. Oops, almost missed that!" So saying the Spaceman grabbed the carafe and left.

Later on, Stanley commiserated with Bonnie.

"What puzzles me, Bonnie, is why go through all the trouble, when I'm only going to be here maybe a month more?"

"Oh, but you've got to be fair! What would people *think* if you had the good furniture and everybody else had the other? And you couldn't give *everyone* the good furniture. My goodness, just think what that would *cost*." Her expression revealed that Bonnie was just now thinking what that would cost.

"No, Bonnie, I don't mean that. I mean, I really don't give a damn what furniture they give me, but *why bother* just for a lousy couple of weeks!"

"Oh, but it *is* important.," Bonnie swept her hand around the secretarial cubicle. "Just last month Ginny Szekely and I thought it would be nice if we had a little rug in here, sort of keep down the typing noise. So we got one. Almost the next day the man from Plant Administration came by and said we had to take it out. We asked him why, and he told us it was a safety hazard. 'A *safety hazard?*' we said. 'Yes,' he says. 'And besides, how would the plant look if everyone put whatever they wanted wherever they wanted it? No, that wouldn't look right, and it wouldn't be fair to the others who worked hard trying to make the plant took nice. No,' he says, 'the rug will have to go, girls.' Then we . . . . ."

"Uh, excuse me, Bonnie, I'm going to be late for a meeting." More confused than ever, Stanley left for his meeting with Ted. Up the elevator, down the hall—hey, what's this? Furniture piled in the hall and sitting in the chair, Blake Dekalb, Manager of Mill Maintenance Engineering, known to Stanley as left fielder on the plant softball team (good hit—no field).

"Hey, Blake, what's up? Taking a little work break?" Inside the office, noises of banging, ripping, and thumping.

"Very funny. C'mere." And taking Stanley in the door, "You're a bright young kid, let me show you something." Inside the workmen had just finished rolling up the carpet, exposing the shiny vinyl tile beneath. Now they are attacking the modular painted steel partitions that constitute the office walls.

"Know what they're doing? They're 'un-managering' me!"

"They're *what*?"

"Un-managering me. You see, first the Spacemen take up the rug, then they turn a nine by fifteen office into an eight by ten by sliding those partitions one foot one way and five feet the other. They take your table and three of your chairs. But what hurts most is when they take your Company Managers' Manual and take you off the mailing list. It's like defrocking a priest or ripping the epaulet from an officer's uniform. And before, where you got to know things a day or two before everybody else, now you wait with the rest of them."

"My God! What did you *do*?"

"Nothing, nothing." Dekalb went on to explain that his small Mill Maintenance Engineering Department had been "consolidated" with Mill Maintenance proper under Ted Shelby. And though he still had the same job, same pay, same functions, he technically was no longer a Manager.

"So, since you no longer need the space to hold meetings, you get the standard staff office. And since the standard hunk of nine by fifteen carpet won't fit in eight by ten they take that too—at least that's how the Spacemen put it. But that sounds fishy to me. I've called Ted . . . ."

My God! Ted! thinks Stanley—the meeting. "See you later, Blake."

"I'm afraid you will have to wait a while, Stanley. Mr. Shelby is on the phone now."

Stan is seated close enough to Ted's office so that he overhears parts of the heated conversation.

"I'm just asking you to get this guy off my back! Won't you just try . . .?

"I know it's not your responsibility, sir, but he's driving me crazy. Listen, last night he called me at two A.M., and I've got to talk with him for an hour trying to explain why he can't keep his old office.

"Yes, I have familiarized myself thoroughly with plant administration procedures . . . .

"Yes sir, I *know* that we make no exceptions, but he says it's not *his* fault that we decided to eliminate the position . . . .

"Of course, I *understand* that it's silly of him to be so upset, I know it doesn't mean anything . . . .

"Certainly, we'd all move where we had to for the good of The Company . . . ."

It seemed to Stanley that this wasn't going to end soon, so he asked Bonnie, "Is there something you can tell me? Doesn't look like Ted is going to be through for a while."

"Sure. I think Mr. Shelby just wanted to tell you that your new assignment has been okayed upstairs, and that you've been assigned new space on the fourth floor, this floor. You can start moving your things into four twenty-one B anytime."

Wow, thought Stanley, fourth floor, with Plant Management!

As Ted's new administrative assistant he couldn't be far from here. So why ask Bonnie, he'll just find the office himself.

Pretty nice up here, thought Stanley, who had just started noticing such things. Carpets, windows, panelling.

"Now let's see . . . four twenty-one. Ah, there it is." Stan approached a large room. "No, that can't be it, that says 'Conference' on the door. Oh yeah. Bonnie said four twenty-one B. Got to be here somewhere . . . Oh-oh! That door says four twenty-one A *and* B." (Actually it read 421A,B.)

Inside a standard (for this floor) nine by fifteen were not one, but *two* low rank green desks, only one work table, two chairs, *no* carpet. A two-man office! The only office like it on the entire fourth floor.

A little, tight ball of disappointment started to form in the pit of Stanley's stomach. What would people think? What about the guys on the softball team? How could he work in here with management people, when they'd know right away he couldn't have much to say about anything?

Stanley had learned a great deal that day. And as with many educational experiences, it hadn't been exactly pleasant for him.

16

LIKE IT IS

It is a fundamental irony of human existence that chance sometimes provides the opportunity for which we otherwise have sought in vain. I can think of no purer instance than Stanley's first two weeks with The Company. Strange, it seems only yesterday. Stanley was right here in the study with me, narrating this ghastly experience much as though it were happening at the time.

"Our second session this P.M. will be given over to familiarizing you with the accounting and inventory system we use here in The Plant. You will be given a capsulized view right from the expert, the chief accountant of our plant, Erno Orne. I hope you will all appreciate how good it is of Ernie to join us this afternoon; he's a very busy man and we're lucky to be able to get this much time from him. I know I'll be listening. Ernie . . . ."

Meeting rooms in mill buildings are not designed with the thought in mind of hosting sixteen bright, new college graduates for eight-hour training sessions in the middle of July. But for lack of alternative, here they were. Orne, a smallish, roundish, balding man, stepped to the front of the room, placed what must have been at least a thousand charts on the easel, and simply started to talk in the purest monotone that Stanley had ever heard. What followed is difficult to put in words, but easy to describe in feelings.

"There are several basic systems we could use— LIFO, FIFO, possibly

FILO, under the right conditions. So let me describe these concepts to begin with." Orne, though obviously relishing the opportunity, betrays no hint of that emotion in the tone or pattern of his delivery. Time passes. Eternity passes. The great exhaust fan whirring in the rear of the incredibly stuffy room hums away in a hypnotic, undulating pattern. Orne also drones on.

"There. Now we are ready to go step-by-step through plant operations. Let's start here with Receiving. Notice that . . . ."

Sweet Jesus Christ! thinks Stanley. *Receiving!* How long will it take to get to Packing and Shipping? The hypnotic beat of the exhaust fan and the heat create a new problem. Anxiety mounts on boredom. I'm falling asleep. That won't do. Not in my first week with The Company, in front of their top management.

More Erno Orne, fan, and heat. Stan digs his nails into his palms. Pain ought to keep him awake.

Stan thinks he hears the words Packing and Shipping but can't be sure of anything in his current state.

Orne, like most accountants, seldom gets the chance to make management presentations. And so he's making the most of this opportunity. Every beautiful detail and nuance of the impregnable accounting fortress protecting the fortunes of The Company should, and *will*, be relished. (Recall our exposition of the dynamics of the presentation in chapter 13, *"By Your Works . . ."*)

"Uh, I see I'm running a bit over. It's five after five. Well, I can cut it off here, or, with about twenty minutes more I can wrap it all up. What do you think, Ted?"

"Oh, by all means finish up. It's fascinating. And that's what we're here for—to learn—right, everybody?"

A murmur of right-right.

Ted's look belies his words, thinks Stanley, but at least he's suffering, too.

Finally, mercifully, it's over.

"Any questions?"

Inevitably, of course, there will be two or three questions. Some guys always want to show their interest and their understanding of the material. But now it's really over—for today at any rate. Only two more days to go.

And now the orientation week is over. Ted, who has been responsible for planning and organizing the sessions is out seeking feedback.

"Well, Stan, I'd like to get your thoughts on our orientation program. You know, things you'd like to see changed or added, general impressions, that sort of thing."

Stanley has a few warmup comments, more to show that he knows what has gone on than for anything else. But finally he cannot restrain himself.

"Frankly, Mr. Shelby, I thought it was pretty awful. Too long, too boring, too superficial in some ways, but too detailed in others. What I mean is . . .."

Stan went on giving some examples of what he was trying to convey to Ted. He wasn't doing a particularly good job, but he was trying honestly to help.

"I find that hard to believe," said Ted, who apparently really did find it hard to believe. "You know, I've talked to most of the others, and every one of them thinks the program was great."

Now it was Stanley's turn. "Well, I find *that* hard to believe. I talked to every one of those people in the hall during break, every day, and there wasn't one of them that didn't feel pretty much the way I do. I wouldn't say they're lying, but they sure aren't telling you what they really think."

"Well, then," said Ted, somewhat regaining his composure. "what would you suggest? From what you say, this hasn't been of much value to you. How would you like to do it?"

Oh-oh, thought Stan. Put your money where your mouth is, in other words.

In truth, Stanley would just as soon have let the matter drop, but Ted wasn't going to let that happen. Training programs are necessary and good, and this man Stanley will have his!

Stanley suggested that perhaps something more personal, more individual, more in depth (of course, those are Ted's words, not Stanley's) would be valuable, and so it was arranged. Stanley spent about a week in every major department in The Plant actually doing some of the work and gaining, as Ted put it "an in-depth hands-on understanding of the departmental mission." And so, even though there was also an ineluctable aura of punishment involved, Stanley got to know every major department head in The Plant. (Being centerfielder on The Plant softball team didn't hurt either.)

Hardly six months had passed when Stan found himself summoned for the second time to Ben Franklyn's aerie overlooking the mill floor.

"Well, son, I've got a proposition for you. Seems that the people in New York are now getting The Program off the ground. They've sent word around to all The Plant locations asking for bright young people to work in The Program. We'll be sending one from here. And yes, everyone seems to think you're the man."

Ben went on to lay out the details of the new assignment, and how they'd be sorry to lose him here, but that this was too good an opportunity to turn down. It was agreed then, Stanley would go.

As the meeting ended, Ben felt the need to impart some fatherly advice to Stanley, who, heaven knows, needed it.

"Son, you've got to remember that the people in New York are the best The Company has. That's why they're there. This is a real chance for you to learn about The Company and how it does business. So listen to them and learn."

And then as a final Parthian shot, the summation of a lifetime's wisdom.

"Remember, keep your eyes open and your mouth shut!"

Good God, thought Stanley, I'm doomed!

And so, all's well that ends well. But what, after all, is the moral of this story? Tell it like it is? Honesty is the best policy? No, not at all. Unmitigated, absolute honesty sooner or later will be fatal. Well then, what? Go back over the sequence of events and see. First of all, Stanley *did* tell the truth, but also he assumed that the others did too. So the net effect was to single himself out. Next, though no credit to him, the particular form of experience/punishment selected made his name the only one of his recruiting generation known in every department of The Plant.

Now, follow this sequence carefully, for it is important. New York goes out to the plant locations to recruit people for The Program. One from each plant and only the best, of course. However, each plant to its own way of thinking *has* only the best, naturally, and so the decision is going to be based on other criteria. And the first of these is—don't laugh—whom can we spare? Well, those who can be spared are generally the new recruits who have not yet earned themselves a spot in the "starting lineup." (You can also send an older failure, but there is some danger with that.) Then how do you make a plantwide decision about which of these young unknowns to select? Of course. Plant management says, "Yes, that young Stanley fellow. Yes, I know him. Bright enough certainly. Yes, he'd be a good man. Fact is everyone seems to know him."

And so it goes.

The important thing to remember is that there exists a vast organizational lumpen-proletariat whose identities are unknown to management, and for them the game is to become known. And it doesn't necessarily have to be for good works either, for most often the name sticks when the event is long forgotten. No, the first step up, and by far the most difficult, simply is to get to the point where a dozen people in middle management know your name. "I don't care what you say about me as long as you spell my name right," is a slightly extreme way of putting it—but only slightly.

17

THE ROPES TO KNOW (II)

The Method actor and the aspiring manager have a lot in common. Perhaps all The Company is a stage after all. With these thoughts Stanley harkened back to his days at The University and to his acquaintances who were "into theatre." One of those, an extremely striking young man, was totally devoted to The Method. We say striking, but you shouldn't read handsome—nor ugly, for that matter. In any event, because his face was unusual this fellow had decided to specialize in a category of roles he termed "brute." And he was *totally* absorbed by this brute thing. How would a brute do this or that, how would he feel, what would he think? Stanley's friend believed that learning to think and feel as the brute did, he would consequently act the part of the brute with authenticity. This also led to many interesting moments, such as the day in the restaurant when friend was considering how brute would eat his dinner. Yes! With both hands, stuffing the mouth. That was it!

Quite a scene.

Later, with The Company, Stanley met another Method actor, though neither of them would have put it that way. At the time Giles Selig was Manager of Applied Psychology at the Portland plant. This encompassed the functions of employee testing, selection, counseling, and the like. Selig was well thought of by management and had received several promotions within plant management. But trouble started when one of the Staff Psychologists from New York questioned his choice of test instruments. Psychologists being a finicky lot, the staff man started looking into Selig's credentials. He found that Selig claimed to have graduated from his own university. Yet no one there had heard of him!

Yes, you're starting to get the idea so we'll skip ahead to the end of the story. As it turns out, Giles Selig has no doctorate in psychology, and probably no degree of any kind. And he has made some errors in judgment here and there during his work—but who's to know? He's in an esoteric specialty, everything seems okay, and he is very personable. It's only when someone who does know takes a detailed look at what he has been doing that the truth finally comes out. For, as they say, he's got all the moves. His impression management is perfect, and almost no one in The Company is both equipped to detect the little anomalies in his actions and also *motivated* to follow it up.

Can't happen, you say? The need for previous references and that sort of thing? Well, let me assure you it did. But that's not the point. The point is an extreme example of how far impression management can carry you. And that is also the point of The Method. Selig believed in himself as a psychologist. He thought, felt, and consequently behaved convincingly as a psychologist.

Now, on a more modest scale this also is the dramaturgy of The Company. Everyone in The Company is acting out a role, calling upon previously socialized responses in ways that seem appropriate to what each one is or wants to be. For the process of defining yourself for others is also the process of defining yourself for you, of getting to know what is comfortable and rewarding—what "feels right." This is why it is a mistake to think of impression management as simply calculated behavior. It is and it isn't. It's what Method is all about. If you get under the skin of the brute (or the psychologist) to his thoughts, feelings, and motivations—well, the rest comes naturally.

Now then, to put all this in the context of the general perceptual principles already outlined.

- Generalized ignorance of the motives and abilities of others
- The necessity of making judgments of others
- The universal propensity for perceptual distortion and filling in
- A striking commonality of previous socialization—de gustibus . . .

Each of these principles is illustrated in the first two stories—*Look of a Winner* and *Friday Go to Meetin'*. People in The Company try both to account for impressions that don't accord with expectations, and to create expectations by impression management. The fact that Mason just cannot account for Ben's behavior in *Friday* is illustrative. Mason is not prepared for Ben's response, and a test of wills develops. Ben knows that whatever it is, it will keep until Monday. Mason knows this too, but that's not the way a hard-hitting executive on his way to the top approaches things. Mason is the boss (he sure is!) so Ben must go. Yet Ben doesn't. Conclusion: something is wrong.

And you know, something *is* wrong. After twenty-six years and three months of putting The Company first, Ben has had it. He is getting older, and he is getting tired. Mason, quite a bit younger than Ben, has been using him badly. Yes, Mason senses it; Ben is in revolt. Well, it will pass; yet the situation is a good illustration of the symbolic meaning of behavior, dress, and speech.

The limitations of the dramaturgical approach are shown in *Sincerest Form*. Stanley's presentation of self is rejected because it doesn't fit the facts or his presence. For even if all the world's a stage there *are* parts that some actors cannot play convincingly. Conversely, the inescapable results of dramaturgy are found in *By Your Works*.

Now, I want to emphasize the point that all this is not lost on people in management positions, and the consequences are illustrated in *Better the Devil You Know*. Management and professional people commonly team up in twos or threes or more and move through the organization that way. This is sometimes referred to by cynics as hitching your coat tails to a rising star (certainly a mixed metaphor), but as I have tried to show, it is a completely reciprocal relationship, and a good way of coping with the problems of having to make judgments under conditions of generalized ignorance.

Which brings us to the central fact of *Spacemen*. Newcomers to The Company generally are astonished—and amused—by the bureaupathic concern accorded to symbols of status and position. I even suspect that *you*, reader, think the point has been exaggerated. *Absolutely not*. But let's not dwell on that point. The issue for you to understand is *why*. And the *why* lies again in our perceptual principles, only this time as a counterbalance. Yes, the two man office, the modest furniture, the lack of carpeting are accurately keyed to Stanley's station in Company life. Just as you can read a harbor correctly through buoys of appropriate shape and color, so too does The Company provide appropriate symbols of status and position. They provide a vital guide to navigation, an aid in avoiding the shoal waters of interpersonal relations within The Company.

Finally, the message of *Like It Is* conveys sage advice to lower participants of large bureaucratic organizations: Better it is to be known for something than not to be known at all.

Let's see now, have I forgotten anything? Yes, and it is an important point too. The point is this: As you and your career move ahead in The Company, for the most part you will be attached to a function— marketing, engineering, production, finance, and the like. You won't realize it, but slowly your whole presentation of self will start to read, "marketing" or "engineering." Your phrases, your way of looking at problems, your dress, and a hundred other little things about you will state unequivocally, "made in marketing"—or whatever.

This is okay and can even be a help in dealing with others in like functions. But what happens when the young manager "made in marketing" starts to work for the executive "made in engineering?" That crisp, go-get-'em impression does not go over so well. "Lacks depth" the boss will say, "given to snap judgments" and "won't take the time to get the facts." Not that this is necessarily true, mind you, but that's the *impression* conveyed. Turn the situation around and the slower, more deliberate, "maybe it will but maybe it won't," approach results in, "can't make up his mind," or "just for once, a simple yes or no," or "this guy would be more effective if he'd concentrate on all the reasons this *will* work instead of all the reasons it won't."

Why is it this way? Because marketing and engineering face problems in characteristically different ways, and mannerisms come to reflect this. If you hit the sales territory hard, think positively, don't take no for an answer, there will be no problem. On the other hand, a solved technical problem is no longer of interest to the engineer, he's got to be thinking about all the remaining reasons why the gizmo *won't* work. See what I mean? So be alert, recognize the link between socialization and dramaturgy, and behave accordingly.

PART III

BUT SOME ARE MORE
EQUAL THAN OTHERS

Introduction to Part III

George Orwell's classic *Animal Farm* is an allegorical tale of social stratification, of the demise of an attempt to establish a classless society. The creatures of *Animal Farm*, having overthrown their masters live by seven commandments, the last of which reads simply, "All animals are equal." All comes to naught, however, when the deceitful and ambitious pigs establish themselves as the new ruling stratum and amend the final commandment to read:

BUT SOME ANIMALS ARE MORE EQUAL THAN OTHERS.

Most of us working in organizations think of social stratification in organizations as an okay thing, as a necessary thing. Achievement is rewarded by promotion, and there has to be an hierarchy of command. There have to be executives, managers, and workers. But mostly we think it's okay because someday *we'll* be up there in that hierarchy, having worked hard to achieve that status and the rewards that accompany it. Through a symmetry in logic we also understand that lower organizational participants are there as well for reasons of merit—or lack of it. The net result in societies and organizations is a layering or stratification into various ranks or statuses, arranged from top to bottom. The assumption, of course, is that these statuses have been earned—that they are *achieved* statuses.

Sociology instructs us that there is yet another kind of status that accounts for social stratification—*ascribed* status. Thus, some members of society are assigned (ascribed) lower social statuses because of beliefs that we hold about them by reason of sex, race, religion, or ethnic background.

Examples? In 1960 many of us doubted that a Catholic, John F. Kennedy, could be elected President. Jokes circulated somewhat later about Barry Goldwater. We knew that the first Jew to be elected President was bound to be an Episcopalian. Because of beliefs that many of us hold about people with certain ethnic and religious identities, these people are ascribed lower social statuses than others. And we don't elect low status people to our most prestigious national office. But surely that's behind us, isn't it? Yes? Then what about the odds on a black or female President? See the point?

Let's look at ascribed status more carefully and see what it means for us in organizations. A few years ago we would have observed that most professionals, almost all middle managers and all executives were white males. On the other hand, most clericals and almost all secretaries were females and mostly white. As a white male professional entering the organization you might simply have taken this situation for granted. And if asked to explain *why* the situation was thus, you probably would have said, "that's just the way it is." If pressed still further, chances are that you would come up with answers that would involve the *attribution* of motives to individuals. Research on attribution theory tells us that typically, when asked to account for some action they have taken, *actors* will explain their behavior as stemming from some facet of the *situation* in which they found themselves at the time. *Observers*, on the other hand, usually invoke some explanation involving the personal *traits* or *motives* of the actor. And this is especially true when the situation is one of failure rather than success.[1] In this case, though, your attribution of abilities, traits, and motives would not be just to single individuals, but to females or blacks *as a class*. These explanations would likely have something to do with motives and goals, based on the assumption that these people are where they are because that is what they want, or because they lack some of the qualities necessary to produce success. Thus, you probably would attribute the status, the organizational situation, of these people to personal characteristics such as ability, motivation, values, and goals, rather than to the situation in which they have been placed.

So pervasive are these explanations that when we witness a case to the contrary we again resort to individual explanations to account for this departure from the general rule. She is an exceptional woman, "thinks like a man," someone will say by way of preserving the more general account. It used to be said of a successful black man that he was a "credit to his race," again by way of preserving the general conclusion that blacks as a class generally are unwilling or unable to make the effort to succeed.

Having established these explanations, the principles of perception outlined in the previous part help us to see what we expect to see, and to interpret accordingly. Women are emotional, passive, and nurturing; blacks flamboyant, aggressive, and undependable. Perceptual distortion and filling in provide abundant support for our beliefs.

Thus we begin to treat people as though the things we've assumed about them actually are true. We protect them from emotional upsets, we protect them from failure, we protect them from stressful responsibility and treat them differently in thousands of other little ways that we don't realize ourselves.

The final act of this ongoing organizational drama is in the observation that people start behaving *in fact* in the way we expect them to behave. What's that? You don't see how our expectations could have that much effect? Don't be so sure. A number of research studies have been conducted on the effect of situational expectations on the behavior of others. Two of these merit brief mention.

In the first, people were assigned at random to one of two experimental groups. These groups differed only in that one learned that despite the fact that their "jobs" were less important and interesting than those assigned the other group, still there would be no hope of "upward" movement for them. The other group, while similarly informed of the nature of their "jobs," learned that movement "upward" was possible, depending on how well they performed. The results? The randomly selected group with no hope of movement spent considerably more time socializing among themselves and criticizing the actions of "management." This despite the fact the experimental situation was rigged so that the two groups were otherwise treated identically![2] The point? They started behaving just as we expect lower ascribed status employees to behave.

The second, and more dramatic experiment, found two groups of college students randomly assigned to the roles of prisoner and prison guard beginning to behave so realistically that the experiment had to be terminated a week early. The experimenter put it thus; he had called off the experiment because of his horror upon the realization that—

> *I* could easily have traded places with the most brutal guard or become the weakest prisoner . . . .

> Individual behavior is largely under the control of social forces and environmental contingencies rather than personality traits . . . . We thus underestimate the power and pervasiveness of situational controls over behavior because: a) they are often . . . subtle, b) we can often avoid entering situations where we might be so controlled, c) we label as "weak" or "deviant" people in those situations who do behave differently from how *we believe we would (italics added)*.[3]

What's that? You're not sure what all this has to do with people like yourself in The Company? Well then, let's take a look. Let's see how these principles apply to the careers of Stanley, Lesley, Claude, and the others as they make their careers in The Company.

18

"HI SWEETIE . . ."

"I thought The Company was sending one of its technical guys over today," he whispered to his secretary, "we've got to get this baby on line *today*."

"Mister Toole, I believe this *is* the, ah—'guy' from The Company."

Chuck Toole, the Mill Master Mechanic at Another Company, was not prepared for that bit of information. "What!? You mean that, that . . . *that's* her?" nodding his head in Lesley's direction. "Christ Almighty. I thought they were going to send someone over who could help us get moving, not some, some . . . ."

Though Toole left the sentence unfinished, his sentiments were clear: not some cute little dolly out of customer relations, he was thinking. "What the hell, might as well get this over. Would you show Miss What's-Her-Name in please, Connie?"

Connie took Lesley's card and introduced her by name to Toole, who in customary fashion immediately took the proverbial bull by the horns. "I'm afraid there's been some misunderstanding here, Lesley. You see, I was expecting one of your technical guys." Without waiting for a reply Toole plunged ahead in his assumption, "Understand, I've got no problem with The Company, I'm satisfied just fine with your service. But we're having this problem in getting the right finish on our impact extrusions . . . but, well, that's not your problem."

"Oh, yes, Mr. Toole, that *is* my problem," Les broke in firmly, "as a matter of fact I've spent most of the past month working on that problem. You see . . ." Lesley went on to explain that somehow or other The Company's design people had miscalculated that stress on the thrust bearing that centered the mandrel . . . .

Well, that's no concern to you. So here's what happened. She went out on the mill floor and expertly directed the millwright crew in the disassembly and the replacement of the offending item. This done she asked for a personal tour of the mill—said tour being part of her "game plan" for every new customer.

And here she really did a number on Chuck Toole and on his counterparts at every other company. They'd stroll down through the bays of heavy equipment, and Lesley would conduct a continual running commentary on the strengths and weaknesses of each machine, together with a barrage of technical questions. Many of the questions she knew would not have ready answers, even from the mill's Master Mechanic. Title aside, he was more of a management person than a practicing technician. The effect was as you might guess. After her first visit, very few of her customers could really say that they liked this young lady very much, but they sure as hell were impressed.

But why was all this necessary, you ask? Wouldn't it just be enough to do your assignment well and have that speak for itself? Lesley knew the answer to that one, unfortunately. The answer was no. For when she had first started out in this business she had traveled with a senior representative, a middle-aged man. His standard routine was to get the task accomplished as quickly and simply as possible and then spend the rest of the visit socializing, swapping stories, talking sports, or whatever he knew to be the interests of his customer. And he was extremely effective. That's one reason why Lesley had been assigned as his trainee.

But when she went out on her own she learned very quickly that what worked for him didn't work at all for her. The first hurdle was that her customers, mostly middle-aged Ben Franklyn types, just flat refused to take her seriously as a technical expert. Of course, Ben evenhandedly also found difficulty in taking seriously "young college fellas" like Stanley.

Anyway, when she completed the task as quickly and simply as possible, they still refused to take her seriously. It was as though they had just witnessed a trained chimpanzee performing by rote a complicated task learned through long and hard practice. A good trick, but only one trick, was the conclusion.

And so she developed her own approach, an approach that carried a large dose of carefully planned impression management. Not an ego-trip, oh no, just the opposite. This was an approach that, whatever else, was calculated to make absolutely certain that her customers had to admit that she knew her stuff. For Lesley had realized early on that she never would be "one of the boys," that it would be a mistake even to try. On the other hand, there were advantages too. Once the initial discomfort had passed, there weren't many men who didn't prefer to have lunch with a clever and attractive young woman.

CAT IN THE HAT

Stanley was sitting peacefully in Lesley's office waiting for her to return from an early afternoon meeting. He hadn't talked with her since she'd been moved to her new responsibility in Corporate Communications. The new position looked like a real opportunity to move ahead, so naturally Stanley wanted to find out how it was going.

Stanley and Lesley had been friends in The Company for quite a while now. Still, he wasn't quite prepared for what was about to happen. But wait, here comes Lesley now.

"You! You're probably just like the rest of 'em. Another sexist! Another male chauvinist!"

"Me?" was about all Stanley could reply weakly.

"Probably," Lesley's tone softened. "Oh, no. I don't really mean that. I know you're okay, Stan. It's just that . . . listen, *listen* to this. Here I am at this meeting. We're getting a project group together to cover Marsh's big research lab dedication next month. We're going to do a whole series for . . . ." Lesley described her excited anticipation of the new job and of how the meeting had progressed.

They are waiting for the Corporate Director to arrive so that the meeting might get underway. And here she is, sitting at one side of the table, prepared as usual with her handful of sharp pencils and a fresh yellow pad. Being new, and knowing hardly anyone there, she's not saying much.

Okay, here's the Director. Let's get on with the job.

Now at this point, and according to Company ritual, the host manager takes orders for coffee; five black, two sugar only . . . .

"Then he turns to me, *to me*, and says in this unctuous voice, 'Would you get these for us, honey. The machine's down the hall to the left.'

"Get these for us, honey?! Who the hell does he think he is? Why the hell should I get his lousy coffee? Just 'cause I'm the only 'lady' in the room? I don't even *drink* the damn stuff!" Lesley was greatly exercised.

Unfortunately, Stanley didn't help much, "Did you?" he asked. It was an innocent enough question, but Stanley just managed to dodge the phone book that sailed his way.

"Yes!" Lesley almost shrieked the answer.

"But why? . . ."

"I just didn't know what else to do. I . . . ."

Hearing the commotion, Pat Jones (The Company's Chief Psychologist) had poked her head in the door and caught the last of the conversation. "Sounds like you're having fun. Look, I apologize for listening in, but I really couldn't help hearing your story. Would you like some advice?"

Lesley nodded.

"I've worked with these guys for years now, and they're really not that bad a bunch. But you can see it for yourself, it's like a men's club around here. Sure, there are women around, but almost all of us are clerks, secretaries, you know. I'm the odd ball. And whether you and I like it or not, those clerks and secretaries do little extra things for them like . . . ."

"Like getting coffee!" Lesley cut in, "So that big jerk figured I was just another secretary! Why? . . ."

"What did you expect? How would he know otherwise?" Then Pat added with a chuckle, "He's more to be pitied than censured, you know. He just assumed that you were there to take notes."

"But what do I do?" said Lesley, "I can't go around introducing myself and saying that I'm not a secretary."

"Oh," replied Pat, "you could. But it isn't necessary. Next time when you're with strangers, just make sure you wear a hat."

"A hat? I don't even *own* a hat."

"Then buy one," Pat countered.

"For heaven's sake why?" said Lesley.

"Ever see a secretary at one of these meetings in a hat?" was Pat's simply answer.

"No, that would be absurd," said Lesley.

"Exactly. Important women wear hats at important events. The boys may not know who you are, but at least they'll understand you're not the one to get the coffee."

What's that you say? You think that's silly advice? Well, maybe so. We really didn't intend it as a serious suggestion, though indeed that *was* Pat Jones's advice. But the point is clear enough, isn't it? Old ways of doing things die hard, and male managers still expect female secretaries to get the coffee and to perform other petty nonwork tasks. And, by and large, they expect secretaries to be females and vice versa. That's what they're used to. Consequently, as a pencil wielding, yellow pad-carrying female, Lesley is assumed to be (a) a secretary, (b) willing and ready to get the coffee, (c) generally expecting to be told what to do, and (d) have the primary job interest of pleasing male authority figures.

Lesley's problem is to short-circuit the process and avoid the accompanying discomfort for all involved by providing unmistakable cues that she is *not* a secretary or other lower participant. And yes, she might wear a hat, but other cues from dress also are important. Finally, in situations where she expects not to be known, she might plan ahead, arrive early, and introduce herself by name and position to each new arrival. You know, that might not be a bad idea for all of us.

20

BITE OF THE APPLE

By Company custom, Personnel and Communications had an office party at year end. No, not an "Office Party," The Company didn't believe in them. This was more like a pep rally. It provided a time for mutual appreciation and congratulations for the good work done over the past year—a time of good fellowship.

Ted especially liked this year-end solidarity ritual. "You know, Stan," he was saying, "there's a bright future for you in The Company. I've watched you grow over the past year, and I want you to know, personally, that Company Personnel is really pleased with the job you've been doing."

At times like this Ted could be really genuine and likeable. Perhaps this was because on such occasions his own ambitions, those of The Company, and those of the people he worked with were all one. No matter. Ted was in an expansive mood.

Spotting Lesley, Ted went over to spread good will, "How's the new whiz of corporate communications," he began. Then, putting his arm around her shoulder, "You know, Les, I think there's a bright future . . . ."

"Would you remind removing *that*?" she interrupted in an icy tone, slipping out from under the offending arm.

"Why, er—I'm sorry but . . . ." Stunned, Ted fumbled for words for a moment, then abruptly walked off. Now he genuinely was angry. A rare thing for Ted. Grabbing Stanley by the arm and dragging him into his office, Ted vented his emotions.

"Just who in the *hell* does *she* think she is. Please remove *that*?! Goddamn right I'll remove *that*. Here I'm just trying to be . . . be, just trying to show her that we *care* about all our people, and she's got to pull some wise-ass stunt like that. I don't give a damn if I never say two words to her again. What the hell do *I* care?"

Boy, was Ted hot, thought Stanley, wondering just what it was that made him so. He'd seen Ted take far more malicious putdowns in corporate staff sessions and stay cool as a cucumber. Finally Ted did simmer down, apologized to Stanley for losing his "cool," and left. Still, Stanley was curious, so when he spotted Pat Jones over by the library he figured he'd get a professional opinion.

As Stanley related the incident to Pat she chuckled. "It would have been worth it to see some genuine emotion from your boss. You know, I think that's at the root of it right there."

"What is?" Stan queried.

"Genuine emotion, feelings. You know Ted as well as I do, don't you? Most of the time he's wearing a mask, playing a part. He's not hurt personally in those meetings, because, well, I suppose it's just a game he's involved in.

"But you've seen him here too. He really comes out from behind that mask at these things. And yes, he's expressing genuine emotion. So in a way he's vulnerable as he seldom is otherwise. That's why when his actions are misinterpreted, as it seems to me they were, why he's hurt, confused, and embarrassed in a way he's pretty much unprepared for." Pat paused, thoughtful for a moment, "Oh well, no real harm done I suppose." Yet her tone suggested she only half believed it.

When Stanley found Lesley she was looking extremely agitated. "I guess I really screwed that up?" Stanley didn't help much by saying that she probably had. Then she continued. "Honestly, I didn't mean to insult him, but I really hardly know the man at all, so why should he be so overly familiar with me? He just gave me the creeps, that's all."

"But he was just trying to be friendly, Les."

"I don't see how you can be so sure," she countered.

"Okay, then don't believe me if that's the way you want it. Anyway, what's the difference if he is?" Stanley was getting a little indignant over what he considered to be Lesley's somewhat puritanical attitude. "Don't tell me you've never had a guy make a pass at you before."

"You jerk, don't you understand?" Lesley exploded. She was greatly agitated and unsure about the earlier incident, and Stanley wasn't helping. "This is business, work . . . my career! *You* (finger pointing) don't have to fight it everyday, trying to convince everybody that you're not just here until you find a husband or whatever. *You* don't have to try to figure out whether someone thinks you're really doing a good job or if he's just trying to get on your good side so he can take you to bed some night . . . ."

"Oh, Les, come on, come off it, will you! You make it sound like the whole damned Company's got nothing on their mind but your body!" Though grammatically a hodgepodge, Stanley's statement conveyed his feelings well. Then suddenly he changed his tone, "Look, would it help if I said that I think I *do* understand, that I think you *do* face a problem that I don't. But could I also give you some advice?"

"Well, what kind?"

"Friendly."

"Okay."

"Look, I think I know you pretty well, but a lot of other people around here don't, and you're getting yourself a reputation as somebody with a chip on her shoulder, a 'libber.' " Lesley started to protest, but Stanley continued, "Hey, it's no skin off my nose, you can do what you want, *you're* the one who's going to have to work with these guys. But when they're looking for people they want to work with in task groups they are *not* going to be looking in your direction. Relax a little. You're a big girl. You know how to take care of yourself."

Easy enough to say, Lesley thought to herself, and probably pretty sound advice. But easier to say than to do. More than anything she wanted to be taken seriously as a career professional in The Company. And to move ahead she had to be able to know that praise for her work was genuine. Still, Stanley was right, too. So what to do? The rules of conduct in the men's hut have been derived from historically male relationships. What now? Ted was embarrassed because he *was* abiding by the rules, and as he saw it, Lesley was not.

Well, folks, what would *you* do?

21

YOU CAN'T BE
TOO CAREFUL

"But don't you *really* think he's overdoing it?" Lesley was saying, "I mean, people don't really think like that any more, do they? At least not *educated* people." The *he* in this case was television's lovable bigot, Archie Bunker. The overdoing was Archie's feisty commentary on the ways and overall worthiness of black people generally, occasioned by his discovery that in particular his new next door neighbor was black.

Lesley's remarks were directed at the group—Claude, Kerry, Ted, and Stanley, Kerry having invited the Technical Personnel and Communications Task Group out for a late afternoon celebration of completion of their final report. As they sat at the table, there big as life over the bar was the umpteenth rerun of *All in the Family*.

As a self-appointed expert in most matters, Ted was the first to reply, "I think that's just the point of the show, Lesley, that's why Archie has to be so obviously ... oh, so obviously working class. It's just because educated people don't think that way."

"Um, I don't think you've got that exactly straight, Ted," Claude said with just a bit of hesitation. "I think what you mean is that educated people don't *talk* that way. And that's a big difference. 'Cause I wouldn't say that they don't *think* that way. Least from what I've seen."

Ted started to protest, but Kerry, who had been doing a bit of reminiscing, cut him off. "From what I've seen too, Claude. Let me give you an example. It's something that happened a few years ago now, and I don't think it could happen just this way now, but I'm sure it still could happen.

"I'd applied for a job as a teaching assistant in the engineering department of Another University, it was in the Midwest. When the time for my personal interview came around I was introduced to the head of The Department. He also was chairman of the committee on committees of the faculty organization, I recall. We talked for a bit, and then he asked me kind of hesitantly, 'Ah, is there some reason why you didn't attach your picture to your application?' I figured that I had done something wrong, and I really wanted that job so I said, 'Well, sir, I suppose I should have, but I was in a real hurry and I didn't have a print handy, so I thought . . . anyway, it really isn't that important, is it? Does it really matter what I look like?'

"With that he got really serious. He moved up a little closer to me so he was speaking right in my face, and he says, 'Doesn't matter, you say? Let me tell you, young man, about a year ago we had another applicant just like yourself, another man who sent in his resume without a picture. From the material he submitted he looked just first rate. Well qualified in all respects. The fact of the matter is we were ready to hire him.'

"With that he moved up even closer, and told me in his most confidential tone, 'Then we had our personal interview with him. And guess what? We found out he was a *Negro*.'

"Funny, he didn't really *have* to tell me that you know. I guess he just assumed that it would help him make his point best. But I've never forgotten that scene. I suppose it's just because it was all so unbelievable."

"To you, maybe," murmured Claude, "but I'll tell you, whenever I'm job hunting I always get the same feeling. Maybe I'm paranoid, but I always feel that they're looking at me as something special, looking for what's wrong with me. It's like a lot of people seem to believe in advance that I really won't be able to do the job so they'd better be extra careful in checking me out."

"Hey, Claude, I didn't know you were looking again," said Stanley, striving to break the tension.

But Ted just couldn't let it drop at that. He *knew* that The Company didn't do those things, and he wanted that said. "Claude, I think maybe that you are being paranoid," Ted began in his best informed/sincere tone, "The Company checks *everyone* out—carefully—whether they are black, white, or polkadot. We make no distinctions. And another thing, we couldn't discriminate even if we wanted to . . . which, of course, we don't," Ted quickly added for fear of being misunderstood. "We can't ask people about race, religion, or their mother's surname; we can't ask for a picture. There are all kinds of equal employment opportunity regulations. You just can't do it, that's all." Ted, now satisfied that he had put the matter to rest, settled back to enjoy the gathering. But it was not to be.

"Now wait a minute, Ted," Lesley began, "I don't know how long it's been since *you* were on the job market, but I've got an idea that there are some things you *don't* know." Lesley wasn't going to let the matter drop so easily. "Stan, how about you, when was the last time you were asked about your 'family plans'?"

Stanley shrugged.

"And how about, 'would you be able to move to another location on a week's notice?' How about that one?"

"Right on, Les," Claude cheered.

"And how about . . . well, not me, but a girlfriend of mine was asked whether or not she used 'the pill,' and even which *kind!*"

"Now, Les, you know *I've* never been asked that," Stanley laughed.

"Well? What business is it of theirs?" Lesley hadn't meant to get angry, but she was.

Poor Ted, he was on the spot, like it or not, so he took up the challenge in his best sincere/understanding tone, "I really *can* understand how you feel, Les, and, of course, those things have not happened to me. But still, those kinds of questions *are* illegal, you know. You could report those people. Have you?" That was nasty, thought Les. But Ted continued, "Still, for the sake of argument, isn't it just possible that those people have a point? What if you're on the job for six months or a year, and then your husband moves? Your organization is just beginning to get some return on investment, beginning to depend on you, and bam! (Ted smashed fist into palm to emphasize the point) off you go. Doesn't the company really have a right to know that may happen?"

Lesley started to protest but Ted cut her off, "No, let me finish, Les. You've had your say. And it's the same thing with pregnancy leaves. How can you hold down a responsible position if you're going to be off four or five months every two years or so?"

"But that's *discrimination*, Ted," Lesley reminded him quietly but forcefully, "you said so yourself."

"That's what the law says, yes, " Ted replied, "but damn it, it's also good business. Look, I don't even know why I'm arguing the point. When The Company says we're going to do it this way, why, that's good enough for me. That's the way we do it. But it just seems to me that nobody really appreciates what The Company's doing for them—what we're giving up to satisfy the law."

"Relax, Ted," said Kerry. He had decided that this had gone far enough. "You're right. That's the law, and that's what we are going to do. And sooner or later that's what everybody is going to be doing. But here, let me ask Stan a question; how many jobs have you held since you graduated from The University?"

Uh oh, thought Stanley, he really didn't want to get dragged into this, "Um, three, I guess."

"In how many years?"

"Little less than five, I think. But look, I'm really happy here, Kerry, I don't see . . . ."

"So let's see then, how long were you on the first job?" Kerry continued, "About a year, I'll bet. And the next, maybe two years. And you've been with us about two. Now tell me, what did those first two outfits get from you, Stan? Did they get a return on investment, as Ted says?"

"Why, er—I guess . . . ."

"Naturally not. Nothing to be ashamed of. You were looking and they were looking. That's just part of the cost of doing business.

"And something else. Sometimes you're happy as hell when someone says they're leaving. That's when you shed those crocodile tears and breathe a sigh of relief. So, Ted, is it really so different? Come on, gang, let's forget this stuff and have another drink. Cheer up, Les," and then as an afterthought, "say, could you move to Pawtucket next week?"

The ensuing laughter broke what was left of the tension so that no one heard Ted mumbling to himself, "I *still* think it's different."

22

MY BROTHERS' KEEPER

Stanley's first assignment in his new position working for Ted Shelby in Corporate Personnel was to "familiarize himself" with the assignments of various others in that department. So it was this morning that he and Claude Gilliam were engaged in the business of doing just that. Claude, it seems, had just been reassigned too, to the Technical Manpower Development Section. Claude's special project was to develop a plan for the recruitment of black professionals.

"I suppose you're going to find this hard to understand," Claude was saying, "but I'm not specially happy about this job. You know, it always seems that folks think I should really want to work helping out other blacks. But hey, I just want to be thought of as another guy, and that's the guy I want to help get ahead. I've got enough problems with that, let alone everybody else."

"Then why, . . ." Stanley began.

"Why did I take it? You've got to know the answer to that, Stan. You don't turn down anything here without having a pretty good reason. And 'I don't want to' isn't a very good reason in The Company."

That having been said Claude's tone changed, "But hey, look here," he said, taking out the notebook with a breakdown of The Company's minority employees by category and location, "See, it's pretty interesting. We've got a goal of about ten percent minority employment, and, if you look at these categories—blue collar, clerical—these kinds of jobs, why, we're doing pretty well. But look here, in the technical and professional categories. Why, we've hardly made a dent here."

"But wouldn't that have something to do with the availability of those people, Claude?" asked Stanley. "I mean, um, well . . . you know what I mean."

"I think you mean what Ted keeps telling me," Claude replied. And here Claude did a surprisingly good imitation of Ted given the short time he'd known him. "I think you'll find, Claude, that The Company has pulled out all the stops in our minority recruiting. You see, it's just a question of numbers. Look, look here. These are the universities where we recruit our best technical people. And look, why, there are only a handful of *your people* (Claude emphasized the words) in each graduating class. Obviously, the competition for these individuals is enormous. So I'd have to say that we're doing extremely well in a difficult situation."

"But that's not an *answer*, is it Claude?" Stanley sympathized. "I mean, what the hell, how does that help when it's your job to improve the situation?"

"Right on. So I thought about it for awhile and, you know, there's got to be lots of places other than The University and colleges like that. Now I know you probably haven't heard of many of them, but there are these places—they call themselves 'Negro colleges'—lots of 'em in the South. So I asked, why not try there?"

"And what does Ted say?"

"He says, 'we have, but the students there just aren't getting the quality education we're looking for.' So I say, 'how's that?' 'Because,' he says, 'our experience shows that most all of them can't get an acceptable score on our standard recruiting tests.'"

Perhaps a word of explanation is needed here. The Company gave tests to all professional recruits interested in a career in "systems." Since, at least at the time, most colleges and universities didn't have a "systems" curriculum, The Company felt it had to do its own selection. Also, Company recruiters had learned that even people with backgrounds in such unrelated fields as English and history might have considerable aptitude for systems specialities. Hence, the battery of tests. But back to Stanley and Claude.

"Tests?" Stanley was surprised, "why I thought everyone knew that tests aren't valid for, um, minorities."

"Stan, don't be so sure about that. Look, the tests The Company gives are basically numerical reasoning, that's all. So if that's the kind of aptitude it takes to pass those tests, why, there doesn't seem to me to be any reason why black people shouldn't have it, too. And the last thing you want to do is to hold to different standards for black systems trainees. Listen, if I've learned one thing in this life, it's that when a white fails, well, that's just another person who doesn't have what it takes. But when a black trainee fails, that's something different, that's just another piece of evidence that *blacks* can't cut it."

"Okay, then, what *are* we going to do?" Stanley puzzled.

"I'm still not sure, but I think I've got an idea. Listen, I've got to go to lunch now, and then I'll be on the road for awhile. Why don't you look me up when I get back?"

Stanley didn't get a chance to talk to Claude again for quite a while. Still, he did learn something of Claude's project by chance one day in The Company cafeteria. Ted and Kerry were sitting at the next table, Ted with his back to Stanley, conversing in a confidential/disturbed tone. " . . . so something doesn't smell right to me about this, Kerry. I'm not sure that it was a good idea to have, well, you know—to have someone with a *personal* interest giving these tests himself without some, er—independent check."

"Then you really think he's rigging? . . ."

"Well no, not really. I don't *really* think he's changing the scores. But coaching?" Stanley didn't learn much more that day. Still, he had pieced together the essentials. Claude had requested and been given permission to administer the tests himself, and not at the testing centers but at the home colleges of potential recruits. The results had been startling. Quite a few of the young people now were passing the tests, some even with top scores.

And what did Claude have to say about all this? Here's what he told Stan several months later. First of all, he pointed out, the testing took place at regional headquarters located in major metropolitan centers. These, especially in the South, were newer, imposing structures appointed in the decor favored by The Company: crisp and businesslike. Also, some felt cold and impersonal. So it was into this environment that The Company brought potential recruits from those small Negro colleges, putting them through several hours of rigorous testing. And by and large, they failed.

"You've got to understand, Stan, that this kind of situation is made for failure. These aren't sophisticated urban kids. And I think it *is* true that their education is lacking in some respects. But look, these tests are designed to get at *aptitude,* not education. Fact is, the tests don't seem to require much knowledge at all. Just a certain kind of ability."

"Then you're saying that you haven't, . . . you're saying that you didn't, um—*modify* the scores even a little?" Stanley still was dubious.

"I don't understand you dudes," Claude replied. "Can't you see how stupid that would be? If I do that, then I'm only setting these folks up for failure later on, and failure where it's going to hurt a lot more. And that's more unfair to them than it is to The Company."

"Then how *do* you explain it?" Stanley persisted.

"Look at it this way, Stan. Suppose you'd grown up black in the rural South. There are two things, at least, that you've got to fight. One thing is that you're sure that the white folks in positions of power and influence aren't going to give you a fair shake, that you're not even going to get a chance. But the other, I think the other is even worse. A certain amount of what just about everybody believes about black folks is going to be buried in the back of your head; just maybe *some* of what they say is true. Maybe you really *can't* do it.

"Anyway, so now they say that The Company wants to hire you—maybe—if you have the stuff. First you say to yourself, to hell with it. Why bother just to be turned down again? But you go anyway, off to some place maybe you've never even seen before. And there you sit in this cold, *un*human place, a knot in your stomach and a lump in your throat. Just another scared black kid waiting to be told once again that there is no place for you."

So that was Claude's diagnosis of the problem and the key to his solution: Provide a familiar, warm, and supportive environment, tested by an official representative of The Company who, by appearances as well as by word believed in your ability and wanted you to succeed.

23

SCARLET LETTER

Why these things happened only on Friday was a matter of some mystery. But there, on The Company's bulletin board appeared a spate of new corporate announcements. Chief among these was that of the elevation of one Anne R. Wood. It read:

> M. M. Marsh today announced the promotion of Anne R. Wood to Corporate Director of Publicity and Communications. Making the announcement Mr. Marsh said, "I feel that Ms. Wood will bring to this important post the energy, dedication, and intelligence that has been characteristic of her in every Company position she has held. As we enter today's new environment of telecommunications . . . .

As Lesley read the announcement her concentration was broken by some *sotto voce* commentary from fellow readers of the corporate tea leaves. One was to the effect that the "boys in communications better batten down the hatches." But another, standing just behind Lesley simply muttered to himself, "Boy, there's one tough broad."

More in annoyance than anger Lesley turned and inquired of the speaker, "And just how do you know that?"

"Listen kid," came the reply, "you can't have been around here very long if you don't know 'Red' Wood. Just ask around." With that he left.

Well now, maybe I'll do just that, thought Lesley. So she did ask around as discreetly as possible, soliciting opinions of the new Director. And what she found was a mixture of dislike, fear, and admiration. Wood was a tough lady, all right, in the opinion of both the women and men who knew her. Just about everyone had a story, too, though one in particular seemed to have found its place in the oral history of The Company.

It seems that a few years ago when Red Wood (incidentally, nobody ever addressed her that way) was in a less influential management position, there had been this meeting between Corporate Communications and Corporate Personnel to "hammer out a policy" on the use of career vignettes of top Company technical people in Company institutional ads. Now Corporate Personnel didn't like this idea, largely because it wasn't their idea. So they threw up a smoke screen of objections as to why it wouldn't work.

"I just don't think you are looking ahead on this one, Anne," the staff man had said, "there are so many areas where we can get into deep trouble—compensation, invasion of privacy . . ."

"No mind. We can handle that," replied Wood, brusquely brushing aside the objection.

Finally, after much pulling and hauling, the Manager of Corporate Personnel Planning came to the bottom line, "All right, okay, suppose we do go along with you on this one, shoulder the risk. What's in it for us? Give me one good reason why we ought to go along." Clearly a direct challenge from personnel.

Red Wood paused for a moment. Then turning slowly and fixing her steely grey-blue eyes directly on her antagonist, she replied slowly and simply, "My good will."

The message, of course, was, "Some day, buster, I'm going to be your boss. So watch out."

But back to Lesley. Having garnered this intelligence, she was a little concerned. She wanted to talk to someone about it, and there was Stanley. "I mean, does it really have to be that way?" she was saying, "Why is it that to get ahead a woman always has to be so . . . so tough. Even the other girls I talked to didn't seem to like her."

"Um, I dunno. I've never really thought about it, Les. Maybe they do." Stanley was trying to be helpful but didn't know quite how.

"But people don't seem to say that about men when *they* move up, do they?" Les continued.

"I guess I never noticed if they did, Les," said Stan, "look, I'd like to say something helpful, but . . . ." Stanley stopped in mid-sentence trying to think about what he thought. He really didn't know any women managers. He knew Ted, Ben—but Ben was special, and Kerry . . . oh, boy, Kerry! "Listen, Les, maybe you're on the wrong track. I don't know if you've ever run into Kerry Drake, but . . . ." With that Stanley related one of his earlier encounters with Kerry (our story *Sincerest Form of Flattery*) and how Kerry spared no verbal abuse when he thought, no, when he *knew* it was warranted.

"But that's just it," Les observed, "it doesn't seem to bother anybody when a guy is 'crisp, hard-hitting, two-fisted,' " Les recited the lexicon of the media people.

But Stanley wasn't listening. His imagination was leaping ahead, "Hey, can you imagine what a female Ben Franklyn would be like, Les? Can you imagine?!" Chuckling to himself he projected a mental image of this cigar-chomping, blasphemous harridan, careening across the mill floor, all the while booming obscenities at cowering subordinates. No, it wouldn't do. It just wouldn't do.

"I think I do see something, Les, but I don't really understand it. A woman just *couldn't* act like Ben Franklyn or Kerry. It . . . it would be out of character. Why, everybody would think she's nuts. So I guess it is true. There's lots of guys who act tougher than your Red Wood. But it just seems more, more natural. So then why? . . ."

"That's just what I'm getting at," Les interrupted, "so why the big deal about women managers being so tough?"

Since by now it was quite obvious that Stanley had contributed whatever intelligence he could to the matter, Lesley decided to look up Pat Jones, the Company Psychologist. Pat listened quietly as Lesley explained her quandary, reflected a moment, and replied thoughtfully, "It may be that there is something there, that it *is* true that women use authority in somewhat different ways than men, Lesley. Maybe we're a little more, ah—covert about it because we're not used to using authority directly. Maybe so. But maybe not. I really don't know.

"But there are some things that I do know that might make some sense to you. Take Anne Wood, for example. What else might she be besides a Company Manager?" Pat paused for a moment while Lesley looked puzzled. "Of course. She might be somebody's lady friend or somebody's wife. She might even be your mother—though she's not quite old enough for that.

"What's that got to do with it?" Pat anticipated Les's unspoken question, "just this. Not only men, but women too, expect a wife or a mother to be a sympathetic, warm, understanding character. Someone who . . . let's face it, someone who will put your good above her own. At times anyway.

"Now what happens when you step out of that role, when you project the Ms. Wood image. Well, you're not crisp, hard-hitting, and two-fisted (Pat knew the same media hype). I'll tell you that. Oh no, you're tough, cold, maybe even bitchy."

"But does it have to be that way?" Les was concerned, "I mean can't Red, um . . . Ms. Wood sort of loosen up a little? Can't she be more um—human?"

"I think you're missing my point, Lesley," said Pat. "Actually, she is more human than you give her credit for. It's mostly that your *expectations* of her are different. And so by comparison to the way you think she ought to act, why, she does seem a bit cold, a bit tough.

"But there's a second thing I know," Pat continued, "and that is that in some ways she can't loosen up, as you put it, because she can't do the same things that people like Ben and Kerry do to make them seem more human. At least she can't do them in this day and age. She can't go out drinking with the boys. She's got to be careful whom she's traveling with, where, and how. I know it's unfair, but you know what the corporate gossips will say—especially when you're a handsome young woman like Wood.

"Sleeping her way to the top, they'll say. They'll try to discredit her ability in every possible way. And that's bound to reduce her effectiveness as a manager. You've got to remember that one of the most important things you can have going for you as a manager is everyone's belief in your ability to get the job done; that maybe, just maybe, this guy or gal is going to be *your* boss some day."

"Let me see if I understand what you're saying, Pat," Lesley began, "because there are so few women in top management, why, everybody figures it's because we women don't really have what it takes to get there or stay there."

Pat nodded.

"So when somebody does, when some woman does make it to the top, then everybody—*including* a lot of other women—looks for some reason to explain it away. Then if they see that you've been going out with the boys, traveling with some other top management, dating somebody from the office, whatever; why then they say, 'she's sleeping her way to the top.' And they say that to explain you away as being no exception to the general rule." Then, after some thought, "Listen, Pat, if a girl can sleep her way to the top, then from what I see around here we must have an epidemic of insomnia."

24

THE ROPES TO KNOW (III)

Having finished this section I suspect that some of you are asking, But what does this have to do with me? For some of you, of course, the answer will be evident. But for others some clarification is needed.

The basic idea of *The Ropes* is to help you to understand what is going on around you in organizations. Therefore, questions such as, How come there are no black or female executives in this company? or Why do so many people seem to have difficulty getting along with female executives? strike right to the heart of the basic purpose of this text. For what I am trying to do here is to provide you with a different perspective, a *structural* perspective on understanding organizational behavior. Put briefly, this approach says that much of what goes on in organizations is not the product of individual abilities, personalities, and conflicts; it is explainable in terms of rules and expectations about behavior that are inherent in the social situation.

Recall that earlier I pointed out that it is typical of observers of the organizational scene to attribute to others just these kinds of individual explanations, particularly to account for failure. In consequence, the obvious facts of social stratification in organizations are likely to be explained away in terms of individual qualities, and we attribute these qualities to entire classes of people.

But there is more to social structure than this. More generally there are expectations we hold for the behavior of others called social roles and norms.

—*Roles* are understandings shared by members of an organization about how people in given positions will relate socially to
others.
—*Norms* are more general patterns of shared understandings
concerning the behavior appropriate to members of a given
group or organization.

Much of our everyday unconscious social behavior is patterned on
roles, how we expect others to behave toward us and how we understand
we should behave toward others. Role relationships form the foundation
of our social lives; how we should dress, speak, act. For example, Jimmy
Szekely will always greet Ben Franklyn as Mr. Franklyn. Ted Shelby
also expects to be called Mr. by Jimmy, who in turn expects to be called
Jimmy by Shelby. And both call Marsh, Mr. Marsh. Notice that role
behavior depends upon the particular role pair involved. Mr. Marsh will
address Ted Shelby as Ted; Jimmy addresses Ted as Mr. Shelby. Of
course, there's a lot more to it than this. The point is that the way we
expect others to act, speak, and dress has a lot to do with our
understanding of mutual roles in a given situation.

Organizational norms are best illustrated by our story in Part II, *Look
of a Winner*. In that episode Stanley had violated some fundamental
norms of dress in The Company. Everyone else takes these so for
granted that they can hardly believe that someone—Stanley—could be
foolish enough to violate them. And that is how norms structure
behavior generally.

What's that? We seem to be getting a little far afield? Just bear with
me another moment. Ask yourself, now, what kinds of roles customarily
are occupied by women in our society. And it would help if you take a
male perspective on this for the moment. For at least in contemporary
organizations, the situation is one of women trying to break into the top
management ranks of male-oriented organizations. Well, then, two of
the customary female roles in our society are those of wife and mother.
Now ask yourself, what are the customary role expectations in the
wife/husband, mother/son (or mother/daughter for that matter)
relationships, and how do these compare with the customary husband or
father roles? Think about it.

Certainly. You would expect mom to be nurturing and sympathetic,
and you would expect dad to be the enforcer. Oh, I know, it wasn't that
way in *your* home. But, by and large, that's the way it is. And
customarily husbands have expected wives to act a great deal like mom.
By the way, don't take my word for it, there's quite a bit of evidence for
these assertions.[4]

And what does this have to do with organizations? Just look around you. Despite the current trend toward liberation, secretaries will make coffee for bosses. Why? Because it's a natural extension of that wife/mother role. You can follow through the rest of the reasoning yourself. The point I am driving at is that these kinds of role expectations structure the work relations between men and women in organizations even though they have *nothing whatsoever* to do with the requirements of the work situation itself. Through the process of socialization into female and male adult roles, our expectations are largely unconscious reflections of the structured adult behavior we have been observing throughout our lives, behavior that most of us implicitly assume to be correct.

My assertion is that problems now develop between men and women in organizations not in the least because—

1. Men simply assume that women will behave in accordance with these customary social roles.
2. Women have little "gut-feeling" for male roles; that a lifetime of learning by observation and emulation is missing.
3. Historically, the work situation has been structured in accordance with male-oriented role expectations and norms.
4. Men infer that something is amiss when a woman doesn't behave in accordance with customary role expectations; they feel uncomfortable.

Men don't like it because they don't know what to expect. And more traditionally oriented women apparently don't like it a great deal either for much the same reasons. Social relations are comfortable and easy when everybody behaves as we expect them to. You can relax and things get done with ease. However, when these structural patterns are disrupted tension develops. Something seems wrong. People don't know why, but they don't like it.

Now then, what I have tried to illustrate in this part are just these things. My hope is that both men and women who read this part will think about these ideas and try to apply them to what they see or have seen in organizations. So let's review them once more.

In our first story, *Hi Sweetie . . . ,* you saw the effect of sex role expectations on Lesley's opportunity to do the job. Because the manufacturing floor is a very-male-oriented world, Lesley had to evolve a strategy of impression management that led her to confront the issue forcefully, though indirectly.

Our next tale, *Cat in the Hat* is similar in many ways. Once again a strategy of impression management is called for. Here, the primary purpose is to forestall those awkward situations that develop from confused role expectations that leave people feeling that professional women are difficult to work with and otherwise a problem for organizations. Note that while impression management for young men in similar situations might also be useful, the situations are not so much based on role expectations as they are on assumptions about lack of experience.

Bite of the Apple illustrates a somewhat different aspect of this confusion in role relations; it is not so much individuals and their personal prejudices that are involved as a generalized set of expectations. After all, that old smoothy Ted gets his feathers ruffled in this one.

The last three episodes illustrate more directly the attribution of personal characteristics to people of lower ascribed statuses, and how our expectations actually influence behavior. (Incidentally, you might skip ahead to part V and read *Praise/Criticism* for another such instance.) In the first of these, we see that special screening procedures often are applied to minority and female recruits. There just aren't many blacks and women in middle and executive management, so recruiters assume there must be reasons. We'd better screen them carefully. *My Brothers' Keeper* illustrates—in what I assure you is almost word for word a true story—the effects that situational expectations can have on people. Finally, in *Scarlet Letter* you get a glimpse of how role expectations can distort perceptions, and in turn how distorted perceptions help us preserve a picture of reality that explains what otherwise might be difficult to explain.

ENDNOTES

1. Lawrence S. Wrightsman, *Social Psychology*, 2nd ed. (Belmont, Ca: Wadsworth, 1977), p.100.
2. Arthur R. Cohen, "Upward Communication in Experimentally Created Hierarchies," *Human Relations* II (1958): 41-53.
3. Philip G. Zimbardo, "Pathology of Imprisonment," *Society* 9 (1972): 6.
4. Wrightsman, *Social Psychology*, p. 464.

PART IV

AN INFORMAL
THEORY OF GAMES

Introduction To Part IV

Having entered the men's hut and learned some of the functions of dress and speech, you are prepared for the lessons of mid-career— lessons for the thirties, so to speak. No longer are you simply responding to the initiatives of others. You are ready to enter the give and take of Company life—to make DECISIONS. In consequence, this and the next part of this book are devoted to games. Not ordinary games to be sure, for this is serious business—analyzing the kind of situation that evokes the words, "Well, Stanley, there's nothing you can do about it *now*." The point to be made is that probably there never was anything that could be done about it. Once in the situation, the outcomes are preordained.

Why is this, you ask? We're all in this together, working for the good of The Company, aren't we? Well, you likely won't ask that, for surely by now you have sensed the thrill of the game, of the competition to outdo others that exists in The Company. And this is as it should be. Let the best man win. That's how Mr. Marsh got where he is, isn't it? Well, isn't it? It *isn't?!* Never mind. The point is that you don't want to make the assumption that your counterparts in The Company are all members of a team, pulling together toward some common goal. What we really have is a large game wherein we cooperate when beneficial and oppose when not. The trick is to be able to analyze the possible outcomes dispassionately, to understand the positions of the other players and choose strategies that guarantee favorable outcomes.

Some help in this endeavor can be had through an understanding of game theory. Now game theory in the formal sense is too restricted to be directly applied by the man of action. But the basic notions and general approach can be applied directly to the "gamelike" situations of interest here. They are gamelike rather than simply decision theoretic because it is usually plausible to assume the presence of a competitor—a malevolent actor who, for his own gain, is waiting in the wings ready to step forward, to point out your failure and claim the reward for ferreting out ineptitude or malfeasance. Hence, here is an informal theory of games: games of man against fate, against a sure but presently unknown antagonist, and occasionally against himself; games where payoffs are to be loaded and probabilities rigged.

You are going to look at several types of games: zero sum, nonzero sum and, in a later section, just plain games. These are mostly two-person games in the sense that there is a player and an antagonist. The antagonist, of course, may be a collection of persons acting as one, The Company, or perhaps chance. Yet the same concepts apply. Let's see what they are.

Payoff matrix. These are the values associated with a particular set of outcomes. In most cases these are subjective—increased likelihood of a promotion, a raise, or the like.

Minimax solution. This is the choice of a strategy that minimizes the maximum loss of the player, the maximum of the minima. It is the strategy that is used universally in the peacetime army, civil service, and by petty functionaries throughout the world. The minimax is immortalized in the slogan, "You can't do anything wrong if you don't do anything," or, if you prefer, "Going by the book."

Expected value. Our games are not games of complete information. For example, a tic-tac-toe player, if he knows the game, can do no worse than a tie. He knows all the possible moves of his antagonist and all the countermoves. Incomplete information can involve either risk or uncertainty. Risk means that all possible outcomes are known, but there is no way of telling which will occur. Subjective probabilities can be assigned to all possible outcomes, however. Uncertainty is different from risk in that the entire array of outcomes is not known. In this situation it is logically impossible to attach probabilities to those outcomes that are known. The fact that people still try to estimate these probabilities is of use in understanding real games.

The expected value of a strategy is a long-run concept. If I behave thus and so in all similar situations, I can reasonably expect an average payoff P. Thus, the expected value of a strategy is the payoff associated with a particular set of outcomes weighted by the probability that this set of outcomes will occur. The error often made by the novice gamesman is that of confusing one-time payoffs with expected values.

Now, it is *absolutely essential* that the corporate gamesman understand this distinction between expected value and payoff, for it explains a great deal that puzzles the average executive. Look at it this way: The Company is concerned with expected values; there's no situation it hasn't been in before and won't be in again. The Company is interested in long-run outcomes. But this isn't the case for Stanley or for Ted or Lesley or Kerry, for that matter. As a Company employee, Stanley is involved in a given situation only once in his present position with his current boss. He must look at each decision as a one-shot occasion. If he blows it he's got no long-term outcomes to worry about, he's through—or so most Stanleys think. Put differently, Stanley looks at the Payoffs, The Company at the Expected Values, and the two can suggest very different actions.

Another feature of our informal theory is that probabilities do enter Stanley's estimate of payoffs. That is, game theory tells us that we must attach a payoff to outcome A under strategy B, regardless of its probability of occurring. But Stanley will tell you that this is silly. A just can't happen if you follow strategy B. What he means, of course, is that the probability of A is so small under these circumstances that he *knows* it won't happen. And so the payoff matrix in our informal theory occasionally has empty cells—no way it could happen.

Zero sum. One player wins what the other loses. Chess, checkers, a debate are all examples. Yet Company games are not likely to be zero sum. Even when one gains and the other loses, the payoffs are not likely to be equal. Therefore, a game is called zero sum simply if it is characterized by win-lose outcomes—another departure from theory.

Nonzero sum. This admits the outcome that both players may win or both lose. Modern organizational therapists try to impress us with this fact by informing us that we can all benefit if we quit infighting, pull together, and become sensitive to others' needs. We should abandon our zero sum outlook. The serious student of games will immediately recognize that general acceptance of this philosophy will make it even more beneficial to himself to find favorable zero sum situations in which to place his corporate colleagues.

An apt illustration of the nonzero sum game appearing in *Scientific American* uses the characters in Puccini's Tosca by way of illustration. The venal Baron Scarpia (also Roman Chief of Police) covets the womanly charms of one Floria Tosca. Recognizing his limited appeal, and being a straightforward sort of scoundrel, Scarpia announces to Tosca that he has her lover, Cavaradossi, in jail and will have him shot unless Tosca agrees to entertain Scarpia that night. Scarpia, for his part, will order blanks placed in the rifles of the firing squad if Tosca consents.

Tosca, herself no fool, and in the quaint manner of times past placing some value on her virtue, has availed herself of a stiletto with which to dispatch the Baron to his final reward. Thus, the payoff matrix for each appears as follows. Each can either keep (yes) or fail to keep (no) his part of the bargain.

Tosca's Payoff

T \ S	S yes	S no
T yes	+5	−10
T no	+10	−5

Scarpia's Payoff

T \ S	S yes	S no
T yes	+5	+10
T no	−10	−5

What happens, of course, is predictable from the fact that both Scarpia and Tosca are minimaxers. Failing to see that theirs is not a zero sum game, and that a coalition solution would produce positive payoffs for both, Tosca stabs Scarpia as the firing squad (no blanks) is heard in the background. Goodbye, Cavaradossi. The problem is that the coalition solution requires that one trust the other, yet the maximum loss occurs to the trusting player. Since neither Tosca nor Scarpia trust one another (with good cause as it turns out) the outcome is the unsatisfactory minimax.[1]

The lessons in the illustrations that follow demonstrate all the preceding features of game theory. In some cases we will make the lesson explicit, in others we leave it to the reader to analyze the game being played and predict the likely outcome. Good luck!

HOLD THAT LINE

Anyone passing through the plant that day would have heard a little drama being enacted in Ben Franklyn's office. In fact, toward the end the volume rose to the point where passersby on the street could have heard it as well.

Ted Shelby IV: No listen, Ben, there's going to be trouble. The union election is coming up soon. You know the men are unhappy with the company union, and if we don't do something in a hurry, it's almost certain to be voted out. You don't want that International group around here, do you?

Ben Franklyn: Well, it's sure not going to help anything to send my foremen to those—what'd you call them, "grill training sessions?"

T.S.: *Grid* training, I said. Ben, you've got to come into the twentieth century. Management training is an investment in good employee relations. What these sessions will cost in time is nothing compared to what the payoff will be. You'll find out the hard way if the men vote out the company union.

B.F.: This new job of yours is going to your head. Getting a product out that door is what got me where I am, and when the chips are down that's all that matters. This employee-relations stuff you're so hot on takes the men's minds off their work. You don't know those guys. They start to figure they're doing you a favor if they put in eight honest hours. Sure they gripe a little, but we do right by 'em. And let me tell you something else. If you think those guys are so ready to fork over dues to some big union, you'd better guess again.

T.S.:   Sorry you feel this way about it; but I think you'd better not forget that the Vice-President for Personnel has said that we're going to have these sessions.

B.F.:   And *I* think there's something *you'd* better not forget, my boy. It's the *line* management that makes the decisions here. And that's me and the Vice-President for Production, not you and those bleeding hearts from personnel. I think you'd better get your organization chart out again, and find out what *staff* means!

On that note, Ted Shelby stalks out of Franklyn's office. Good old Ben has laid down the law once again. He is one guy who cannot be pressured to do anything he doesn't want to do.

But Ted Shelby, perhaps cowed for the moment, is certainly not defeated. A couple of days later, a memo appears on Ben Franklyn's desk.

CONFIDENTIAL MEMO

To: Ben Franklyn, Mill Superintendent
From: Edward W. Shelby IV,
           Office of the Vice-President for Personnel

It is the opinion of the office of the Vice-President for Personnel that our new program will be a strong step toward preventing the election of the International union. In a recent discussion you indicated an unwillingness to participate in this program.

The purpose of this memo is to inform you that we see a real likelihood of success by the International union in the coming election, and should you continue to obstruct our efforts to improve employee-management relations, you will in large measure be responsible for what happens.

cc: Mr. Marsh

Following a few more exchanges of this sort, all with appropriate copies, lo and behold, several weeks later Ted Shelby is giving a kickoff speech to a conference room filled with Ben Franklyn's foremen. What happened?

If the facts are reviewed it becomes clear what happened. The Office of Personnel has no direct authority over Ben Franklyn, true, nor can they take every decision directly to Mr. Marsh. But by sending the memo (with a carbon to Mr. Marsh) Ted Shelby put Ben Franklyn in a position where he really had no choice but to go along with the program. The two payoff matrices, Ted's and Ben's, show why this is so.

Ben Franklyn's payoff matrix:

Does the training program go?

		YES	NO
Is the outside union voted in?	YES	−2	−30
	NO	−4	+4

Ted Shelby's payoff matrix:

Does the training program go?

		YES	NO
Is the outside union voted in?	YES	+2	+2
	NO	+5	−5

The goal here is to prevent something bad from happening—the International union getting voted in. If nothing happens, this is good. The whole incident will be soon forgotten, and the memo will remain buried. This is because "not happening" is not an event like "happening," and since it doesn't actually take place it doesn't require an explanation. From Ted's standpoint, if Ben okays the program, and the union doesn't get in, that is Ted's highest payoff; he got what he wanted, and he can claim that it worked—+5 for Ted. If Ben doesn't okay the program, and the union doesn't get in, well—logically we have to suppose he's lost what he might have gained: −5. But everyone is happy with the outcome so no one is going to dig up that memo.

From Ben's standpoint, if he goes along with the program after his earlier refusal, and the union does not get in, he loses some face: -4. If he doesn't go along with the program, and the union doesn't get in, he's second-guessed the situation correctly—give him and his foremen +4 for avoiding some grid training.

But look at what happens if the union *does* get voted in. If Franklyn went along with the program, give Ted a +2: he did what he could after correctly foreseeing the danger, but next time they'll have to go with a better program. Now, if Franklyn *didn't* go along with the program, Ted digs out the memo. *He* did what *he* could, but Franklyn sabotaged him. Ted still gets a +2 for a good try, and maybe more because Franklyn can't afford not to listen to him next time.

And if the union gets voted in after Franklyn refuses to go along with the training program, Ben is in a bad spot indeed. Ted's memo has pointed out the danger of not having the program, and made sure to publicize Ben's position. Ted also saw to it that the payoff associated with this position was exceedingly large by making executive management aware of the situation with his carbon copies. Ben now has relatively little to gain by not going along with the program, but potentially he has plenty to lose, if, after his refusal, the union does get voted in. It is a priori his fault (at least in appearance—he will certainly have some explaining to do), and that is worth -30—at least. If the union gets in after Ben goes along with the program—well, unlike Ted, he *is* responsible for the management situation in the plant—too bad Ben, good try, but -2.

For this sort of reason, statements to the effect that staff has no direct authority are misleading. It is true that staff has no *direct* authority; but this doesn't mean that staff doesn't have ways of exerting its will. Ted gets his way, by managing to seize upon a situation in which his success is guaranteed. And he has done this not by appeal to higher, and direct authority, but by carefully structuring the situation so that Ben's minimax and his "maximax" just happen to coincide.

26

EXTRA EFFORT

Mr. Marsh is just concluding his address to The Company Foremen's Club. Most of plant management is there. "Extra effort," he says, "is what made The Company what it is today. Don't take failure as a final answer. When it looks like all is lost, that's when you should come back and try twice as hard. I'm sure you all remember the time we fell behind on . . .etc., etc."

During his speech Mr. Marsh has alluded to production difficulties on the M-Machine line, making it abundantly clear that he wasn't happy about the fact that the plant had not met the deadline. As usual, things had been held up in production engineering. Typically, the development engineers hadn't given much thought as to whether the machine they'd designed could easily be produced, and in this case, it couldn't. So for weeks the project had been hung up in production engineering, waiting, among other things, for a few key decisions from the development people.

Because of these problems Dr. Faust had been called in as a management consultant to "get things straightened out," and rumors were out that heads would roll unless things got straightened out pronto. Stanley, Faust's former student, was assigned to help Dr. Faust get the paperwork together.

"The President's office wants to get to the bottom of this," said Ted Shelby with the concerned/crisp tone that he had decided was best for this situation. "I've been given the authority to open whatever doors may be necessary to help you get us out of the woods. Stanley, your job is to see that Dr. Faust gets whatever documents and clerical support he needs. Don't forget, this is our chance to put in that little extra effort and beat this problem." With his last remark, Ted Shelby strode decisively from the room.

"Well, what do we do, Dr. Faust?" asked Stanley.

"First of all, dig out all the correspondence, weekly progress reports, expenditures, and whatever other documentation looks relevant. Pull it all together and bring it to me."

About a week later Stanley brought in a stack of papers. "There's something funny going on, all right," he said. "You know, I was on that project, and it's a fact that lots of Ben Franklyn's production engineers were just sitting on their hands doing nothing. He was waiting for some decisions on the M-Machine from the Development Section. But look here; he's had his production engineers on *overtime* for the last two months, nights and Saturdays! If you want to know where the problem is, it's right there. Franklyn doesn't care about how he spends The Company's money."

"Stanley, you've got a lot to learn," said Dr. Faust. "You've just proved again that education doesn't begin until after the Baccalaureate."

"What do you mean?" said Stanley, bewildered. "You're trying to tell me that having people sit around on overtime with nothing to do helps The Company? You'll never get me to believe that."

"No," said Dr. Faust, "what's wrong is something else, probably unavoidable, but no one's fault really. I'll try to make that clear in my report, although I don't expect they'll believe it. They'll wind up pointing the finger at someone; they always do no matter what. And that's what Ben Franklyn knows that you don't know."

"I don't understand what you're driving at," said Stanley.

Dr. Faust paused to light his pipe. "Tell me what you would have done if you were in Ben Franklyn's shoes."

"That's easy," said Stanley. He is always eager to tackle the things he knows least about—and maybe that's why. "It's obvious from this pile of correspondence that Ben Franklyn knew all along that this would happen. See, here's his early memo to the Office of the Vice-President of Design and Development. He called it perfectly. So, if I were him, ..."

"He," Dr. Faust interrupted.

". . . so if I were he, I'd simply take this memo, make X many copies, send them around to everybody concerned, and I'd be home free."

"Wrong, dead wrong," said Dr. Faust. "That's a good strategy only if someone *else* has the responsibility for getting the job done. If that's the case you circulate the memo to show that you warned him but he wouldn't listen. Now let's say that Ben Franklyn tries that. He says, 'I told you all along that this project wouldn't go.' Then what?"

"Oh, I get it," Stanley exclaimed. "Then they say, 'Ha, this guy never really tried. He never put in that extra effort to push it through. He never believed in it from the beginning. What we need in that job is someone who carries his part of The Company load, not some backbiter who points the finger at somebody else when he never did his own share in the first place.'"

"Now you've got the idea, Stanley. How about the overtime?"

"Let's see . . . Ben can't just say that he's tried his hardest, he's got to be able to *prove* it. He knows that what they'll look at is the records, and that the records don't show what his people have actually *done*—just how many hours of overtime they've been paid for. So he had his production engineers sitting around forty hours per week plus ten extra hours on overtime so that he can say . . ."

"Exactly!" said Dr. Faust. "When Shelby makes his report to the President's Office, Franklyn will be spotless. He'll be on record as having given his . . . (here Faust winced a bit) . . . ah, 'extra effort.' Yes, it cost The Company some money, but he did all that he could. Here, let me diagram the payoff matrix for you. These are the possible outcomes, and . . ."

But here, why don't you test your abilities as a payoff matrix diagrammer? Fill in the empty cell.

Success of M-Machine Project

		Meets Deadline	Fails to Meet Deadline
Franklyn's Performance	Gave Extra Effort	+4	0
	Didn't Give Extra Effort	+8	?

Did you put in a −20 or a −50 in the empty cell? Actually, anything over −15 is appropriate, depending on the circumstances. The only way Ben can lose big is by not making that extra effort and letting the project fail. Maybe it wasn't his fault, but if he hadn't even *tried* . . . *and, if he had tried, maybe* it wouldn't have failed.

So Ben makes sure that he looks good. As far as The Company is concerned, Ben wasted a little money, but as far as Ben is concerned, he's still got his job.

27

GHOSTING FOR GAIN

What follows is a simple, yet instructive application of the principle of the nonzero sum game. This game is easily played, taking advantage of a universal principle: Busy executives are too busy to write all their own memos. Sergeants write those letters signed "The Commanding General" just as obscure staff specialists write those magazine articles attributed to Mr. Marsh. And, of course, the President of the United States has a staff of ghosts who contrive his most moving phrases, his most powerful speeches.

Let's see how our informal theory can be applied in the game of ghosting for gain.

One of Ted Shelby's most productive ideas as assistant to the Manager for Personnel Development was his Subordinate Readiness Program. That is, it was productive for *Stanley*. Inconceivable? Here is how it all transpired.

Ted Shelby himself wasn't that enthusiastic about the Subordinate Readiness Program. The idea came to him one day as he leafed through an article xeroxed from the *Academy of Management Review*. The title of the article first caught his eye, "Managerial Subordinacy: A Neglected Aspect of Organization Hierarchies." "Every manager a subordinate," it began. Intrigued, Ted read on, " . . . a management course on 'Effective Subordination' might be difficult to sell," the article pointed out, "yet the full implications . . . have been mostly overlooked in management thinking, research and education."[2]

Well, now, here was an Opportunity, no question. Though just a slight change in approach might be necessary. Hmm, let's see—yes! (1) All the programs we have now deal with *management* training; (2) management means getting people to do things you want them to do; (3) what about the people who have to *do* those things? (4) ergo, why *not* have a training program for *subordinates*, for secretaries, foremen, and the like?

Amazingly, Kerry Drake (the Production Manager) also favored this program. Not that he was worried about getting his subordinates to do what they were supposed to do; that has never been a problem for Kerry. What *he* liked about the program was that, unlike the other programs Ted Shelby customarily inflicted on him, this one at least left his *managers* alone. And he couldn't see Ted Shelby doing anything to the rank and file with this program that might result in any permanent damage.

So neither Ted nor Kerry felt strongly enough about the program to want to do much about it himself. Kerry, as usual, just didn't want to be bothered with Shelby's nonsense. And Ted was more interested in *management* training programs— the higher the level the better. You spend your time with other executives, not subordinates, is one of Ted's rules of thumb.

The next day Ted Shelby got together with Stanley. "Stanley," he said in his earnest/executive tone, "I would like you to handle part of our new Subordinate Readiness Program for me. I've been getting it underway, and now it's to the point where we need someone to keep it on course—schedule room arrangements, make sure that all the materials for the sessions are in order—that kind of thing. Won't take much of your time, and it'll sure take a load off my back. Tell you what, why don't you hop over to production and ask Kerry if there's anything more that needs to be done on this end. And you handle it. Naturally, I'll be available if you need a decision," Ted concluded.

With that Stanley marched off dutifully to get things lined up with Kerry. But Kerry himself had little time for this kind of thing. In truth, he *endured* rather than supported Ted's programs, and only because he was quite well aware that his own effectiveness rating would suffer if he couldn't show some kind of ongoing personnel development activity.

"Since you're Shelby's liaison on this, Stan," Kerry began," I wonder if you could also do some things for us—scheduling, room arrangements, that kind of thing. I know you're plenty busy already, but Jimmie (administrative assistant) is tied up completely on the inventory right now, and I'd really appreciate your help. Why don't you draft a memo from me to Shelby saying that as far as we're concerned, things are ready to go."

And so the memo was sent over Kerry's name, nowhere mentioning Stanley's own involvement. Just a day or so later Ted pulled out his memo from Kerry and handed it to Stanley.

"The first thing I'd like you to do is answer this. Kerry says he's ready to go. Tell him so am I and that next week is fine, if he can line up the conference room for Thursday and Friday. I'll handle getting the word out to his people. Oh, and one other thing; he's really cooperating with me on this program, and it's something I'd like to encourage, so make sure we take a positive tone on this." (Ted used phrases like "positive tone" to avoid having to do the work of figuring out what he really wanted.)

Stanley took the memo back to the office and looked it over. It was the memo he'd written for Kerry the day before! Well, answering it should be simple enough, and by way of "positive tone" he added at the end: "Incidentally, it looks like this program is really shaping up well. Keep up the good work!"

Two days later Stanley again was in Kerry's office. "I see you've got everything lined up for that program of Shelby's," Kerry told him, "and I'd like you to draft another memo for me, telling him when and where. He's being pretty good about this program—said that he was impressed with the job that we're doing—so let's try and encourage him. Put something in the memo about how I appreciate the effort at his end; that should do it. There's one thing that bothers me though. He has a session scheduled for Subordinate Sensitivity, and I just don't see how I can spare the people for that one. Any ideas?"

"Maybe there's some way he could do that session while everybody's on the job," Stanley suggested.

"Hmm" said Kerry. ". . . put that in the memo. Make sure you get that 'On-the-Job' business in the title. That will appeal to him. Here's his last memo, for reference."

Stanley could scarcely believe his eyes; it was word for word the same memo he'd drafted for Ted two days before! He didn't say anything about it, but did just what Kerry had asked him to do, On-the-Job Subordinate Sensitivity he called it. And when it came to the part about complimenting the effort at Ted's end, he made sure to be duly complimentary.

So a couple of days later, Ted Shelby calls Stanley into his office and says, "Kerry came up with a great idea—On-the-Job Subordinate Sensitivity, he calls it. What a concept! Teach our people while they're on the line! I'd like you to draft a memo for me right away telling him this looks like a real breakthrough, and that I'm all for it. Say, and send a carbon to Mr. Marsh's office; we might as well let him know what a dynamite program we're putting together here and what a great job Kerry's people are doing on it." He gave Stanley Kerry's last memo, which Stanley really didn't need, having written it himself only a couple of days before. Stanley was only too happy to take pencil in hand and....

By now you've got the idea. Stanley is bouncing good things about himself back and forth between two people whom it is clearly to his own benefit to impress. And, not knowing of Stanley's involvement at the other end, each is genuinely impressed. Stanley is getting good mileage out of this.

Is Stanley being dishonest here? No, not really, because if he weren't doing a good job at both ends he couldn't get away with this sort of trick. And if he *is* doing a good job it doesn't really make any difference whether he says so or Kerry says so, as long as Ted Shelby *thinks* Kerry says so—and vice versa.

The occasion won't often arise where you find yourself writing such memos back and forth. But often enough you will find yourself writing material in which it is easy enough to slip in a good word on your own behalf. As long as it is grounded in truth, what is the harm? Being a nonzero sum game, one person can win without anyone else necessarily losing. And you have very little to lose yourself, no matter what happens.

Finally, drawing on the lessons of *De Gustibus*, remember the value of the file and the personnel dossier. Even when memory has long since faded (a year or two perhaps), those letters in Stanley's personnel folder will give eloquent testimony to his competence and, hence, his readiness for the next management "opportunity."

28

WATCHDOGS

On the staff of every well-run business you will find several watchdogs, and some businesses have quite a few. As a general rule, it seems as though the larger the enterprise, the greater the proportion of watchdogs to productive people. The Company, being a large enterprise, is no exception to this rule.

The term *watchdog* is used in jest, but the behavior of these people is very like that of their canine counterparts: If you violate the rules, take care! Watchdog will get you. No questions asked. Don't bother with appeals to kindness, reason, or good fellowship, because these won't get you anywhere, The watchdog's behavior is a pure example of what we illustrated earlier in the Tosca game. Watchdog plays zero-sum only; the coalition strategy escapes him.

Let's look at two examples of Company watchdogs in action.

EXAMPLE 1

Kerry Drake and Ted Shelby are sitting in Kerry's office having a heated discussion, and Stanley is taking it all in. Kerry says, "The trouble with The Company these days is that they've got too many of these staff wiseguys right out of management schools in the Vice-President's office. They look at the title on their door, and they get power-crazy. They like to tell you what to do, but they just don't understand the problems we have out here."

Ted answers, "They're only doing what the Vice-President for Finance wants them to do, Kerry. Listen, they are very bright people. You think they'd be in those jobs if they weren't?"

"Sure they are," says Kerry. "That's why they do things like what happened this morning. My project is going over the budget a little bit, so this kid tells me I've got to cut back. Cut back? Why, I'm funded for next year at twenty-five percent more than this year. This project is taking off, and the only reason I'm over budget is that we ran into a few problems that we couldn't have figured on anyway. But, other than that, we're right on target. So this staff kid comes and tells me that I've got to transfer twenty people to another project!"

"Transfer?" says Stanley. "Can't you find the money someplace else?"

"Oh, certainly," replies Kerry with an edge of irony in his voice, "I suppose I could lease some of our equipment to Another Company." Then, more seriously, "Listen, you guys know what a product development project is all about. Ninety percent of my budget is personnel, so the only choice I have is to cut personnel costs. And that means *permanent* transfers out of this project. You know Company policy on transfers. No phony paperwork transfers just to make budget. So I can't hide 'em and I can't hire 'em back in four months (the next budget year). I've got to transfer productive people off the project permanently! It's crazy! So next year I bring in twenty brand new people and lose at least six months while they learn the job . . . *plus* the new people I'm budgeted for anyway!

"Go ahead, go ahead. Tell me *that* makes sense!"

Ted says, "I guess you shouldn't have gotten into budget trouble in the first place."

"Thanks for the advice," says Kerry.

Later Stanley asks Ted Shelby why something which obviously is as wasteful to The Company as Kerry's having to transfer his men is allowed to happen.

"Stanley, my boy," says Ted, "I've been in that position myself. Let me tell you what happens. Now, you've seen Kerry's problem. But he's only one program director. Every program director in The Company is exactly the same. They all have something they want to do, and they all figure that if they stretch their budget a little bit, it won't hurt anything. And every one of them has the same story: 'You'll kill me,' they say. 'I'm on the verge of the biggest breakthrough in twenty years, and all I'm asking for is a lousy two hundred K.' But there are hundreds of these guys out there, and there's only one of you."

"Yeah, but we both know what's going on with Kerry," says Stanley. "He's got a good case."

"Sure," says Ted, "some of those guys *are* right, and you *do* have a few dollars to play with for overtaxed budgets, but when you're working out of the Vice-President's office, you can't know the details of every project. And as Kerry likes to say, you just don't have the time to separate the unfortunate from the incompetent. Every one of those bandits is *very* convincing, and what's more, just like Kerry, every one of them genuinely believes he's right. But if you work for the Vice-President for Finance, your job is finance—the Budget, and only one thing is expected of you: Make that Budget! You don't and your boss is in trouble with Mr. Marsh. And if he's in trouble with Mr. Marsh . . ."

Ted didn't finish. It didn't seem necessary.

EXAMPLE 2

"Just finished my paper on the reliability problem," said Stanley. "I'm going to send it off to *The Journal* this afternoon."

"That's great," said Lesley, "Communications okayed it with no trouble, eh?"

"Who?" Stanley asked.

"Communications," Les explained, "is the department responsible for The Company's media image. Before anything goes out from Company employees, they have to approve."

"But there's nothing proprietary in my paper," said Stanley.

"Well, then you've got nothing to worry about, but you still must have it approved."

Later in the week Lesley saw Stanley shaking his head in disbelief. She asked him what was wrong.

"It's incredible," he said. "They won't let me send this out. One of those idiots in Communications said that it wouldn't look good for The Company to admit that it has a reliability problem with the Model M-Machine."

"I don't blame them," she said. "Why did you put something like that in your paper?"

"But I *didn't*," said Stanley. "I didn't say anything like that. Here, see for yourself."

He handed Les the paper, whose title was about as long as the text: "A Note on Reliability Analysis for Certain Machines of the Model M Class with Relaxed Restrictions on the Allowable Distribution of Parameters."

"Must be quite exciting," Les remarked.

"So this guy says, 'I don't think we should say that, because it seems to me that this directly implies that we have reliability problems with our Model M—and that certainly won't do The Company's image any good.' Well, it was clear to me that he didn't know the first thing about any of this, so I told him, 'Look, The Company wants us to publish papers like this, and it's good for our reputation, not bad.'"

"What did he say to that, Stan?"

"He said, 'That's for *me* to judge, not you. And *I* can't see how saying that our products are unreliable is going to help anything. But I'm not trying to be difficult, and by the way, I'm *on* the Committee to Encourage Technical Publications. Tell you what; you rewrite this taking out all the references to reliability, and I guarantee that we'll put it through.'"

To understand the watchdog and his behavior, think of a sentry standing guard in a war zone. As far as the sentry is concerned, there are only two types of people—friends and foes. He hears a suspicious noise and shouts, "Halt! who goes there?" The noise is still there, but doesn't identify itself. The sentry can either shoot at it or not shoot at it. If he shoots, and it is a foe—good. If it is a drunk from Company C—too bad, but the guy should have known better than to be out there like that. If he doesn't shoot, and it is a friend—thank goodness. But if he doesn't shoot, and it is a raiding party . . . well, that's the ball game. The moral is: Don't play games with sentries, because if they're doing their job, you'll get shot at.

The situation is similar with regard to Company watchdogs. Take the communications example; the first thing to realize is that the watchdog isn't playing against Stanley. All Stanley has done is create a situation for the watchdog in which there is an unknown but foreseeable antagonist who will come forward waving a copy of *The Journal*, opened to Stanley's article, and saying, "This could hurt The Company's business. Who let this out?"

Stanley himself is safe. His perfectly predictable reply will be: "Watchdog okayed it." So, from watchdog's viewpoint, the payoff matrix looks like this.

		Decision to let article out	
		YES	NO
Suitability of article for publication	YES	0	−5
	NO	−30	0

If the watchdog okays a suitable article, or nixed an unsuitable one (defining *suitable* and *unsuitable* with reference to after-the-fact problems, or lack of them, engendered by the article), he gets the usual reward for doing one's job and not getting into trouble—nobody notices. If he rejects an article which really ought to have been okayed, he may take a little flack from Stanley, or from someone else who might accuse him of being overzealous. But, if he lets an article out which later causes trouble— −30! This is what he fears, and minimax is the order of the day. Wait a minute, you say, poor watchdog has no positive outcomes. And now you are getting the idea. At the very best he has nothing to gain by saying yes, but plenty to lose.

What annoys Stanley is that the expected values—The Company's viewpoint in this situation—are quite different. All the watchdog can see is the possiblity of −30 and goodbye, so probability doesn't enter in. But The Company will still be around, even if the watchdog isn't, and its outcomes are weighted by probabilities; let us say, 1 in 10 that a problem will occur, and 9 in 10 that it won't. Also, The Company would get a payoff from Stanley's article, say +4, but nothing if watchdog says no. We leave it to the reader to derive the best strategy for The Company based on the expected values.

The financial watchdog is in a slightly different situation. Again, he is not playing against Kerry Drake, but what sociologists like to call a "generalized other." Kerry takes it personally, and he is wrong to do so. Minimaxer watchdog knows only one thing: Exceeding the Company budget equals −30, and he's dead. No expected values, just a one-time payoff. And if he says yes to everybody, this is a certainty. Furthermore, he doesn't have much time for each individual case, and in any event he's no universal genius, so his only truly objective decision rule is to say no every time. If the project manager has a good enough case, let him take it up the line. Funny how seldom *that* happens.

But, you say, it looks like the watchdog again has only negative outcomes. Why would anyone want such a job? Why? Because they wanted to be decision makers, and because they failed to understand the nature of the situation at the outset; something that shouldn't happen to you.

29

BACK TO THE DRAWING BOARD

There was a time when Kerry Drake was the Chief of Airframe Design, when The Company had a heavier investment in aircraft than it does now. Ted Shelby was on his staff, and one day Ted came in and exploded, "How does it happen? Every damned time we build a prototype structure, it comes out overweight! And *this* time it's serious! Would you believe that we are fifteen tons overweight on this one?"

"Sure," said Kerry. "You guys in stress analysis see only part of the picture; you're only specialists, all wrapped up in your arithmetic ...."

At this point Stanley came in. Ted turned to him and said, "Stanley, you worked on this latest model. It's fifteen tons overweight. How does it happen?"

Stanley thought for a moment. "I don't really know," he said. "It seems as though those guys in design don't really care about the weight problem. Let me tell you about one of them I had a go-around with just a little while back. I saw a paper on some new techniques of stress analysis, and it had something on a new process for forming members which have twice the strength of members formed the way we've been doing it here. So I go to the guy in charge of B Section—one of those old timers who've been here forever—and I say to him, 'How about trying this new technique?" He looks through the paper for a second or two, then looks me right in the eye and says, 'Will you guarantee it will work?'

"So I tell him, sure—here are the calculations, look on page one thousand forty-five—but I can tell he doesn't understand the first thing about it. So he says, 'I don't mean all those *numbers*. I mean, will it work when it's up there?' Well, Ted, you know what that section chief is turning out in there. It's the same as MOD 1, but about twice as big. So I say to the guy, 'Look, that component you're turning out there is about twice the allowable weight limit.' So he says, 'Well, what's five pounds? And I *know* this one will work.'

"So I tell him that the one I'm showing him will work too, and you know what he asks me? He wants to know would I guarantee the structural analysis of the *whole section* if we used the new process! So I say, 'Wait a minute. That's not my job, it's yours. This design meets your specifications just fine, and beyond that it's not my responsibility.' "

"That's right!" Ted broke in. "Our job is to provide better components, not to guarantee his work! But hell, they'll never use your new design anyhow. They don't have the technical knowhow to evaluate your design, and they're afraid to try anything new. Kerry, you ought to get some young blood in that section."

Kerry held up his hands. "I've tried, I've tried. But putting airframes together is a pretty cut and dried thing, and all the bright kids want to get into something where they can try all that stuff they learned in college. My guys can't keep up with them, technically."

But the real problem here is not that the people in Kerry's group are getting technically senile. What we have, in fact, is a good example of the effect of *diffused responsibility*. Let's look at the airframe designer's payoff matrix.

		Airframe Design	
		New Way	Old Way
Component Performance	Part works	+5	−5
	Part fails	−40	Probability Zero No payoff estimated.

Obviously, the object here is to make sure the part works. If it works, but is a little overweight, that isn't nearly the disaster for the airframe designer that would occur if the part fails. And since he already knows that parts made the old way work, he knows also that there is no real danger of failure if he keeps on doing it the old way.

But more to the point, if there is some sort of part failure, it can be traced directly back to the specific source—that is *him*. And what is five pounds? Not much by itself, though by the time you multiply it by a hundred section chiefs and a couple dozen different parts each, you get an airframe design that is fifteen tons overweight.

However, *that* malfeasance cannot be pinned on any individual. The responsibility for it is diffused over hundreds of people. Who is going to lose his job over five or ten excess pounds?

Let's take a look at another, somewhat different case. This happened when Kerry was the chief of the reliability section, and Ted Shelby was the project director for the design and development of a new desktop computer. As project director, Ted made the decisions on the allocation of funding. Kerry, from his position, wanted some money for designing a high level of performance reliability into the new computer, but he was never able to get it, because Ted simply wouldn't give him what he needed for that purpose.

This seems to be rather irresponsible on Ted's part, because after all, a designer should certainly want to insure that his product is going to work for a good long time once it is in the field. In some ways it is, though we also have to look at the situation from Ted's point of view.

In order to get Company funds allocated to a product development project, the project head usually has to promise a little more than he can deliver in terms of performance (what the product will do) and scheduling (how long it will take to develop a product that will do that). This is simply because others competing for project funds are also engaged in limited lying about their proposed projects. Inevitably, the project manager comes down to the wire behind on those promises, and if he is going to come out with his skin intact, he will have to take time and money from somewhere else in order to meet his commitments.

Scheduling can be checked against a calendar; and if the product doesn't meet the performance specifications, punishment is swift and sure. *But*—problems associated with reliability won't show up until the product has been out in the field for a year or so—and the product won't even hit the field until it's gone from design through manufacturing to production and distribution.

Oh, you say, but isn't a reliability test part of the development process? Well, yes it is, but somehow the results of those tests always seem inconclusive, with problems that will more or less take care of themselves "when we go into full scale production."

And this is why Kerry Drake's product reliability section never can get support to do the job that was promised. Ted simply takes from his budget the time and money allocated to reliability design and uses it in a crash effort to meet his promises on schedule and performance. And this invariably happens despite top management policy statements and associated marketing campaigns emphasizing ideas like "Our product is so reliable we haven't yet found out how reliable it is."

What the project head knows is this: If his design doesn't meet the immediate specifications, he's had it, right here and right now. But in two or three years, even if there *is* a problem, he might have been promoted, gone to a different company, or otherwise managed to get far enough away from the scene of the crime. And after that length of time he probably can "selectively forget" how the problem developed. Or maybe they'll be so busy trying to solve the problem that they won't have time to look back into its history.

This is an example of *deferred responsibility*. You put off facing the music as far into the future as possible, under the assumption that you may never have to face it. And this is a reasonably good assumption. In a large organization, the situation is so fluid that there is a good chance that parties to the crime will be elsewhere by the time it is discovered. And problems, as often as not, are associated with the job, not with whoever was occupying it at some time in the past.

30

SUNRISE SERVICE

It was a trying time for everybody, the year The Company built its new extruded expandrium plant in Pocatello. Finally, the business office, the planning office, the architects, and Top Management got everything ready, and construction was begun. Ben Franklyn was to be plant construction superintendent, and Ted Shelby and Stanley were his staff. Their task was to coordinate the efforts of the contractors, the mechanical engineers, the electrical engineers, and the operations people.

Soon they found that this was not easy, and about a month after the ground was broken, Ben found it necessary to call a staff meeting. "I don't like the way this project is going," he told Ted and Stanley.

"Yes, in fact, I analyzed the situation yesterday myself," said Ted. "As I see it, there's a problem in getting everybody together on what's to be done."

"Listen," said Stanley, "I can tell you *exactly* what's going on. One of the electrical engineers comes and says that his group needs another generator installed. So you go to the mechanical engineers to see about the structure to house it, and they're busy working on the ventilating system, and anyhow they can't do a thing about the generator structure until the contractor hires some ironworkers. So you go to the contractor, and he's busy on the main building, and anyhow, he can't submit any plans until the operations people okay the specifications for the generator installation. So you go to the operations people, and they're busy making modifications in the materials flow charts, and anyhow they can't pass on the specifications until the electrical engineers explain to them why they want the extra generator in the first place. All those people have their own priorities and their own schedules, and none of them worries very much about the others."

"That's right," said Ben, "but what are we going to do about it?"

"How about a meeting?" Ted suggested. Ted likes to have meetings.

"Meetings!" says Ben. "We've wasted enough goddamned time already!" Ben doesn't like to have meetings. But then he thinks for a moment and says, ". . . but you know, maybe that's the answer. We'll get together and figure out what everybody is going to do . . . each morning before work."

"But work starts at 7:30," says Stanley.

"Well, an hour should be enough time," says Ben. "We'll meet every morning at 6:30 to coordinate the day's activities."

"Wait a minute," says Ted, who doesn't like meetings *that* much, "if we can't get those people together now, we certainly can't get them together when we're all half asleep."

"Never you mind," says Ben. "I know what I am doing."

Ben schedules a series of meetings every morning at 6:30 A.M. for the foremen and engineers from his various groups, and he notifies them all that they are expected to be there. For two straight weeks they *are* there, and though not happy about it, they do manage to solve some of the problems.

The first meeting of the third week, Ben begins by saying, "I can't say how pleased I am about the progress we're making in getting this project straightened out. In fact, if things go well today, I don't know that there is any reason to have a meeting tomorrow morning."

Things go beautifully that day, and Ben skips a day on the meeting. The next meeting ends with Ben saying, "I don't see why we can't just coast until next week, the way things are going. You people are really hitting it off now, and as long as you've got the project under control like you do, we don't really need to meet in the mornings. Let's see how things go, and maybe we'll have a meeting next Monday morning."

As it turned out, everything got going so smoothly, and kept going so smoothly, that next Monday's meeting was the last "sunrise service" that anybody had to attend for the duration of the project.

Why did such a tactic work? Could Ben Franklyn do anything but generate hatred by requiring his people to attend a meeting at 6:30 in the morning? Well, in the first place, he demonstrated that he meant business by showing up himself at all those meetings. In the second place, he made it quite apparent that all they had to do to quit having those meetings was to get together and coordinate their efforts.

There once was a labor problem in the mining area of South Africa. The Europeans certainly weren't going to work the mines, and the Africans saw no reason to. They were happy enough without money, and they didn't need the things that it would buy. The solution seized upon by the government was the imposition of a "hut tax" on the Africans. Money was required to pay the tax, and the only way to earn money was to work in the mines. The government had, as one of them put it, "provided a gentle incentive to labor."

That is exactly what Ben Franklyn did.

31

THE ROPES TO KNOW (IV)

In keeping with the theme, this perhaps, is a more personal message than will appear at the conclusion of other parts. These are do's and don'ts addressed to you. Pay attention.

I will now state explicitly what has been illustrated implicitly by the examples—a fundamental truth of The Company, known to older hands but generally escaping the newcomers. To wit, the best decision is no decision at all. You can't accept that? Well, yes, you are right that "decisions theories" abound, and that university professors and others who should know better mouth barbarisms such as "decisioning" in descriptions of "how to do it."

But what you don't realize is that the very *best* "decision makers" make no decisions. Let's see how this happens. First, take the instance of complete information. Alternatives are known, and suitable values can be attached. The task is simply to pick the best alternative. This might be called a *good decision* in the vulgar sense, but is really no decision at all. Who would do otherwise? Even computers can handle that kind of thing.

A second type of situation involves risk. Again the possible outcomes are known with probabilities attached to these outcomes. Is this a decision? Obviously not. Again you pick the best one, and if you've got any sense your choice is the minimax. But again this is no decision. Our friend the computer can do it too.

So we are left with the case of uncertainty—possible outcomes not all known, and obviously their probabilities also unknown. Now this is the area for the decision maker; he's got something to decide now. The Company wants to move on this project and some things are just not known. Someone is going to have to make some choices, some decisions, say "do this" or "do that." And this is our point; the real pro won't touch this one. He will find a way to let the other fellow take the risk, while making sure that it is he who stands to gain. He will leave the real decisions to someone else.

The function of this informal game theory section is to help you to recognize these situations, to serve as a basis for tailoring real decision situations for the ultimate decision maker. This is what Ted Shelby did for Ben Franklyn in our first example involving the union. Ted made sure that Ben would have to make the decision he wanted, and that he, Ted, would be credited with saving the situation if nothing happened. Of course, Ben would take the loss if it did. Good work. No decision on that one, Ted.

Ben did about the same thing in *Extra Effort*. Had he been foolish enough to think of himself as a decision maker, he could have sent out a memo pointing to what was wrong, saying that he'd said all the while that this was going to happen, and calling for action. He could have decided to try to make it right. No. He just keeps on doing what he's been doing all along—with a little extra effort. Don't worry, Dr. Faust will make sure that the right records come to light; Ben will get some credit while another head rolls.

And so you should be starting to see the power of passivity in real decision situations. The key is to structure the situation, or simply pick it right, and let happen what will. Let's look at some more examples. I have already discussed the strategy of pinpointed responsibility—Ted and Ben in our first story—but that's useful only when you can be sure that the other fellow is held responsible. Then you want to bring the outcomes about as soon as possible and pocket the gain. But what happens when you're the one who has the responsibility? You say that you would rather not have it? Well, that's not realistic, so your guiding principles in this case must be those of diffused or deferred responsibility. Diffused responsibility is the more preferable of the two, being more flexible.

Here again you avoid having to make the decision, for only by deciding can you be pinpointed as the responsible party (there will always be others trying to do this for you, so why go out of your way to help them?). In practice, diffused responsibility means avoiding final stages or not having responsibility for the entire project. In practice this can usually be accomplished by parceling out the work to other organizational units or by calling on specialists to handle various phases of the work. Ted Shelby likes to get "the best thinking of all our people on this." Of course, you'll want to be involved in *big* projects—the "broad sweep"—and this of itself is quite a help. The principle of diffusion is working at its best when you have arranged to get credit for your own successful part of the work, while the failure is diffused among many.

Deferring responsibility is obviously a less desirable alternative (there is some possibility that you'll be called to account), but it is based on the same principle. Again, a decision can serve no other end than to pinpoint responsibility: "Mr. Marsh, this machine can't be built to the specifications we have. We've got to . . ." No. No! Don't do *anything*, let it coast. You did your best under the circumstances, didn't you? Of course. And you know that everyone else plays the same game. Don't you be the only one to get burned. Make sure that you have taken care of those things that will show up *now*, say on the first product test.

To continue, you also have the principle of coalition to help you. This is when parties recognize that they can gain through adopting a nonzero sum strategy. Of course, this is not so easy with a bunch of minimaxers. But one way of ensuring coalition behavior is to adopt the approach used by Ben Franklyn in *Sunrise Service*. And no decision is required here either. What Ben did was to find a way to provide the diverse groups who had to get the job done with a "gentle incentive" to form a coalition. Inducement to coalition again has no negative outcomes—an outstanding passive strategy. Nice work on that one, Ben.

There can also be an implicit coalition. Stanley worked this nicely in *Ghosting for Gain*. His only official involvement was memo writing about the good job he was doing. Certainly no decisions necessary here. Stanley has formed an implicit coalition with both Kerry and Ted—doing their "grunt work" in return for the opportunity to say some nice things about himself. Not a common opportunity, but a golden one!

All right, you say, I see your point. Perhaps you are right: The best decision is no decision. But there are still a couple of things bothering me. How do I recognize a situation in which a real decision is called for?

Relax, it's easy. From time to time you will be aware of a situation that seems to cry out for action, yet no one seems to be stepping forward to seize the opportunity. Watch out; this is the first warning sign. Next, find out what you can about the reputations of the people who usually wind up handling this kind of . . . ah . . .. opportunity. None of them highly regarded, thought of as not having the stuff to handle real responsibility? That ices it. Don't go near this one. You don't see the point? You think this sort of situation should be a good thing, not too difficult to do a better job than *he's* been doing?

This is a typical mistake made by amateurs. Most all of the people who fail in a management job do so not because they are incompetent, but rather because the job itself is impossible. Sooner or later the job will be changed, but don't count on it happening sooner. A far better strategy is to seek a position where the incumbent is generally regarded as a brilliant success (though not too brilliant). Chances are that no one has realized the position is a lead pipe cinch, and if you play it right they won't find it out during *your* tenure either. So it goes.

Oh, you say there is still another thing that bothers you? Ah, yes, the "heroic decision maker." There are, in the folklore of every company, stories of heroic decision makers, stalwarts who by design made real decisions under conditions of great uncertainty and were right. And they did this time and time again.

Yes, such people exist, but to accept them too literally is one of the most persistent of human delusions. Admiring such heroic decision makers makes about as much sense as admiring the heroic pennies that manage to come up heads in each of the twenty tries comprising the usual statistics laboratory experiment. No, you wouldn't do that. Of course you wouldn't. But somehow people feel it essential to impute special abilities to the human pennies of The Company who have comparable records of achievement.[3] And human decision makers have the added advantage of contriving to make a decision look correct after the fact, using the simple expedient of working like the devil to make it come out right. (A comprehensive discussion of this principle is presented in Part VI).

This completes the message of Part IV, but for one final note. Yes, there is the possibility that someday your own well-being and that of The Company will finally coincide. This is the case for Mr. Marsh. In this situation you must look at expected values and long run outcomes, not payoffs. In consequence of this your whole perspective must be different. Having used these lessons to get you where you are and to insure that you stay there, you must completely reverse your logic. You must guard against their use, relentlessly ferret out instances of the application of game strategy, disarm the offenders and expose the game. You must punish the minimaxer and reward the man who is guided by expected values. But it's difficult to do. Somehow a principle learned too well . . . .

ENDNOTES

1. Social psychologists have spent a great deal of time trying to solve this problem labelled as the prisoner's dilemma.

2. Andre Laurent, "Managerial Subordinacy: A Neglected Aspect of Organizational Hierarchies," *Academy of Management Review*, 3 (1978): 220. Earlier readers of *The Ropes* might note that in 1977 Ted actually anticipated the publication of this article.

3. See Karl Deutsch and William Madow, "A note on the Appearance of Wisdom in Large Bureaucratic Organizations," *Behavioral Science* 6 (1961): 72-78, for a confirmation of this reasoning.

PART V

MORE GAMES

Introduction to Part V

Some of the more "formal" games situations that occur in large organizations have now been covered; but if you have ever tried to play a game of poker with real people according to the principles of formal game theory, you might know that this approach to games has its limitations.

Circumstances that pit man against man, or man against The System, can be analyzed in terms of nonzero sum, expected values, pay-offs, and minimax. But there are other types of conflict—man against himself, or man against nothing in particular—for which the formal concepts are inappropriate, but which nevertheless fall under the rubric of "games": that is, situations which have predictable outcomes, winners or losers. In fact, often these situations have predictable but *unintended* outcomes—self-*un*fulfilling prophecies, so to speak.

Serendipity has become a popular term in recent years; it means the process of looking for one thing and finding another. Invariably this term is used in connection with fortuitous outcomes, like falling into a cesspool and coming out with a diamond in your hand. But the history of mankind reveals that "neg-serendipity" is much more common: we look for diamonds and fall into the cesspool.

There are hosts of examples. Achieving better crop yields with insecticides, people have managed as well to pollute the globe. In wiping out diseases, we created the "population explosion," and by the year 2030 we'll be stacked two-deep. The indispensable message of Christianity was spread to the nether cultures together with the epidemic diseases that quickly dispatched them to their final reward. A tidy package! Well, "you can't win for losing," and "hoist on your own petard" are old sayings.

The point is that innocent, well-intentioned actions have likely caused more grief than anything done by people who were basically evil. Though undoubtedly a reason for this is that there are considerably more well-intentioned people than evil ones. Frankly, the point is about the same as that of the Greek tragedian; or, if you prefer, Shakespeare ("The fault, dear Brutus, lies not in our stars, but in ourselves"). We move inexorably to a fate of our own making, all the while contriving our actions to achieve quite different ends. The theme of the chapters in this section is this inherent propensity of man to louse things up for himself.

And what do these philosophical verities have to do with Stanley and his cohorts? Well, they are people, and that alone qualifies them to take part in all the grief that people perpetrate on themselves. But more importantly, they are members of a large organization, one which has certain goals, beliefs, practices, and rules which direct the activities of its members. As human organizations go, businesses are relatively rational. They and their participants pursue limited sets of goals in limited contexts. And what each can do by way of pursuing these goals is fairly circumscribed. Surely, the organizational innocent might say, businesses are not as subject to tragedies as the rest of mankind.

Ah, but they are. For the definition of tragedy is an outcome preordained by the nature of those to whom it happens. Take, for example, the way that achieving success can insure failure—the principle involved in the extinction of the dinosaur and the dodo. These beasts adapted too well to their environment. The environment changed, and their highly specialized forms became liabilities rather than assets under the new conditions. Or, put another way, they became captives of a very special set of environmental conditions; no good elsewhere.

Also, too much of a good thing, indiscriminantly dispensed, produces the opposite of the intended result. "Me thinks the lady protesteth too much . . . ."

And, rules and procedures intended to guarantee favorable outcomes perversely result in something else. We set up a measurement system to reflect high productivity and find that our people quickly learn how to beat the system, to look great on the measures while actually producing less. Or, to our horror, we find out that ultimately the steps necessary to look good on the measures cannot help but bring about a decrement in the real thing, the thing they were supposed to reflect.

The chapters that follow are illustrations of these principles. You'll see in every case that the actors are well intentioned, not malevolent. They are trying to do only what is expected of them, trying to do their best given the perceived circumstances in which they find themselves. However, their imperfect understanding of the overall consequences of their actions brings about a failure of some sort. And many times these mistakes, once made, are discovered too late to be corrected. By the time their outcomes are clear, too much has been invested to do anything but ride them out to their bitter ends.

When Shakespeare wrote that our faults are not in the stars but in ourselves, he might also have added, ". . . and in the little games that we can't help playing."

32

COWBOY

Time was when business used to bring me to Pawtucket now and again, and I would stop by to check on Stanley's progress. Thinking back on it, I suppose Stanley's first real career problem came as a result—of all things—of success. I recall one incident vividly.

Ben Franklyn and Ted Shelby were having one of their go-arounds, and this time the bone of contention was Stanley himself.

"No, you can't have him," said Ben. "He's the best damned computer man we've got."

"But this would mean a promotion for him," Ted pleaded.

"From this unit to the Personnel Office? That's your idea of a step up? Listen, Stanley's got a future in computers. Anybody can push papers in the Personnel Office, but . . . you ought to see what Stanley can do with that computer. I didn't think they were good for *anything* until Stanley took it up. And there's no way I could possibly replace him. You can't have him. Period!"

When the computer was first installed, Stanley was fascinated by it. He took a one-week company seminar, then got a couple hours of computer time to play around with. He had a natural talent for programming, and the next thing he knew, he was handling the data processing for Ben Franklyn's unit. His reputation got around quickly, because in those days people were still impressed by someone who could make a computer do anything at all. People in the plant got to know him as Ben Franklyn's "computer genius."

Stanley still likes to work the computer, but he's at the point where he'd really like to move on to something else. He isn't unhappy, he's not going to do anything rash. He's content to work with the computer day in and day out, and as long as he's there, he's going to do the job in the only way he knows—as well as it can be done. Ben knows it, and he has managed to make Stanley the highest-paid computer man in The Plant.

The problem is that Stanley may never be anything else. Ben has kept him there so long that most people think of Stanley and his computer as an inseparable team. Only rarely now will someone like Ted Shelby think of some other kind of job for him. Usually, it's: "Oh yes, Stanley, our young computer genius. No, I was thinking of a different type." Or, "Well, there's no doubt that Stanley is a capable man. Still, he's never moved out of that computer job. Maybe that tells us something, eh?" So it goes.

The lesson here is that indeed it is possible to be too good at something. Not that this is always a problem: John Wayne undoubtedly enjoyed his lifetime of cowboy parts (sometimes, of course, wearing an Army or Marine uniform, but always the same part). Yet most people enjoy doing something different every now and then; if a person fits his "type" too well, that's not going to happen.

Look at John Wayne: What if he had been cast as a thug, or as a werewolf? Who would believe it? Who could watch the movie without saying, "What's that cowboy doing, sprouting hair and claws when the moon is high?" And it wasn't too long ago that an actor committed suicide because he'd played "Superman" on television so long that he was unable to get any other roles. Tragic but understandable; what other role can Superman play?

So, "Ben's computer genius" is stuck with his role unless there is some drastic change in the situation, or unless he manages to put his foot down before it is too late. Jean Stapleton came within a hair's breadth of being "Edith Bunker" forever, but she realized what was happening in time and escaped, being killed off to end the TV series neatly. Maybe Stanley will wake up in time and elbow his way out of being typed, but it isn't that easy, because there is a guaranteed level of reward associated with the "type," and to try to break the mold throws a person into a very uncertain situation: what if he *can't* do anything else?

What I am talking about is the preordained failure of success. It comes from not knowing when to quit, from being too good at something that someone can label with a good word or phrase—"our man in Paducah," "computer genius," "cowboy."

And it can happen also to departments or even to entire organizations. The Company once hired a young operations research specialist to introduce new management techniques to all their plant locations. This young woman in turn hired herself a couple cohorts, and they went to work. In the beginning they had trouble; every plant manager was skeptical about new procedures he didn't understand. Every now and then they got acceptance from a department manager to install some sort of special system or other, but general acceptance was elusive at first.

In the early days the "operations research team" would sit and dream of the time when they might get a shot at designing an entire plant. That was the only way to do it, after all. But in the meantime they were building a substantial record of novel, effective applications.

Success eventually arrived. They got to design the entire system at the Portsmouth plant, and their system worked just great. No longer was plant management asking, "What is O.R. good for? What can these guys do?" Now every one in The Company knew; they wanted a system just like the one at Portsmouth. No, don't you guys change a blessed thing; give us one just like Portsmouth.

In fact, the whole endeavor was so successful that the operations research group persuaded The Company to come out with a Company Standard for Production and Inventory Control Systems—just like Portsmouth. And each plant hired its own Operations Research Specialist, reporting directly to the plant manager and responsible for maintenance of The Company standard system.

Now it wasn't long before the two young assistant operations research people departed in search of more "creative and challenging opportunities," and the creator wondered where she had gone wrong, for it was clear that the whole O.R. scene in The Company suddenly was very dead.

And where had she gone wrong? Well, her first mistake was in wanting success too badly, and in defining success in the shape of an epic achievement. Her group succeeded, in the sense that she had defined, and in doing so they lost control of their achievement. Each plant manager hired his own O.R. person, loyal to himself, and at that point had all the O.R. he needed. Why send problems back to the staff O.R. group, when he now had his own O.R. person, who *also* knew something about production (and who was sympathetic to the local management point of view—he'd better be). What the plant manager had now was just fine—no new ideas, please. As it is, it will be years before we "get the bugs ironed out" of this system.

And so the original Operations Research group lost control of the thing it created, losing it by virtue of being too successful. That plantwide system at Portsmouth has its equivalent in the cowboy part . . . just fine, no changes, please.

33

PRAISE/CRITICISM

Ted Shelby opened up the morning session of participants in the Phase Three, Section II, Group 1 of the "Subordinate Readiness Program: Production Workers." "Gentlemen and ladies," he said, "Stanley has come in this morning to take over this session. He is our expert on manager-man relations on the assembly line, and that is the topic today. Stanley, the session is all yours."

Stanley, finally having broken from the stifling embrace of his personal iron-maiden, the Computer, has been working with Ted for almost a year now. But he still bears the imprint of his technical background. To put it bluntly, he isn't the world's greatest showman. He knows his stuff, but he has trouble putting it over. At every opportunity he seeks security in charts and numbers, and had tended, as he evolved this session over the months, to build more and more charts and numbers into his presentation. He doesn't have to engage his audience if he just talks facts, so he would read the numbers from the charts, poke at them with a pointer, and say as little as possible about what they meant.

"... and so we see here that Class A assemblers who—and I quote: 'accept instructions eagerly and intelligently'—have a tendency to move up faster in pay grade than those who do not. Eighty-seven percent of assemblers who scored lower than twenty-five percent went up a grade in less than six months, compared to only forty-three percent of assemblers with scores higher than fifty percent. Remember that low scores indicate high instruction-acceptance, and that high scores indicate low instruction-acceptance. That is, where the chart is going up, it is actually going down and, etc., etc., etc. . . ." Stanley really worked very hard at his sessions, but sometimes it was painful to watch.

Stanley's troubles were not lost on Ted Shelby, and given the situation and his responsibility for it, you might have thought that Ted would have tried to straighten Stanley out early in the program. But Ted didn't like interpersonal conflict, and Stanley was pretty defensive about his sessions, not being sure that he wanted to do that kind of thing anyway. Criticism from Ted would be certain to precipitate a confrontation; he knew that Stanley's reaction would be something like: "What do you mean, 'go easy on the numbers'? Look, I'm the expert on this topic, and what do *you* know about it? What makes you think your way is better anyhow? If that's how you feel, you can take your Subordinate Readiness Program and shove it, for all I care. I'm going back to production where we talk facts, not B.S."

Ted simply had no stomach for that sort of thing. People like praise. Accentuate the positive. Catch more flies with honey than with vinegar, etc. So from the very beginning . . . "Good show, Stanley. The way you handled that question about Subordinate Responsiveness was terrific. It was your *best talk yet.*"

This went on for almost a year when Stanley finally burst into Ted's office and said, "I quit! You must really think I'm some kind of idiot!" Stanley hadn't been drinking, but he had been indulging in what Elton Mayo quaintly termed *pessimistic revery.* He was really fuming. "The very first time I did that session you said, 'Good show, Stan.' Okay. I knew it wasn't that great, but I appreciated your wanting me to feel good. The next time you told me it was better than my first one, and I think it was. But, it's been how many times now? And each time . . ." Stanley mimicked Ted's most super-sincere delivery, ". . . your *best talk yet,* Stan." Well, if the last was my best then the first one was *really* lousy, and you've been lying like hell to me right from the beginning!"

Modern management textbooks tell us that praise is an important motivator: a pat on the back is as essential as a dollar in the pocket. But like most principles, this one can be carried too far, and must be tempered by another, not-so-modern principle first delineated by Aesop in his fable concerning the bored shepherd boy who cried "wolf" too often.

People catch on if you don't mean what you say, and pretty soon they start discounting your words. Inflation and overuse rob your praise of its value.

* * * *

When Stanley got back to Pawtucket now and again he invariably stopped up to see his old buddies on the fifth floor. Today as he entered the big drafting room, Claude Gilliam and Lesley were having a heated discussion. Stanley approached the pair with some circumspection, not knowing what he might be getting into.

"I don't get it, I *don't* get it. You'd think Claude would get a kick out of this. Why is he getting so excited?" Lesley was talking half to Claude and half to Stanley. It turned out that Lesley had just been chewed out by Kerry Drake—who is an expert at that. Lesley was willing to admit that she was wrong, that Kerry had a good point, but Lesley didn't see the necessity of Kerry's doing it the way he did. Stanley, of course, knew that Kerry had only one way, and that was it.

The spat developed when Claude commented that Lesley shouldn't complain, that she actually was very lucky. That sort of thing never happened to Claude. Lesley was in no mood to take any needling, especially when it didn't make any sense to her and so, well, we've already noted the result.

Hearing all this, Stanley made an attempt at reconciliation. With as much good humor as possible he recounted the time that Kerry really skinned him on that construction job. But while Lesley and Stanley laughed it off, Claude became even more angry.

"Sure you think it's funny. But then, how could *you* understand?"

Uh oh, thought Stanley. Here we go with that "black experience" stuff again. Stanley had gotten to know Claude well enough in the past to have a couple of friendly arguments about that sort of thing. For Claude was one of The Company's first wave of "equal opportunity employees." This was a way of saying that if The Government hadn't found ways of making The Company hire black professional people The Company probably wouldn't have got around to it for some time. Nevertheless, in fairness to The Company, once they decided to do it, they were going to do it right. And they were trying.

It isn't that The Company never had any black employees, even professional black employees; but typically they were "white" blacks. To say it another way, except for the accident of color of skin there wasn't any difference between them and the rest of the people in The Company. But Claude was Black; Black in speech, dress, appearance, and in a thousand and one minor things that told you that Claude hadn't had a close white acquaintance until he became a student at the Polytechnic Institute. But back to Stanley, Lesley, and Claude.

"No, you *don't* understand. You don't understand because nobody's ever treated you the way they treat me. Look at Ted. Know what I am to Ted? I'm Ted's nigger." (Stanley and Lesley blanched at the use of the proscribed word.) Claude enjoyed the reaction.

"That's the way he thinks about me, I mean." And pointing to Stan, "He thinks about you as you. But me, all he sees, all he can think of is that I'm a black man. No, I don't mean it that strong—but it's always there.

"And you know what, he's scared to death of me. What if I fail? How will it look? They'll think he can't get along with Equal Opportunity Employees. (Claude added an ironic emphasis.)

"Why the hell is he so afraid I'm going to fail? I got through Tech okay and everything I got, I got the hard way—working my ass off to learn what all you dudes knew in high school. So what's he so worried about?

"I'll tell you. He's worried 'cause I don't talk right. I don't sound right, and I don't act right. I guess I don't look too good to him either. That's what I mean when I say how could you understand. How could you?

"Ted just *knows* there are things I can't do, so he's not going to give me the chance to fail. He does what he thinks is helping me out. They all do, more or less. Don't give me anything too tough to do. Make excuses for me. No criticism. Never, *never* chew me out. See, I'm just not going to get the chance that you dudes get, so how do I learn? Everything I do is always fine. And then, finally the time comes when I've been here a while and I've been promoted—and when that time comes they turn out to be right after all. I can't do these things 'cause no one's ever let me and no one's ever given me an honest reaming out when I've screwed up. Then they say, 'See, just like we thought. It's the way it is with them.' "

And there you have it. Unfortunately Claude is right on target. So our stories have a message at several levels. The first is that expectations often produce the result. Ted *is* prejudiced. Not in a conscious, nasty, malevolent way; no, it's unconscious, well-meaning, and stupid. The crazy thing is that Ted, as in all the affairs of The Company, wants what The Company wants, wants black professionals and managers, wants Claude to succeed. The irony is that Ted *is* trying to help Claude, but he is afraid that Claude will fail and he doesn't want that to happen. So the way he helps only ensures that, sooner or later, Claude *will* fail.

And that is the second message, the theme of consequences contradictory to intentions. No one ever was aided by withholding the opportunity to fail and a subsequent honest appraisal of the reasons for failure. False praise to avoid interpersonal strife eventually will engender strife, just as withholding the opportunity to fail denies final success. The common element in each is lack of what learning psychologists call "knowledge of results." For how else are we to learn? So Ted, first with Stanley and then with Claude, and through different motivations, has denied each the thing he honestly sought to promote—success.

34

HELLFIRE
AND BRIMSTONE

"So I'm sure that you will be as surprised and concerned as I by the findings of Dr. Faust's study of subordinate readiness in The Company."

One of Marsh's staff aides was concluding his introduction of Faust to a staff briefing session. Faust is now reporting on the part of a nationwide study of subordinate readiness conducted right here in The Company.

". . . so to capsulize the findings for you, we have a workforce that is becoming pervasively dissatisfied with dull, unchallenging, and repetitive jobs. And not only do we have bored, alienated assembly line workers—'the blue collar blues'—we also show widespread 'white collar woes' and serious job dissatisfaction or even despair at all occupational levels up to and including managers."[1]

With this salvo fired off, Faust had sufficiently awakened his audience to continue with his findings.

"Our earlier studies show that *fully one-quarter* of our workers express some level of dissatisfaction with their work. And now we find that *only twenty-five percent* of these same workers would choose similar jobs again if they could."

Stanley took mental note of the careful use of "fully" and "only."

Faust intoned on, "Compare this to the fact that only one-half of our group did not express some level of dissatisfaction on at least three of our twenty selected job attributes. Furthermore, . . ."

The last lost Stanley completely.

Finally Faust concluded, "Any questions or comments, gentlemen?"

"Yeah, listen, since it's my boys you're talking about, I may be a little closer to this than the rest of you guys." Ben turned to the assembled group. "I don't know about you, but Faust lost me after the first couple minutes. Only one thing I *can* see, and that's the glass is always half empty as far as Dr. Faust is concerned.

"Here, since I'm an old mill hand myself, let me read you something from the *Times* one of my personnel guys brought me. It's about the whole thing that we're looking at a part of here. Here's what your U. S. Labor Secretary thinks about it.

" 'This issue of job dissatisfaction has been overblown and is largely a creation of pop sociologists and their media sisters under the skin.' "[2]

Ben stumbled a bit over the words, but he obviously savored the message.

Faust was quick to retort, "An obviously bureaucratic whitewash. Of course, they'd have to say that, otherwise they'd have to do something."

Of course.

Now, it was Ted's turn for his best sincere/balanced tone.

"Ben, I think we all agree that the study's conclusions may not be fully supported by its data and it may in fact be off by quite a bit, but if it is anywhere near the truth, we had better start thinking about the implications."[3]

And, of course, not the least of these implications was an increased urgency attached to Ted's subordinate readiness program.

Later, Stan caught up with Ben Franklyn on the mill floor.

"Ben, I don't think I understand. The men here don't strike me as *that* unhappy, yet you can't argue with Faust's data."

"Who can't? Come on over here by Jimmie Szekely.

"Jimmie, how long you been here in the mill? Twenty-eight years? And how long you been an oiler? Fourteen?

"Lemme ask you a stupid question, Jimmie, What kind of work would you try to get into if you could start all over again?"[4]

"Don't get no chance to start over," was the answer from the round, oil-smeared face.

"Now, come on, what if you could really do anything you wanted?"

"Uh, well, if I could do anything I wanted I sure as hell wouldn't be doing this. But, you nuts? What's a guy like me gonna do anyway? Listen, I'm glad I got a job."

They left Jimmie talking to himself.

"See what I mean?" said Ben. "Listen, if *fully* one-quarter of those guys would *keep* doing what they're doing, then there must be something wrong with *them,* not the other guys."

"Then why do Faust and the others . . . and worse, why do those staff guys in there listen to it?"

"I'll tell you why, it's just like the preacher at this little church my folks used to take me to."

Big help, thought Stan.

"This preacher was all hellfire and brimstone. Jesus, to listen to him you'd think you were living in Sodom. But every Sunday he'd pack 'em in. And you know, the ones who came needed it the least. Each one to himself knew he was doing okay, meanwhile the world is going to hell in a handbasket. So they feel pretty good about it, see. Lots of trouble and sin out there, and their neighbors' going to get theirs for sure. But them, they're okay. And it's a good show.

"But suppose he did the opposite. Nothing to get excited about. Pretty soon folks would stop showing up."

"Ben, I'm still not sure I understand."

"Sure you do, look at it this way. Faust and his guys can go one of two ways—what you just saw or the opposite. They can't mix the two together because then there's no 'message,' and nobody listens.

"Suppose Faust gets up and says everything's just fine. And better, we've got a 'highly motivated' workforce 'cause *only* one-quarter of our mill grunts would choose the same jobs. Shows 'high subordinate readiness' he'd say. The glass is half full, *not* half empty. So, don't worry about a thing, and nothing needs to be done. Nothing at all. Everything is A-okay.

"Well now, just what do you think would happen then?" Ben obviously was neither looking nor waiting for an answer. "I'll tell you what would happen. First thing, you wouldn't need Faust anymore. And the next thing you'd have is a lot of unemployed staff guys."

Ben savored the thought for a moment.

"So that's why you see what you see. They've got to keep the pot boiling just like the preacher. Plenty of hellfire and brimstone. And it doesn't worry those staff guys any more than it does the preacher's congregation. Hell, it makes 'em feel good. Their jobs are okay, and they can bleed a little for their—what do they call 'em—'alienated workers' and get paid for it to boot. Oh yeah, I think it's very easy to understand."

35

DON'T ASK

Thinking back on it, if it hadn't been for a peculiar turn of phrase by Mr. Marsh, Ted Shelby might never have become the author of The Company's Subordinate Readiness Program. But I find the incident precipitated by that phrase instructive for other reasons.

Perhaps you will, too.

"Hey, Stanley," said Ted Shelby, "would you take care of this for me? I'm pretty busy, and I think it's something that you can handle as well as I." He gave a sheaf of papers to Stanley.

Stanley shuffled through it off-handedly. "What do you want me to do?" he asked.

"You can figure it out," said Ted. "No problem."

Later in the day Stanley looked at the papers more closely. At the bottom is a seven-page xeroxed article from *The Academy of Management Review* on "Managerial Subordination." Attached to the article is a small mound of paper. Leafing through to the bottom Stanley finds a brief note from The Office of the President addressed to the Vice-President in Charge of Personnel. The three by five stapled to the memo says simply, "Ralph, please exercise on this at your earliest opportunity. Marsh."

Layered over Mr. Marsh's three by five is another from The Office of the Vice-President in Charge of Personnel, this addressed to the Personnel Director. This says, quite directly, "Sheila, let's exercise on this. Ralph." And atop this is attached still another memo, from Personnel Director—Corporate Staff, which says: "I think we ought to 'exercise' on this at our earliest opportunity. Sheila." This memo is addressed to the Director of Management Development.

The penultimate layer is the memo from the Director of Management Development to Ted Shelby, which says: "Ted, I'd like you to 'exercise' on this. This is something Mr. Marsh wants now."

The final link of the chain connecting Stanley and Mr. Marsh comes from Assistant to the Director for Training Programs—Edward W. Shelby IV. It says: "Stanley, please 'exercise on this.'"

Stanley is puzzled by the word "exercise"; it doesn't make any sense to him in this context. So he takes it to Lesley, and the two of them puzzle over it for half an hour. Still, they can't come up with any plausible notion of what any of those people mean by "exercise on this."

Finally he goes back to Ted Shelby. "Ted," he asks, "just what in God's name did you mean when you said 'exercise on this'?"

Ted is smiling at him. "Why, Stanley, I'd have thought that a smart fellow like yourself would have been able to figure that out."

"No," said Stanley, "I don't have any idea at all, and it seems as though nobody else around here knows either, judging from this cascade of memos.

"What *does* it mean?"

"I don't know," said Ted, "and you're probably right that nobody else does either, except maybe Mr. Marsh."

"Well, then why didn't anybody ask him what he meant, why pass the buck all the way down the line?"

Ted leaned back in his chair. "Let me answer that question with a little story." Edward W. Shelby IV had a lot of stories about The Company. "Back during the war most of our buildings were thrown up in a hurry. Pawtucket had just been completed—one of those corrugated steel jobs. I was there with my dad when Mr. Marsh (Sr.) went on an inspection tour of one of those buildings. You know the kind, corrugated sheet bolted through the structural members, so naturally the nuts on the inside show, and naturally they turned every which way. Well, Mr. Marsh says, 'That looks terrible!' And that very night the plant manager sends in a crew on overtime to straighten out the nuts and get them all turned in alignment. A week later, they were all like ducks in a row."

"I don't get the connection." Stanley looks really puzzled now.

"The point is that no one wants to ask a question of the top management above you. If you have to ask a question, the implication is that either you are stupid (because you didn't understand what he said) or that he is stupid (because he didn't make himself clear.) So when Mr. Marsh says, 'That looks terrible,' he might have meant the nuts, or he might have meant the whole plant, and he might not even have meant to be taken seriously. But the plant manager wasn't about to ask and take the chance of looking foolish."

"Oh," said Stanley, "then all those people passed that memo down in the hope that somebody below them would know what the people above them meant by 'exercise on this.' "

"Right," said Ted, "but after I gave the memos to you, I got some ideas. It's about time that I came up with some sort of program, and this looks like as good a bet as any. We know that Mr. Marsh likes it—or at least, he knows about it. And that's good enough for me." Ted took the cascade of memos back from Stanley and went to his desk to start drawing guidelines for his forthcoming "Subordinate Readiness Program."

We already know how the "Subordinate Readiness Program" turned out—very profitably for Stanley. But that is another story. The moral of this story is more for the Mr. Marsh's of the world than for the Ted's and the Stanley's: "It is easy to abuse your power." Since subordinates don't want to be put into the position of questioning what the boss says, the boss must be careful lest his offhand remarks be put into effect. And even more important, he's got to be aware that the Shelby's and Stanley's who work for him have stopped asking questions, that they are likely to get a great deal more "exercise" than he ever intended if he doesn't take the trouble to make himself clear.

36

SPEND IT, BURN IT...

It was indeed a strange scene that Stanley happened upon: Ben pounding his fist on the desk and Kerry beside him, roaring with laughter born of incredulity.

"Uh, excuse me, I thought maybe Dr. Faust was here." But as Stanley turned to leave, suddenly Ben thrust (threw would be more like it) a thick triplicate form across his desk to Stanley.

"Here, what the hell do *you* make of this thing? I'll be damned if *I* can figure out what's on these people's minds."

Stanley eyed the form for a minute and then, "Looks to me like it's a request for price quotation from The Agency."

"I think we have already figured out that much," put in Kerry. "We want to know what they want."

With these new instructions Stanley read it again. "They want . . . a tape, demolition, high precision (a plus or minus .001 tolerance), stainless steel, nondestructible . . . Right?"

"See," said Kerry with a grin, prodding Ben on the arm. "You can read. That *is* what they want."

"Yeah, I can see your problem," interjected Stanley. "It beats me what they'd use something like that for."

"Oh, no," returned Kerry, "that's not our problem. I know exactly what they want to use it for, because I used to do the same thing myself with a piece of rope. You see, when I was an Army engineer one of our jobs was to blow up enemy bridges. All you needed was a piece of rope, some dynamite, and the ability to swim. The rope had a series of knots tied along its length, and you'd swim out in the dark, wrap the rope around the piling and count the knots. For every knot you'd use a stick of dynamite. And that's what this tape they're talking about is supposed to do. The job of that piece of rope. But Jesus Christ—stainless steel, etched markings fully calibrated to hundredths of an inch—it'll cost them an arm and a leg and they won't even be able to use it at night. What's more, it says they want a thousand *prototypes* for field trial!"

"Wait a second," the light of revelation was shining in Stanley's eyes. "That RPQ is from The Agency, and this is the end of the fiscal year."

"What in the *hell* are you talking about?" Ben had his fill of nonsense for the afternoon. "I'm trying to find out about this idiotic request for price quotation, not about the time of year."

"All I mean is, well, maybe you're looking at it the wrong way. See, we used to do this kind of thing all the time when I was at The Agency. They had me working in Purchasing. Everybody called it 'Spring madness', since that was when it happened. The main thing was to get rid of it anyway you could. I'm surprised that people didn't just put it in a trunk and sink it in the Potomac, since that would have been a lot cheaper and easier than what we ended up doing. But I guess you really have to have a receipt to show what you did with it . . . "

"Hold on," Ben interrupted. "What's this 'it' you're talking about? You mean . . . "

"Money," Stanley completed the sentence.

"But it just doesn't make sense." Ben was now more puzzled than annoyed. "You say these people are *trying* to spend a lot of money on something they don't need? And they want to do it *now*, and they wouldn't want me to show them how to get the same job done for a tenth the cost?"

"Oh, I don't think they'd care," answered Stanley, "but you wouldn't get their order. They'd have Another Company do the work. But why do you say it doesn't make sense?"

"But that's no Goddammed way to run a business," Ben exploded. "What possible sense could it make to throw money away?"

Faust, who had arrived just a minute earlier, and seeing that Stanley was becoming somewhat intimidated, came to the rescue. "Perhaps I can supply a little, ah—perspective, Ben. We at The University work under a very similar system, though the amounts are far smaller. What you must understand, Ben, is that we, and they, are not running a business. We are, shall we say, providing a service. But just as you do, we work on a yearly budget. And so does The Agency. Now if it's an important agency—and certainly The Agency is—the justification of this budget will be laced with statements about how important, how very crucial it is for The Agency to have these funds. Now let us suppose that at the end of the year—June 30th—The Agency has not spent the funds so urgently needed for such important work. What happens when they submit the next budget, once again supported by the same arguments justifying the need for that much money?"

Stanley had to restrain his answer, for obviously this was one occasion when Faust's Socratic exercise was meant for another. Kerry, for whom the whole thing had been a joke from the beginning, was chuckling at the new revelations and so it was left for Ben to answer. "I can see what happens all right, even though I don't think it makes any sense. The head of The Agency is in trouble. Someone's going to say 'you must not be doing the job if you didn't spend all your money.' Or they might even say, 'looks to me like you never needed that money in the first place. Now the boys at Another Agency ran out last year so . . . '"

"Precisely," Dr. Faust was pleased that the lesson had taken so well. "So you must see that running The Agency is quite *unlike* running a business. One cannot grow unless one overspends. It is most necessary to show that one needs more money each ensuing year for there is no profit and loss statement to show how well one is doing his job."

With that Kerry, shaking his head and still smiling, turned to Ben, "Let's see that RPQ again . . . Hmmm, stainless, high precision, nondestructible, M1-A1 . . . all righty." And then, putting his arm around Ben's shoulder, "Ben, know something? They've come to the right outfit."

37

MADE TO MEASURE

Ted Shelby, the Staff Director of Sales Management Development, is delivering the wrap-up pitch to the new members of the headquarters sales staff group. Twenty bright, young trainees sat attentively.

"Let me say once again that this is your big chance," Ted began. "Each one of you has been sent here to sales division headquarters by your branch manager to learn how the game is played. Each one of you has been selected for your outstanding record. Every one of you in this room is a potential division manager. This is your opportunity to see the planning side of this business, and you've got to make the most of it."

Twenty heads nodded in unison. A pleased murmur filled the room. Ted continued: "As you know, the name of the game we're in is *Competition*. We're the best, and that is what we're going to stay. If you've got no stomach for infighting, you don't belong in this league."

Twenty competitors nodded; yes, they had.

"It's not just a matter of doing the same outstanding job we've been doing. It's not enough to have a crisp and hard-hitting approach anymore. There are new management tools being developed to increase effectiveness, and measurement, gentlemen and ladies—*measurement of results* is the name of the game now. It's not enough to do our best. We've got to know how good our best is."

With that profundity Ted wrapped up the final session. Stanley, whose assignment as Ted's assistant required that he sit in with the

group and take notes, had scribbled tersely on his note pad, "Measurement Important." Another of Stanley's duties was to check on the
progress of people who in the past had received the ministrations of
Ted's developmental programs (again measurement). Consequently,
following this session Stanley was off to the Seattle sales office to
interview one Willa Diehl, now the Assistant Sales Manager under
Kerry Drake.

Kerry was not happy on the occasion of that visit. (Not happy?
Perhaps that is an understatement.)

"You," the word drilled Stanley squarely through the chest, "and the
rest of you at division, and *especially* that damnfool Shelby, are
responsible for *this*!" Kerry now waved an eight and a half by eleven
floppy covered notebook at Stanley's face.

"See this? It's my score card. Count 'em; forty-four different monthly
reports. Yesterday the division manager called me and said that I was
two months behind in my 'Subordinate Readiness' report. *Subordinate
readiness?* For Chrissakes, I've got so damn many reports to keep track
of that I don't even know who all my subordinates are, let alone how
'ready' any of them are!" Stanley inadvertently retreated a step before
Kerry's wrath.

"Let me tell you something. Now I've got forty-four of *these things*
(Kerry contemptuously shook the sheaf of reports in his hand), but just
three years ago I only had four. That's how many—four! Net, percent of
quota, deliveries, and accounts receivable. That's all I had then, and
that's all we need now!

"I used to know where my business was. I even had time to get out
there and do a little selling myself. But now it seems like almost every
month I get another one of *these*. Here! This is the latest—Subordinate
Readiness with Intermediate Milestones Program. How can *I* know
where I stand on my Subordinate Readiness Program, when I'm not
even sure from month to month what it is? Now I've got to add someone
just to take care of it. I'll tell you one thing, I'd sure like to meet the damn
fool who thought up this last wrinkle." Stanley thought, you already
have. For that program was the brainchild of Will Diehl, as everyone
called her.

Oddly enough it turned out that Willa was just as concerned as Kerry.
After assuring Stanley that things were going rather well for her and, in
turn, getting Stanley's assurance that the author of the new program
would remain anonymous, Will Diehl held forth at some length on
the problem.

"Kerry's right, you know. But when I worked up the program it never
occurred to me what I was doing until I got out here on the receiving end.
Look at what you're doing at headquarters, even Ted. It all starts with
Ted, you know. He wants some recognition just like the rest of us; he
wants to get ahead too. So he points to something that I guess is

necessary. He says that there is a lot of staff work that has to be done, so why not combine it with the management development function so that our sales people will get to see the thing from the headquarters perspective. Why not? So what we do is take the best salesmen from the field, bring them to headquarters, and get them involved in sales staff work.

"Now I don't know if you understand what that's like, Stanley, but let me tell you. In the field you're in the thick of the action, doing what really counts; it's exciting. Then, just like that, you're in with a bunch of staff zombies from headquarters, up to your neck in paper and telephones. Nothing's ever finished, and it seems like nothing is ever accomplished either. One day is like the next. No offense, but good lord— would anyone be there if we could possible avoid it? So finally, you've got only one question: How the hell do I get out of here?!" Just the thought of it seemed to bring a note of anxiety into Willa's voice.

"The question is—what it really boils down to—what do I have to do to get someone to say, okay, she's ready for the next assignment? I'll tell you what you do. You do what Ted and a bunch of other guys did. You dream up a program, get to talk to some of top management in the process, and pretty soon when the next chance comes up—well, they all know you and so it's your turn."

Yes, thought Stanley, and along with Willa Diehl was the inevitable program. For she found out pretty quickly that the best way to do it was to develop a new, crisp and hard hitting program, to be responsive to The Company's new needs in the "changing business environment." And you needed measures to go along with it . . . "it's not enough to do our best. We have to know how good our best is." Hence Subordinate Readiness with Intermediate Milestones Program—SRIMP.

The point I am trying to make here is that the result of this arrangement is inevitable; that under the conditions I have described, programs designed to improve sales management effectiveness and accountability have just the opposite effect. Kerry will get his reports filled out one way or another—in this case by the person who developed them. But the facts will be mostly "guesstimates" with an occasional sprinkling of lies. Consequently, it becomes more difficult than ever to find out how someone really is doing.

But why inevitable, you ask? Surely there are other ways of gaining attention. Yes, of course, that is true. And it is true as well that not everyone uses the route of program development. But keep in mind that these are young people on the move. An extra year seems like a lifetime. Remember too that they are all salesmen and good ones. So what could be more natural than to sell—to sell a program and yourself with it. If modern management tools are the hot product today, well, that's what we're selling isn't it? Finally, it is not until you get back into the field as assistant manager that you get to see the overall impact of the thing.

After all, yours was just one little program, wasn't it?

And so this is where Kerry Drake is found, laboring under the burden of SRIMP and its near and distant relatives . . . a whole list of programs necessary to fit The Company to the changing business environment, and incidentally, to promote a number of desperate staff misfits away from division headquarters.

38

PROPHET WITHOUT HONOR

" . . . so what we find, managementwise, is that fully eighty percent of our management subordinates who, as we put it—start from SCRATCH—will, over a period of five years be promoted more often and achieve higher levels of compensation than a comparable group not so selected."

What's Ted up to now? He's pushing his latest program, "Subordinate Career Readiness Assessment and Training Centers—SCRATCH" (with the H added to form the acronym). Right now he's presenting his ideas to a group from engineering, production and personnel including Ben, Kerry, Dr. Faust, and Pat Jones. Faust has been Ted's consultant on this one, while Pat is attending as the company's in-house expert on industrial psychology. Lesley's there too. She's been working with Ted on the communications package. That "Start from Scratch" slogan is her invention. But here, let's listen to Ted. He's only just begun his pitch.

"The key to this approach," Ted continued, turning to his next flip chart, "is realism; realism in the situation, in testing and in the rating of performance.

"First, it's a group situation. That's the *management* situation, isn't it? And then we use a number of different tests and procedures. But most of our tests aren't really tests at all. Mostly we're simulating the kind of situations that practicing managers find themselves in. Those are the tasks we rate our candidates on." Ted went on describing the group problems and the simulated manufacturing problem.

"It seems to me that what you're really doing here," Ben broke in, "is getting a bunch of staff psychologists to sit around and try to decide whether a guy knows how to manage from watching him work on a couple of dummied-up problems. Is that it? And that this is supposed to tell me *better* than watching my guys work on *real* problems what their *management potential* is. And you want me to believe that!"

"Now just a minute, Ben," Ted shot back. "I knew you were going to say that. No, that's *not* what we do." Now, mustering up his best crisp/urgent tone, "As a matter of fact, Ben, our raters—the people who are making these assessments—are a group of high potential middle managers themselves. Don't you see, that's the beauty of it! These are the very people who are *best* qualified to make these kinds of assessments."

"Maybe so," replied Ben, "but I still think that this is a line responsibilty. For the life of me I can't see why we always need so much help."

"Maybe I can help clarify the situation somewhat, Ben. I believe that I have more direct experience with these assessment centers than has Ted." The voice was that of Dr. Faust. "Pardon me if I'm wrong, but I think you are, ah—somewhat in error in the belief that these people are going to tell you whom to promote and whom not. No, this is intended strictly as a *staff* service. Ted's SCRATCH staff will provide you with a quantitative, objective appraisal of the managment potential of each candidate, together with an assessment of strengths and, ah—shall we say 'future developmental objectives.' How you use this, what you do with this information, is entirely up to you."

"And no one from New York is going to be after Ben and me to see how well these high-potential characters are doing? Is that right?" Kerry sounded skeptical.

"Well, yes and no, Kerry," said Ted. "Naturally we'll want to follow the progress of those identified as high potential future top managers. But no, as Dr. Faust has outlined, how you *use* the information we give you is strictly up to you.

"Still there's another point that I think we are overlooking," Ted continued, "and that's the truly *objective* nature of these ratings. With this program each of our top managers will have a way of comparing his own subordinate's promotional readiness to those of similarly placed subordinates throughout the company." Ted grew almost lyrical in description of the absolute fairness of the system, and how talent perhaps now buried by circumstance would be brought to light and justly rewarded through promotion and "increases in compensation."

Up to this point Pat Jones, who probably knew more of these things than anyone at the table, had been silent. Even so, Ted had been eyeing her uneasily, for she had a way of asking the most impossible questions. Well now, here it came.

"So as I understand this, Ted," Pat began, "what you are offering us is a way of increasing the validity of our managerial selection procedure for middle and top level management. Correct?"

Ted nodded.

"And by validity, I take it, you mean the extent to which people who get higher marks in your procedure show higher levels of performance?"

"Well, er, yes. That's about it, Pat," Ted was hedging.

"*About* it?" Pat pressed on.

"Why, you know that we've never had any really *objective* measures of managerial performance, Pat. You know that as well as I do. Heck, that's one of the main reasons we've developed the SCRATCH program, so we will have some better idea, some more *objective* idea of who our top managerial subordinates are. Why, that's just the point of all this." Ted was afraid he could see where this line of discussion would lead.

"I know, I understand all that," Pat bore in, "but my question is, how do you *know* this is any better than the way we do it now? How *have* you validated your procedures, if not against direct and objective measures of performance?"

"I think that you will find that we have used the usual measures, Dr. Jones," Faust stepped in to rescue the floundering Shelby, "Number of promotions, number of merit salary increases, and supervisory ratings of future potential. We have achieved validity coefficients as high as point five zero with ratings of future potential, for example. I believe that you can see . . . ."

"Hold it, Doc," Kerry interrupted, "you and I have known each other quite awhile, right? And I usually think you make pretty good sense, right? So do I really understand? It seems to me that what we're doing is this: first you're asking Ben and me to tell you who's good and who isn't so good, so that you can figure out whether this SCRATCH program of yours really works. And if it does, why then you'll be in a position to tell us who's good and who isn't good. What's more, you'll even tell us who has . . . what'd you call it—high potential—so that we'll know how to rate the future potential of our managers so that . . ." Kerry threw up his hands, lost for words.

"It's lifting yourself up by the bootstraps," chuckled Ben.

Pat, sensing that the situation was getting out of hand, that the entire idea of systematic performance appraisal might be thrown out with the bath water of the SCRATCH program, decided to restore some sanity to the situation, "People—Ben, Kerry; I think we're in a little over our heads in the technical issues of this program. Remember that we do use testing procedures in limited ways right now to help us improve our managerial selection. They work. And we do use performance appraisals of all employees right now: executives, managers, subordinates, workers. Flawed as they may be, they *are* better than nothing. so that's not the issue here, as I see it."

Then turning to Ted in a somewhat surprisingly conciliatory tone, "What Ted, here, is trying to do is not something that hasn't been tried before. And, frankly,I think we ought to support this effort—on a *limited, experimental* basis," Pat emphasized the words. "The value of these procedures is not that they produce something that we haven't had before, but rather that they can help us make systematic and objective the kinds of procedures that now may be haphazard and subjective.

"The risk is not that managers will ignore the recommendations that Ted will make. Oh, no. The real risk is that they'll use it as a crutch to avoid the gut-wrenching responsibility for making those hard decisions. So, as Ben says, it becomes part of a boot-strap operation where 'subordinates' with high assessment ratings are therefore given high performance ratings and in turn receive more merit increases and promotions. No, the risk is that the same kinds of impression management that may help candidates get higher ratings on the simulated exercise will also be mistaken as performance by their own management. So what you're left with is not prediction, but self-fulfilling prophecy."

39

SIC TRANSIT

The early morning fog had not yet lifted as Faust strode briskly to his morning engagement. Somewhat behind, Stanley struggled to keep the pace. Quite likely the difference in pace was attributable to the encumbrance of flip charts and the inevitable paraphernalia of the "presentation" that Stanley was lugging along.

Just off The University campus stood The Institute, a modern two-story building with a distinctly academic facade. Stanley, as Dr. Faust's student, would accompany him occasionally on these junkets as a kind of apprentice—if for no other reason than to carry the necessary equipment. On this particular occasion Faust was providing The Institute with some bits and pieces of esoterica pertinent to a current project. The arrangement worked well both for Faust and The Institute, since the client paid not only for Dr. Faust's efforts but contributed as well a modest management fee added on by The Institute—presumably for the value of knowing where to find Dr. Faust.

"How does a place like this get started?" Stanley asked, with a mixture of hope and admiration, thinking that the knowledge might be useful in the future.

"That's difficult to say, but it wasn't too long ago, ten, fifteen years, perhaps. The Director and I were colleagues in The Department at The University. Naturally, you wouldn't remember, but the Government was interested in certain kinds of research at the time, and the Director and some of my colleagues obliged. It was a pleasant and, ah—fruitful relationship which evolved into a full time career for them. Of course, the Head of The Department didn't see the good in this for The University and so he asked my friend to cut back these activities somewhat. Now my friend and another colleague were, ah—irritated by this kind of interference so . . . well, in short . . ." Faust swept his arm panoramically about the building which they had just entered, ". . . this is the result."

Looking about him Stanley saw lots of people—all looking quite busy—and lots of offices—all suitably fitted out with academic-looking inhabitants. This scene prompted Stanley's next query, "What do they do now? I mean, how do they keep this thing going?"

"That is difficult to say exactly. I know that it is virtually all Government research, for that is the nature of the field they are in. And, of course, that is where the contracts are. But I believe that there has been a change from what the Director and the original group were doing. The program has changed as Government needs have changed. I believe that it would be accurate to say that they are in the business of doing research that the Government wants done. In systems, of course."

"Well, whatever it is, they must be doing it pretty well because they've really grown." The evidence for Stanley's observation was indisputable.

"Yes, I suppose so, but in this kind of work, it is grow and die."

"Uh, Dr. Faust, you said grow *and* die. Of course, you mean grow *or* die, don't you?" Now, you would have thought that by this time Stanley would have learned that Faust, even in casual conversation, did not speak imprecisely. This realization would have spared him an occasional verbal barb from his mentor.

"What I meant is precisely what I said," Faust noted coldly.

Now seated outside the Director's office, waiting for the appointed time, Faust emphasized his displeasure by focusing his attention straight ahead. Stanley succeeded in choking back the impulse to say that Faust's earlier comment made no sense, so perhaps he was learning. He replied instead, "I'm sorry, but I just don't understand."

"Yes, of course." Then, "We do seem to be a bit early, don't we? Here, leave the charts with the secretary, and we'll have a cup of coffee in the cafeteria." Faust suddenly brightened. Obviously he'd had an idea that pleased him.

"Here, sit down. You have looked about you quite a bit since we arrived. Let us test your powers of deduction, shall we?" Naturally, this was not a question. "Let us say that you were my friend, the Director. You have left The University and established this business. You are involved in Government contract research. Now then, what is your first concern?"

Stanley pondered the question for a minute, for he had just been reminded that it was risky to answer Faust in haste. Then, "Well, I don't know about your friend, but *I'd* be worried about where my next meal was coming from. It all seems kind of risky to me."

"Yes, certainly. Even granting the fact that my friend is considerably more self-confident than you are, that would be his concern as well. Now then, what would you do?"

"Okay, I'm not sure exactly *how* I'd do it, but I would make sure that we had work. I guess I'd bid on a lot of jobs hoping to get enough to keep going."

"Quite correct. Go on."

"Uh, I can't. What I mean is, do I get the jobs or don't I?" Faust's look indicated there would be no immediate help on this question. "All right, I see. Yes, it's obvious that I do get these jobs because this place is here, isn't it?" Stanley's face brightened with the pleasure of successful deduction. "In fact, I guess we get more than . . . . Yeah, we get more than we bargained for. And that puts me in a tough spot doesn't it?"

"And?"

"And—and so I need some help. I suppose I go back to The University, offer a few young professors a big raise, and they do the work."

"Yes, quite right. Now what do you suppose happens next year? You realize, of course, that Government contracts are funded on a year-to-year basis."

"Why, the same thing, I suppose. Only now you've got these new people who feel the same way you did when you started off. Sure! So the whole process repeats itself! And the year after that, too!"

"So you see, do you? And what kind of growth model does this suggest to you?"

"I don't think I follow you, Dr. Faust."

"Do you think it would be arithmetic, or . . . ."

"Oh, I see. Oh no, the model would more likely be geometric. At first you have two, then the two need four, or even five, then eight. No, it wouldn't be arithmetic."

"Well, now, what else does this model imply?"

Stanley's look stated eloquently his puzzlement. Faust relented a bit, but only a bit. "Look around you, who are these people?"

"The people who work here, I guess." Stanley's brilliant observation was met by silence. Then, after almost a minute, "Uh, I guess you mean *what* are these people? And then I suppose I do see what you mean. They're not all research scientists, that's for sure. There's got to be secretaries, clerks, technical support . . . ."

"And there are managers, managers' managers, and executives as well. You must not forget that either." The time for the appointment was drawing near and Faust, wishing to finish the game, felt he could not depend entirely on the speed of Stanley's mental processes. "Then let us restate the original question, 'What does this model imply about changes taking place in the organization?' "

"Oh, sure, I see. It means that you've got lots of kinds of people that you didn't have before. Yeah, and the growth of these other people is even faster than the researchers. Sure. Every four or five researchers need a section head, and the head needs a secretary, and they've all got to communicate with one another, and you're bigger now so you have to make sure that there's a permanent record of that communication in the file. Sure, you get a whole bunch of management and clerical people that you never had before."

With this Faust reached out for a paper napkin and drew a circle on it.

"I am fond of this metaphor as an illustration of the process. The research staff," said Faust ringing the circle again and again with his pencil, "grows as the periphery of the circle, but the supporting management, technical and clerical staff, grows as the area—expands as the square of the periphery, as it were. Therein lies the problem."

"But doesn't it stabilize, come to an equilibrium?"

"Seldom. How can it stabilize given the dynamics we've talked about?" Now brushing the pencil back and forth within the center of the circle, "Who pays for this? Someone must. For this reason projects are asked to 'tithe' to pay for the supporting staff. In direct consequence project costs go up. And as a further direct result, contracts become more difficult to win. Then there are the vicissitudes of the economy." The look in his eye revealed that Faust now was conversing with himself. "Most of these Institutes bloom in the economic spring, then flourish and grow in the ensuing summer. But there are the autumns and winters of the economic cycle as well. What happens then?" Stanley understood once again that this was not a question.

"Several things," continued Faust. "First, with the added costs induced by the incaution of good times one is less able to compete. So one assembles his management team and sets forth some new rules. Nonproductive groups, one says, will cease to exist. Each group must carry its own weight. One's understanding of this message, of course, is that it will spur activity. Aha, but the activity it spurs is the, ah—defection of those research scientists who best can make it on their own. They leave and start the cycle anew. They feel, and rightly so, that they will be better off on their own, without the burden of excessive management and staff.

"So now we enter the final phase of the cycle. Strangely, the organization cannot stabilize itself on the downward trend because it divests itself of management and supporting staff more slowly than it must. Once again, the process is inevitable. Executives and managers have come to enjoy being executives and managers. They tend to resist the inevitable. One might say that for this reason a certain amount of misrepresentation of the health of the organization takes place at this point. Next, all have become accustomed to the luxury of technical and clerical assistance. And while these people are cut, to be sure, they are never cut in the same proportion as they were added when the organization grew.[5] Finally, you have the fact that the first rats to desert the sinking ship are, ah—shall we say the brightest and healthiest rats. And so inevitably the organization will die."

"You don't mean that all these Institutes eventually go under, do you?" Stanley's question brought Faust back to reality.

"Did I say that? No, you are right. That would be an overstatement. No, sooner or later spring returns to the economy and some will survive. But some, the ones that have grown fat and sluggish, will not. Some will meet a natural death, and the corporate wolves will devour their share of the others. It all depends. But the basic cycle is there. That is all I wanted to illustrate."

Toward noon, following their appointment, Stanley looked about him with new vision as he accompanied Faust to the street. Yes, there were an awful lot of people here. Outside the fog had lifted, replaced by a beautiful clear, crisp day. Yes, there was no doubt about it. There was just a hint of autumn in the air.

40

THE ROPES TO KNOW (V)

The games just illustrated are not games in the usual sense of players competing with one another. They are games of people against fate. Much in the sense of the Greek tragedy, our players are inexorably drawn to outcomes preordained by the circumstances. If there were one message in this section it would be that too much of a good thing is no good. And if there were a second message it would be a turnabout of the old saw—nothing fails like success.

Take the example of the experimental psychologist's white rat. The rat learns that by pressing a bar he can provide himself with a sesame seed (which he likes). "Operant" psychology says we are "reinforcing" this bar-pressing behavior with the seed. Rat keeps pressing, and psychologist keeps reinforcing. Finally this behavior (perhaps for both rat *and* psychologist) becomes so ingrained, so habitual, that the little creature keeps on pressing the bar long after the seeds have ceased to flow. Rat has become "conditioned."

Rat's ultimate reward for his faithful performance is also instructive. Since he is no longer "naive"—he's got this "behavior set"—he is useless for other experiments and is summarily dispatched to his final reward.

What has this got to do with Stanley and The Company? Consider the Stanley of *Cowboy*. He starts toying with the computer. Ben finds out, likes the idea, and gives Stanley a new position. Sesame seed one. Stanley sees the gain in this—finds the situation rewarding—and continues to develop his computer skills. Ben also sees the gain and keeps up the flow of metaphorical seeds. Pretty soon Stanley is "our computer expert" and he's at a dead end with little more to gain. No more seeds left. But he keeps on with his computer because that is all he can do now; he's overspecialized, lost his flexibility to adapt, and in some instances (like our rat friend) his ability to survive organizationally.

Now, the stories have been developed from two underlying themes. The first of these has to do with the consequences of overspecialization, of overadaptation to a particular set of organizational circumstances. The second has to do with the unintended consequences, the remote—or better yet, the *systems*—consequences of organizational strategies. Though these are distinct themes, they come together as one in many instances. This happens particularly where specialization is used as a strategy for achieving success.

These themes have been explored from the standpoint of systems consequences for both the individuals involved and for the organization as a whole. And the stories are illustrative of the fact that overspecialization, overadaptation to one organizational role, is likely to produce systems consequences dangerous to both individual and organization. So in *Cowboy* and *Praise/Criticism* Stanley and Ted, respectively, found a good thing and stayed with it. But in doing so they became inflexible in their behavior. Each in his own way became less effective through his diminished perspective. The consequences were unfortunate not only for themselves but for other individuals as well.

Don't Ask and *Hellfire and Brimstone* are special examples of the impact of individuals adapting to immediate and specific needs, of doing exactly what is called for to meet current requirements. When Marsh says "exercise" on this, don't ask. Obviously he knows what he is doing, it's our job to interpret. So countless hours are lost in fruitless search. Somewhat differently, the inevitable result of the "morale" survey is to uncover discontent. After all, good news is no news (to reverse the epigram). So individuals behave in predictable, though perhaps dysfunctional ways.

Perhaps even more important are the consequences to organizations as a whole of this tendency of individuals to adapt and make the most of particular sets of organization circumstances. In *Made to Measure* and *Spend It, Burn It* are examples of people adapting to the organizational environment and doing so creating real problems for The Company and The Agency. The Agency, in fact, is a classic example of dysfunctional adaptation. To promote sound fiscal management, the government decrees that funds cannot be carried from one fiscal year to the next. (An exercise for the reader might be to examine the organizational consequences of *not* doing this.) But the consequences of this particular strategy have been illustrated; get rid of that money somehow or you're going to have to answer some embarrassing questions. *Made to Measure* is an example of a similar process where again consequences accrue not so much to the individuals involved but to the organization as a whole.

Prophet Without Honor illustrates the same theme in a different way. Because it is easier to measure promotions and merit increases than it is to measure performance, those "assessment centers" wind up simply confirming management's subjective guesswork rather than challenging it. And finally, in *Sic Transit* there is an example of the organization as a whole adapting to a narrow set of circumstances and in consequence coming to grief. Prosperity for The Institute came as a result of finding a particular set of business opportunities to exploit. Not only was there a particular environment, but a particular host as well. The analogy of organization to organism becomes complete.

Let's take these themes and expand them further by still broader analogy. Borrowing from biological theory, let's look at two strategies for organizational survival. The first of these is "adaptive specialization"—finding a particular set of organizational needs and becoming outstandingly proficient in meeting them. The second is "adaptive generalization"—being able to do many things, to fit in anywhere.[6]

Biology teaches that adaptive specialization is a cul-de-sac, the end of development and growth. Once you've adapted completely to an empty ecological niche it's the end of the road. This was the case for the dinosaurs and the dodo. And there are social counterparts in the mining and canal towns.

Overadapted organisms are in an evolutionary trap. Having specialized so completely, they have lost their ability to cope with major changes in the ecological system to which they are adapted. Similarly, changes in the social or organizational system displace overspecialized individuals. Mining and canal towns struggle to find a new reason for being. Government research contractors diversify, aerospace engineers go back to school and get MBAs.

In the second method of survival—adaptive generalization—the individual survives and prospers because it can exist under a wide range of circumstances; it fits many ecological spaces. For this reason, the little mammals made it when the dinos didn't.

Wait a minute, you say. You seem to be getting lost in analogy. All this talk about mammals and dinosaurs; what does this have to do with my career in The Company?

Well, yes, I am getting a little far afield. You should see what adaptive specialization is, the business about the cowboy parts and The Institute, that sort of thing. So your question must be, what do you mean by adaptive generalization? The answer is two things really, for it works a bit differently for individuals and organizations.

Once again return to our bar-pressing rat. He likes sesame seeds, so the seeds can be used as an incentive for rat to behave in such a way that makes it possible for him to obtain same (be rewarded). Psychologist sets up a very simple system—press the bar and get the seed. That's it. Not surprisingly, rat learns and adapts completely to this very limited ecosystem.

People also respond to incentives. If it's bar-pressing that's being rewarded—well, press away! Of course, the situation is more complicated than this. There are many kinds of incentives, social as well as economic, and there are disincentives, too. Avoidance behavior results from disincentives; remember the minimax. So what is being said is that, by and large, people in organizations pay attention to the consequences of what they do and try to arrange things so that these consequences will be as rewarding as possible with as little risk of "aversive stimulation" (being chewed out by the boss, for example) as possible. Simple, isn't it?

Well, what is not so simple is the prediction of the long-term consequences of this behavior for both individual and organization. And that is what is important here. For *individuals*, adaptive generalization requires the moral fortitude to defer the immediate gratification attending specialization while investing in new, additional skills. This is what nature did for the early mammals who consequently could prosper in many environments.

The consequences for *organizations* are somewhat different. Oddly enough, the basic difficulty seems to stem from a lack of appreciation that a man truly is an adaptable beast, with a strong tendency toward metaphorical bar-pressing. Specific, limited, and concrete incentive situations act to focus individual behavior on a specific, limited repertoire of activities. This is the analogy to adaptive specialization whose consequences have been described. Diffuse and general incentive schemes focusing on a broad behavioral repertoire do quite the opposite; lead to adaptive generalization and retain organizational adaptability. It is this adaptability that avoids some of the long term undesirable systems consequences described.

So in closing remember that the real issues here are the game of man and fate, and avoiding the fate that lies in store for he who would follow the strategy of adaptive specialization. Flexibility—adaptive generalization—is your course. Yes, learn how to use the computer, but don't go so far as to become expert at it. There will always be others for that. Your job is to know how and where to fit the computer into the work of other specialists. It may take longer, but you'll never go the way of the dodo.

ENDNOTES

1. Excerpts taken directly from *The New York Times,* December 22, 1972, p. 1.
2. Ibid., p. 14.
3. Ibid.
4. Ibid.
5. Since the initial publication of *Ropes,* new research has been published that completely supports Dr. Faust's observations on growth and decline in organizations. See Jeffrey D. Ford, "The Occurrence of Structural Hysteresis in Declining Organizations," *Academy of Management Review* 5 (1980): 589-598.
6. These terms and the basic argument are taken from Dunn, *Economic and Social Development.*

PART VI

SKATE FAST OVER THIN ICE

Introduction to Part VI

As Stanley moved through the ranks of The Company, he came to be aware of a particular quality of Ted Shelby's. Ted wasn't one to admit he didn't have the answer to a critical question, nor was he one to let a dearth of convincing arguments dissuade him from taking positions he felt were advantageous. So on occasion he would be heard to skim quickly over major points on his way to his final conclusion. On these occasions, Stanley would say to himself: "That's right, Ted—when you're skating on thin ice, you'd better skate fast. Because if you stay in one spot too long, you're going to fall through."

Now, if this principle holds true for skaters on ice (and it does), then it is doubly true for corporate skaters. To wit: when you reach the stage where you are involved in making real decisions, you will want to avoid being in one position too long where some minor miscalculation may catch up with you. That is, you'll fall through. Actually, everyone falls through now and again, but organizationally speaking, this is least likely to happen to the fast moving executive—the one who moves fast through projects, fast through the organization, and fast through personal interactions where results or outcomes are defined for future reference.

An earlier section discussed decisions and why you should avoid having to make them, if possible. But I also said that it is not realistic to believe that you always could. In fact, about the only way to move up through an organization *is* to make decisions. So, this chapter is concerned with decisions—not *how* to make them, exactly, but how to make them pay off.

Now, one of the most important factors in decision making is the situation in which the decision is evaluated. This is where the skating comes in. You may skate fast (1) before the fact, (2) during the process, or (3) after the fact.

Skating fast *before the fact* means setting up the situation in advance, providing a proper payoff matrix and keeping things moving and fluid. You should be ready to jump in and take credit for a situation that is shaping up profitably.

Skating fast *during the process* has to do with continually being aware of possible outcomes. Keep an eye on developments, and be ready to declare the job well done and pass it on to the clean-up squad. Be sensitive to various indicators that the ice is cracking so that you can get the most out of the situation before moving on to a new "opportunity."

Skating fast *after the fact* is not only unavoidable, but mandatory. You may find that you are saddled with a decision, a situation when you can't evade doing something. This might appear to be a terrible responsibility, but not necessarily. There are many situations where some fast footwork will not only save the day, but even reap rich rewards. All you need do is to define the favorable outcomes as part of your program—for example, pointing to someone else's work and showing how its success logically derives from your decision.

These lessons will be elaborated shortly.

But, you say, this sounds very self-serving, and that's not my style. I'm basically a team man. I'll do well for The Company, and The Company will do well for me. I'm a builder not an opportunist, and you seem to be suggesting . . . .

Yes, I recognize the impulse, and it's a sound one. If it weren't for the builders we'd still be sleeping in caves. But this is about succeeding in an organizational environment, and perhaps you need to be reminded of the distinctions among a bricklayer, an engineer, and an architect.

Now, skill and competence are unquestionably required to be a successful bricklayer. But do you really want to spend your life executing the details of other people's schemes and designs? Well, maybe you do. But consider the engineer and the architect. The architect is the artist, the conceiver, the shaker, the mover. He operates under the dictum of: "I'll give you what's best for you, not necessarily what you think you want." His sweep of imagination and boldness of concept mark his place. Surely you can visualize his organizational counterpart.

The engineer is expected to take the architect's conception and show how to realize it. The engineer will lay out the details, design the structural members, and so forth. His responsibility is for the working plan. By now, of course, you see the relationship: the architect's job is done after the broad sweep. If the final structure doesn't turn out as envisaged, then it's the engineer's fault; he didn't have the stuff to bring the grand vision to fruition. On the other hand, if the structure is a success, who gets the credit? How many of Frank Lloyd Wright's engineers can you name?

The architect moves from project to project, he is done when the design is complete, not waiting for the actual building to go up. And this is your role. Engineers sometimes do without architects, yes that's true. And although this is reasoning by analogy, it's also true in organizations. Organizations have many metaphorical engineers and few architects. And, typically, for some reason or other these "engineers" seem not to feel any need for "architects"—so don't look to them. No, look to other people in The Company with vision—to Mr. Marsh and his key advisors. They'll listen to you.

Once you've adopted this course, then it is but a simple matter of keeping your skates sharp, and success must follow. These lessons should help.

41

STITCH IN TIME

When the devil are they going to finish that thing! It seems to me that they have been putting up that new building forever. Not that I care, understand. But the incessant clanking, hammering, and honking is not suitable accompaniment for my work.

Still, the sight of new construction brings back some interesting recollections. This incident must go back many years now. Stanley had been with The Company perhaps not more than one year at the time.

It was his first really big assignment with The Company, working on the construction of the Portland plant. Not only was he given some major responsibility as Kerry Drake's assistant (Kerry was construction superintendent), but it was a brand new plant, on a site about 3,000 miles from New York. All in all, it was an exciting occasion for Stanley.

But there were some problems at Portland, and Stanley was discussing these with Kerry.

"Now, how're we doing over at B Building, Stanley?" asked Kerry. "Still having problems?"

"I'm afraid so, Mr. Drake," said Stanley. "In fact, construction hasn't even started. The contractor says he has to finish up in A Area before he can move his men."

"Listen, we can't take that kind of answer from him," said Kerry. "Did you point out to him that he's already behind on B Building? The construction schedule calls for that to be finished by the end of the week!"

"Well, yes, I did," said Stanley. "But then he says that he would have finished with A Area except for that goof-up of ours. He told me that he could get to work on B if that was what we wanted, but that it would cost us some extra money."

"He's got us there," Kerry admitted. "Listen, I want you to . . ." Just then the phone rang. Kerry answered it. Ted Shelby from New York was on the line. "Ted? Fine. How's the weather back there? Oh? Is that right?. . . oh, Mr. Marsh? . . . plant schedule, eh? Urgent? . . . you've got a list you say? Most important buildings? . . . okay, fire away . . . B Building . . .?"

Stanley blanched. They were in for it, sure as hell. When Ted found out that the ground hadn't even been broken, Marsh's watchdogs would be all over the place in a couple of days, fouling everything up and generally making life miserable.

". . . No problems there," said Kerry ". . . I'd estimate B Building at about eighty to eighty-five percent completed. Oh, say eighty percent just to be conservative . . . yeah, things are going very well, we've been getting in some good licks the past couple weeks . . . "

Stanley couldn't believe his ears. Had Kerry Drake gone crazy?

". . . yeah, we've been pushing it hard since your last visit, Ted . . . well, I'm sure glad that Mr. Marsh will be pleased . . . . Say, one other thing, Ted, we've been pushing this thing so hard that we got a little ahead of our construction plans in A Area and . . . ."

Stanley listened in awe as Kerry neatly wrote off their goof, came up with some extra money, and got a pat on the back besides. When Kerry hung up, Stanley said, "Kerry, uh—don't get me wrong, but I couldn't help overhearing your conversation with Ted Shelby, and . . . you *do* know that we haven't even started on B Building, don't you—I mean, like we were just talking about? I mean, eighty percent complete? What if Mr. Marsh or Ted Shelby comes out to check?"

Kerry laughed out loud. "Son, there's no way I can be worse off than to tell Ted Shelby exactly what is going on out here. And I mean that. Those staff guys have never built a damned thing in their lives. I know what I've got to do, and I'll get it done. Mr. Marsh knows what he's doing too, but he has to work through his staff jackals. They're all afraid of him, and they take everything he says at face value. Listen, if I'd told Ted that we haven't even started B Building, he'd go straight to Marsh's handlers, get them all stirred up, and we'd be finished. Every damned staff smart alec in The Company would be telling us what to do and tripping all over themselves. We'd never get the job done. Besides, even if they decide to come on out now, let's say they start thinking about it tonight, nobody would arrive for a week anyhow. Get the contractor in here, Stanley, and we'll start moving on the shell of B Building; we've got the money for it now. And, what the hell, those staff guys can't tell twenty-five percent finished from seventy-five percent finished, or eighty percent either, for that matter."

The moral of this chapter is: "Lie to your boss when it suits your purposes," right?

Wrong. At least mostly wrong. The moral is: "Manage the situation." Let's try another illustration, from another context. Bill Whyte—the William F. Whyte of *Street Corner Society*—has a story he likes to tell about the restaurant business—"The Crying Waitress," he calls it. There's a particular restaurant in a big city, a place to go to get something to eat and then get out. It's a very busy place, not some gourmet hideaway. People don't go there for the renowned cuisine, but because it's quick and convenient.

Being hectic and crowded at dinner, it's tough on the waitresses. One of them, Nancy, just can't take it; things are always going wrong, orders are getting mixed up, customers are nasty—and she ends up in tears just about every day. Another waitress, Magda, does okay. She gets through the evening with relatively few problems, no tears, and pretty good tips besides.

How come? The easiest explanation is that Magda can take it, and Nancy can't. But that's too easy, and Whyte was never much of a one for personality theories. So he looks a little closer at the situation, at the way that Magda went about her job . . . .

Stanley has had one hell of a day, and to top it off, didn't leave his office until 6:45. He collapses into a booth, exhausted. Magda is right there. "Good evening, sir. Tough day? How about a drink? Martinis are the special tonight—a double for the price of a single."

"Uh . . . " says Stanley. "Well, I . . . uh, I really like manhattans better."

"Sure. I'll get you a special martini that's so special, it'll be a manhattan." Off she goes. She knows the bartender, so she gets Stanley a double manhattan for the price of a single. While he's drinking it, she comes back. "Like to order, sir? The prime rib is terrific tonight . . . " Why not, Stanley likes prime rib as well as anything. And so it goes.

What Magda is doing is managing the situation. She keeps the customer from having to think too much, makes the decisions for him. After all, most of her customers are indifferent anyway; they wouldn't be at that restaurant if they were gourmets. And they're tired, to boot. The truth is, they'd *rather* that the waitress would make the decisions for them, and if she can get a drink into them first, so much the better. The less muss and fuss, the happier they are.

So that's the plan of attack: drink first (double if possible), suggest what's available and fast, rather than what's best, or, worse yet, what the customer *really* wants (most of them don't have a real craving for anything on the menu, at least not until after they make their choice.). But always manage the relationship so that the customer doesn't finally set his heart on a dish only to find out after considerable time and anguish, that they're all out of it, or that he'll have to wait another half hour till it's ready.

To survive onslaughts of staff busybodies, Kerry Drake manages his relationships with them. To get through a hectic dinner hour in one piece, Magda manages her relationships with the customers. And to skate fast over thin ice, you had better do the same. This is a very fundamental and practical principle: define the situation for the other. Don't worry about who is *supposed* to manage the situation; *you* manage it.

42

SUCCESS STORY

Stanley looked at the headline on the front page of *The Company Clarion* with wide-eyed amazement: "Mill Hand to Vice-Chairman of Board in Ten Years." Incredible! thought Stanley. With increasing interest, Stanley read the story beneath the headline.

> Beginning his career with The Company as an operator of an expandrium extruder in the Pawtucket plant, Mr. C. Marsh Bell was, after three months on the job, made foreman, then three months later was promoted to assistant mill supervisor at the plant in Pawtucket. During his six-month sojourn, the mill achieved a rate of production that still stands as a Company record. He was then selected as marketing manager for expandrium products in District 7 of the Southwest Region, where he set a sales record that has never been equaled, before or since. His next promotion, after one year, was . . .

It was a fascinating article, and Stanley could see why Mr. Bell has risen so far, so fast. Obviously a man of talent. Up and up and up he had gone, each time with longer tenure—Assistant Marketing Director for the Western Region, Assistant to the Plant Manager at Punxatawney, Corporate Director of Personnel, Assistant Vice-President in Charge of Systems and Components, then to Vice-President in Charge of Personnel, before finally being made Vice-Chairman of the Board.

Fantastic! thought Stanley. How lucky we were to land a guy like that! What if he'd hired into Another Company? Then Stanley noticed another story on the front page, a short biographical sketch of the new Vice Chairman of the Board.

> . . . son of Mr. and Mrs. Coolidge M. Bell (the former Miss Belle C. Marsh of Scarsdale, N.Y.) . . . Best School for Boys . . . Choate . . . degree from Dartmouth . . . traveled extensively in Europe before joining The Company . . . family well known to employees, dating back to the merger of Bell Products and Marsh Industries into the present corporation, The Company . . . .

Stanley suddenly felt that he understood a few things that had been puzzling him scant moments ago. But still, Mr. Bell had done the job—set records in all of his assignments, as a matter of fact. He may have had a few advantages in getting his foot in the door, but clearly, given the chance, he had shown that he could perform. Yet there was a lingering doubt in Stanley's mind, borne of his observation over years with The Company that not many things happened by accident.

Then he heard Ben Franklyn ambling down the hall, muttering to himself: "Well, well, well—little Cooley Bell finally made it . . . records at Pawtucket—har, har . . . . " Ben obviously was enjoying himself. Then he looked up and noticed Stanley.

"Hey, Stanley," he said, waving his copy of *The Company Clarion,* "did you read this? Just goes to show you, stick with old Ben and you'll get places fast—har, har. See, little Cooley Bell was my assistant supervisor at Pawtucket . . . and look where he is now!"

Little? Cooley? What is this, thought Stanley. Ben doesn't usually speak of top Company management so irreverently. "Sorry, Mr. Franklyn," he said, "but I don't think I get the point."

"Sure you do. *C. Marsh Bell. . . . "* Ben spoke each syllable with exaggerated diction, ". . . was the most successful assistant mill superintendent I ever had. And did I work my ass off to make sure that happened! Listen, the Old Man . . . " (here he was referring to Mr. Marsh, Senior) " . . . himself brought little Cooley into my office. He said, 'Ben, you and I have been business associates for years (that was his very words, 'business associates'), and I believe that you know more about mill operations than anyone else in The Company. I'd like you to take young Coolidge here and teach him all you know about the business. Don't spare him. He's a bright lad, and he's got a future in The Company.'

"Well," said Ben, "I may not have a college education, but you don't have to hit me over the head twice to give me the idea. The Old Man was telling me that Cooley was going to make it big, no ifs, ands, or buts about it."

Something still wasn't right. "Mr. Franklyn," said Stanley, "tell me—the way you call Mr. Bell 'Cooley,' it sounds like you don't like him."

"I like him fine," said Ben. "He turned out to be a swell kid. But you know, I don't think that there was ever one day in his life that he had to work hard. I don't think he knew how then, and he probably still doesn't. But I'll give him credit; he never acted like he felt he was better than the rest of us, and the men liked him. He could take a joke, and dish one out too. Still, I was glad as hell when he left. Sometime when you get down in the Southwest Region, ask old Kerry Drake about those sales records that Cooley set. Betcha Kerry slept for a month after his star assistant got promoted—har." With that, Ben wandered off.

It was tough for Stanley to figure. Ben didn't seem to resent Mr. C. Marsh Bell, even seemed to like him; but he obviously didn't *respect* him. And that probably accounted for his strange attitude, for his calling him "Cooley" instead of "Mr. Bell." Ben knew why C. Marsh Bell was where he was, and he was honest enough not to pretend. Stanley reflected that Ted Shelby would have no trouble at all mouthing the appropriate, "Mr. Bell."

Why does The Company go through a charade like this, when it causes a fair amount of trouble for everybody concerned? Well, for one thing. The Company would like to have everybody believe that hard work and talent (in that order) are what it takes to succeed. And as a general rule this is true. But what do you do with the C. Marsh Bells? Left to the vagaries of Company life, there is a chance they wouldn't make it on their own. Also, it is quite impossible for an ordinary Company manager to have a normal relationship with a subordinate who is a nephew of the President and the son of the Chairman of the Board. So you can't stick him somewhere in The Company and let him work his own way up. And since there is a deep family involvement and a well-founded loyalty to The Company, you wouldn't want to have Cooley working for Another Company; that wouldn't be right either.

How about taking up law or medicine, you ask? Well, that's not everybody's cup of tea either. So The Company has to make it look as though C. Marsh Bell has made it on merit . . . or at least, even if he's made it because of who he is, he *could* have made it on merit if he hadn't been who he was. Hence, the job experience and the records. And The Company is smart to do it this way, for even though there will be cynical interpretations very few people will really know for sure that it happened that way. And those like Ben who do know won't talk about it much except on those rare occasions when the temptation is just too much to resist.

Finally, no harm is done anyway. Cooley will be charming and well-connected as a member of the Board. He can carry his share of the corporate load by making speeches to Kiwanis, Rotary Club, and various civic gatherings—duties which must be performed by somebody. He will be loyal, and he'll represent The Company well. Of course, he'll never be president, comptroller, or any other key position where he might botch up something important; that is, unless it strangely turns out that he really *does* have what it takes.

43

THE RATING GAME

Ben Franklyn's hearty voice droned on in the distance. ". . . So it seems to me that we are all in pretty clear agreement that Drew Bolt is our man for spot number 52. He's not been with us long, but those of us who know him can already see the kind of job he's capable of, and . . . "

Stanley is observing the annual merit ranking session at the plant in Pawtucket. The task at hand is no less than the rank ordering of 238 Level Two production engineers. What is rank ordering, you say? Well, the job of the assembled management group is to take those 238 engineers and assign a number from 1 to 238 to each and every one of them. Number 1 stands for the very best Level Two engineer in the plant, number 2 for the next best, and so on down to the anchor man, number 238 (the worst . . . or, ah, that is, "least best").

But, why would The Company indulge in a questionable exercise like this, you ask? Simply, because it has to give promotions and salary increases, and it would like to give them to the people who deserve them, and not give them to the people who don't. So, if you are one of those engineers, and you are ranked number 1 or 2, you'll get a promotion and a fat raise; but if you're number 237 or 238, forget it; it's been a bad year, and you've had your warning.

Oh, that's not what you mean? You want to know why it is necessary to go through a procedure that, at first glance, strikes you as impossible? Then the best thing for you to do is to hear what Ted Shelby has to say about it. In fact, right this minute he's talking to Management Development Session 6, Level 1: New Managers. Come on, let's go have a listen . . .

"As all of you know, The Company believes strongly in rewarding superior performance. We want to have our top people where top people belong—in the management of The Company.

"Now, none of us is infallible; don't get me wrong, we're as good as they come in this business, but we're human, and we do make mistakes. But when it comes to judging performance, we can't afford to make mistakes. We want our best horses in the lead team. Of course, the work of technical professionals is hard to put numbers on; our own judgments are inclined to be subjective; and since most of us like to give someone the benefit of the doubt, our individual ratings tend to be a bit high. When we found twenty percent of our people rated 'superior,' fifty percent 'above average,' twenty-five percent 'average' and only five percent 'below average,' we knew something had to changed. Seventy percent 'above average,' and only five percent 'below average'?

"We found our way around these problems with our MERIT system—MErit Ranking in Teams—and I'm pleased to say that I had a small part in developing MERIT.

"What are the advantages? *First,* by ranking we know exactly where each one fits. Oh, I know, there won't be much difference between, say, forty-three and forty-four, but at least we do know that our best thinking indicates that number forty-three is a better performer than number forty-four. *Furthermore,* the team aspect means that all our managers who have worked with the individual have had a chance to input their knowledge. In summation, we now have a sound, scientific procedure here, instead of the old 'seat-of-the-pants' game that we used to play."

What Ted meant in his reference to "the team aspect" is the fact that all sixty or so first, second, and third line plant supervisors participate in the final ranking sessions. It is a group effort, to be sure, but to a person witnessing the spectacle, there is some reason to be skeptical of its description as a "team" effort.

And Stanley was witnessing the spectacle. Part of his role in the CATCHUP program is to "familiarize and orientate" himself with Company procedures. Specifically, he happened to be on hand to "familiarize and orientate" himself with the procedure by which Drew A. Bolt arrived at spot 52 out of 238.

"I think we've made some real good choices in our top twenty spots," said Ben Franklyn as he began his nominating speech, "and I've got a guy here who belongs right up with that group—Drew Bolt. No, he's not a five or ten, but I think he's our choice for number twenty-one. He's worked for me for six years now, and I know he's done a job, etc., etc. Here's a letter from etc., etc. If you look at his record you'll see that, etc., etc. Who'll second my nomination?"

"I'll second it!" says one of Ben's old cronies.

"Any discussion?" asks the chairman.

There is plenty of discussion, the gist of which being that Ben Franklyn must be crazy. There are plenty of better people for that spot. In fact, one of them is nominated and voted in. "Okay," says Ben, "I respect your judgment, but I still think that you are making a mistake."

Now they are down to position number 35, and Ben pops up: "Okay, I've paid attention to your arguments, and while I'm not happy about it, I'll be willing to accept position number thirty-five for Drew Bolt. Any seconds?" A different buddy of his seconds the nomination. "Well, as we've already gone over this pretty thoroughly, I guess there won't be any need for discussion this time," says Ben. "Certainly there's no question now about his qualifications for a spot as low a number thirty-five." But there is discussion, culminating in No Deal. Ben looks stricken.

Ben gets up again, at position number 50, and Stanley is worried. He's never seen Ben like this. Ben is a beaten man, and that's not the Ben Franklyn that Stanley knows. "Listen, folks," says Ben. "It seems that I've done something terrible to Drew Bolt here today. I can yield on your judgment that he's not our number twenty-one man, and I guess you're all convinced that he isn't number thirty-five, although I don't agree. But fifty? Number fifty spot for Bolt? Yes, I've hurt this man's career, I can see that now."

My God, thinks Stanley, I never thought I'd see the day when they took all the fight out of Ben Franklyn. This is tragic. Can't these guys see that they've really screwed him?

Ben went on: "Somehow I guess I just haven't been able to present his case for him, haven't been able to show you the job he's done for us. Maybe by matching him up against our top ten guys I put him in the wrong light. Okay, okay—maybe he's not our very best, but he's still a top man. Look, we're down to spot number fifty! Come on. If we've got any sense of justice we'll etc., etc., etc." Stanley, in spite of himself, gave a little quiet cheer when Drew wound up a number 52. Poor Ben, he thought. Well, he won't make this kind of mistake again.

At the end of the day the meeting adjourns until tomorrow, when MERIT is to pick up again, at position number 162. As Stanley is going back to his office, he overhears Ben Franklyn talking and joking with his buddies. "Yes sir, we did all right," Ben is saying. "All in all, a good session. What about Bolt, hey? Now tomorrow, we've got young . . . "

What is this? wonders Stanley. Has the strain been too much for Ben?

What this is, is this:

Rule 1: If you don't take care of your own people, nobody else will.

Rule 2: Take care of your own people, and they'll take care of you.

Rule 3: Any successful manager is a good actor, and the less he looks it the better an actor he is likely to be.

The fact of the matter was that Ben figured Drew Bolt for a solid 70, and anything better than that was pure gravy. The problem Drew had was that he had worked for Ben so long that nobody else knew him very well. So Ben went into his act. First, he brought him up often enough to associate him with the top candidates. Then he acted terribly disappointed that he had to settle for spot number 52—31 spots lower than he'd shown he'd expected. This latter tactic is to mollify the pack of jackals who are sure that everyone is cheating (which they usually are).

The point here is that no system can put precision into a process that is inherently imprecise. And the managers who learn to beat System A will have little trouble in figuring out how to beat System B, C, and D. After all, systems are only systems—that is, something that a shrewd person can figure out how to beat. In this case, the system was beaten by Ben's manipulating the expectations and definitions relating to "his boys." On pencil-and-paper rating systems Ben would routinely rate his average people as "better-than-average," and his better than average people as "superior." If Ted Shelby tries to make the system "more scientific" by having everybody rated as to separate attributes—"creativity," "initiative," "personal appearance," and the like—Ben will simply rate his people as excellent on those attributes that really count ("performance," "initiative," "responsibility," and the like), while rating them as average on those that don't count for much ("personal appearance," "punctuality," and so forth). That way, it looks like he is being "objective"—who would believe him if he rated his people as "excellent" straight across the board?

And who with any sense would do it any other way?

44

THE PEARL

"But Another Company's *doing* it, I tell you. Doing it and beating us right in our own backyard!" The CATCHUP (Company Approach to Technical CHange and UPdate) task force is having another meeting, this time on the feasibility of CARP (Cybernation and Automation Readiness Project). In addition to the CATCHUP regulars, also present are some of the top technical people in The Company, and several of Marsh's top staff aides (Marsh's "handlers," as they were known)—in this case the corporate technical staff boys.

"You may *think* Another Company can beat us on this, but you couldn't be more wrong!" This is a reply to the claim from one of the corporate staff types by Kerry Drake. He continues. "*We* can't do it, *they* can't do it, nobody in the whole goddamned industry can do it! Yes, I *do* know that we have the technical knowhow to completely automate and cybernate a manufacturing plant. But I know some other things, too. I know I can pay a guy a few bucks an hour to carry pieces from one machine to another and feed them in with the proper order and orientation. And I also know that it will cost a million bucks to design a machine to do the same thing, plus many bucks an hour for a technician to keep it running right. That's what I know for sure!"

Another of the corporate staff boys says, "If that's so, then how is Another Company doing it?"

"They're not *doing* it, goddamn it! They're *trying* to do it," replies Kerry. "Can't you get that distinction through your thick skull?"

"Well, Kerry," says another of Marsh's handlers, "at least they've got a better attitude about it than what we seem to have here. And listen, I don't think you understand how badly Marsh wants this." Ted Shelby's attention had been wandering, but no longer. His ears perk up as the staff man continues. "Mr. Marsh feels that CARP will symbolize The Company's technical excellence in the market place. In our position we can't give our critics anything to shoot at. And if Another Company beats us on this. . .."

Ted knew an Opportunity when he saw one. The remainder of the meeting became a process of Ted's getting himself appointed as operating chief for CARP, despite continuing protest from the assembled technical hands. Ted told them that he saw a way to get this thing done, but that he would need special powers to round up the facilities and technical talent to push ahead. It finally was agreed that this could be done if Ted's project proposal and schedules looked okay to The Corporate Review Committee.

The meeting broke up, and Stanley caught up with Ben Franklyn as he was leaving. "What do *you* think about this, Ben?"

"I think what Kerry thinks. That's something I've learned over the years," said Ben. "If it's something to do with production engineering and Kerry says it doesn't make sense, then there's no way it's going to work. We're going to lose our ass on this one . . . ."

Yet, in not too long a time at all, the following memo was circulated:

To: All CARP Personnel

From: CARP Project Director

The first product line is on stream at our experimental facility at Flagstaff. You will be proud to know that we beat our schedule by six days. Our permanent facility at Phoenix is seventy percent complete, and we can look forward to a startup date there in three to four months.

Looks like we are well ahead of Another Company now.

(signed) Ted Shelby

cc Mr. Marsh, et al

In the ensuing months, Ted generates furious activity—technical missions, conferences, plant visits, the whole works. Experimental activity at Flagstaff is furious. Demonstration lines are set up, and a steady stream of Company brass comes to see them in action. A beautiful new "facility" at Phoenix is now complete, and fifty percent of the equipment is installed. Everything looks great. And each new accomplishment is, of course, heralded by a flood of memos.

Even so, there are doubters. Some people, for example, are saying that it's one thing to run individual lines under total automation, maybe even two or three lines in tandem, but an entire manufacturing plant is another matter.

The Company Clarion thought enough of the event, and some related events, to feature it on the front page.

SHELBY TO TAKE OVER AS CORPORATE MANAGER OF PLANS AND CONTROLS

Edward Wilson Shelby IV will be leaving his successful project CARP for a new responsibility in Corporate Plans and Controls. In announcing this promotion, the office of M. M. Marsh cited the pressing need today for a comprehensive, company wide program of plans and controls for the medium-term outlook. Shelby's experience as prime mover for CARP makes him the obvious candidate to head up this new program. In Marsh's own words, "we've an urgent need to take a long, hard look at tightening up our budgeting procedures and making crisper, more hardhitting decisions . . . ."

So it was that Ted Shelby was separated from CARP at the penultimate phase. People said it was tough luck for Ted not to be able to stay on long enough to realize the fruits of his efforts. But Ted himself seemed stoical enough about it.

And then there were the few who knew that Ted had himself been instrumental in developing the need for, and philosophy of, the new Office of Plans and Controls. In fact, he had pretty much created his new position. Dr. Faust was one of the people who knew this, and he was sharing his observations, as he sometimes did, with Stanley.

"But what did he really accomplish, anyway?" Stanley was saying. "You know as well as I that what Ted mainly did was to stir a lot of people up, create a lot of publicity and make some good people awfully unhappy. And now he's leaving. Who's fooling who around here? The real work of CARP is still to be done."

Faust puffed at his pipe—his way of preparing for a pronouncement. "Well, Stan, I do know that, and then again, I don't know it. The end of this story hasn't been written yet, that's true; and when it is, you're going to learn another valuable lesson."

Stanley wondered what *that* might mean, but it was obvious that Faust wasn't going to elaborate any further at present. Faust continued:

"But let's take a look at what Ted *did* accomplish. The first thing one has to recognize is that organizations like The Company are full of Cassandras. It is always easier to find a dozen reasons why something can't be done than it is to find one good way to do it. I don't know why this should be so, but it is. Perhaps no one wants to fail, and *before* you do something the possibilities for failure are more obvious than the possibilities for success. But one will never do anything unless he tries, so someone is necessary to get things stirred up—a shaker, a mover, an irritant. I call it the 'pearl theory.' " Faust paused to let the proper questions form in Stanley's mind.

"Now, if you leave an oyster alone, it's a commonplace thing. It's content. But you put a grain of sand into him and he gets all stirred up. It starts him working, and the result of his labors will be a pearl—something far from commonplace. Analogous to this, consider The Company. This commonplace corporate oyster needs a grain of sand now and again to bring out a pearl of accomplishment. The grain of sand doesn't make the pearl all by itself, but on the other hand, the pearl wouldn't happen without it."

Faust looked quite satisfied with his explication of his "pearl theory." Of course, he hadn't pointed out that not every grain of sand results in a pearl, nor that not every oyster lives through the process.

45

MOST VALUABLE PLAYER

"I've called you all together today to announce an important personnel change." The Pawtucket Plant Manager continued, "Our good friend and Mill Superintendent, Ben Franklyn, has just been named Superintendent of our new automated facility at Phoenix. Congratulations, Ben, this is a big opportunity for you. I'm sure we all remember when . . . " Here he went into a warm reminiscence of Ben's accomplishments and the good times they had all had together. Ben seemed pleased by the speech, but he didn't say much about his impending opportunity.

Now let us look to *The Company Clarion* for the story of how Ben's big opportunity worked out. Over a six-month period, such statements could be found in *The Clarion* as:

> . . . Franklyn will be taking over from Edward W. Shelby IV, with responsibility for making Project CARP fully operational . . . .

> . . . There has been some unavoidable delay at Phoenix due to problems encountered in articulating the man-machine interface . . . (which meant that the old mill hands in plant operations were having none of letting a computer do their jobs for them).

... Full realization of the potential of the CARP project at the Phoenix facility will be delayed until current problems with system breakdowns and unreliability are licked ....

... The presidents representing four union locals having jurisdiction over the Phoenix plant were in agreement that key items in the upcoming contract negotiations would involve current problems with displacement of jobs and new job categories ....

... Another Company recently announced that it has dropped its project of cybernating and automating a production facility, leaving The Company without any significant competition in this vital area ....

...The decision has been reached to operate the new facility at Phoenix as a semiautomated plant, with several model lines operated on a fully cybernated basis ....

There were a number of rumors floating around The Company regarding the CARP project at Phoenix. A lot of people were surprised at just how much Shelby had been on top of it. After all, if an old hand like Ben Franklyn couldn't bring it off, Shelby must have had more management talent than had previously been suspected. Too bad they'd transferred Ted.

Another story was that The Company had put out so much publicity on CARP, mostly through Ted Shelby's doing, that there was no choice but to follow through, then salvage what it could. And with The Company, there were always the legal considerations.

At any rate, Ben Franklyn finally ended up more or less off the hook. The consensus was that it had just been too big a job, even for Ben. The technical boys were heard to say, "We told you so," but not too loudly. As for Ben, it was back to Pawtucket with a suitable Company announcement about changes in plans.

"What I don't understand," Stanley said to Dr. Faust, "is how they let Ted Shelby get away with this fiasco. He got the whole thing started with a bunch of promises he didn't have to live with. I don't know why we didn't keep him on CARP to see it through. I'll bet he knew all the time that it wouldn't work."

"I wouldn't jump to any conclusions about what Ted Shelby did or did not believe," said Dr. Faust. "In fact, my opinion is that he *did* believe there was a chance of success. But that's beside the point. You can't leave a man like Shelby in one place too long, he's too valuable."

"Too valuable?!" Stanley choked. "You've got to be kidding! Here's a guy who goes against the best technical brains in The Company, promises something he can't deliver, creates a hell of a mess, but takes the credit before he bails out to save his own skin—and you say he's *too valuable* to leave on the job? The only reason he took it on in the first place was because he knew Marsh wanted it so badly he could taste it."

Faust let Stanley stew for a moment while he paused to light his pipe. His final pronouncements were always more effective when preceded by time for thought punctuated by puffs of pipe smoke. Eventually he began. "Stanley, once again you've got the facts but you've missed the point. First, let's give Ted credit for what he's good at—hustling. And let's not forget that the technical people aren't always right either. They tend to forget the fact that once one has made the decision to go ahead he often finds ways of getting the job done that had never occurred to him earlier. Let's say that there is an added motivation to find a solution.

"Also, there are certain projects that, from the perspective of top management, are too important not to take a crack at. That is where the value of a Shelby must be appreciated. Make no mistake, Ted knows how to bring people together and get the ball rolling. And yes, I know that he isn't so good at following through, but there are others to do that. You need someone who is willing and ready to take risks, to bet on the long shots—and also, you must protect him from the consequences of his failures."

"But what if everybody did that?" said Stanley. "What if . . ."

"I wouldn't worry about that," said Faust. "First of all, there aren't many people who are willing to take that kind of risk. And besides, The Company wouldn't let them."

"But I thought you just said . . . "

"What I just said was that you need *people* like that, not an organization like that. Obviously one can't afford to have everybody running around, stirring things up. You evidently have forgotten some of our previous discussions. Look, it's not so much that there are right and wrong decisions, because, after all, enough energy and enthusiasm in following up often can make right decisions out of what by all appearances were wrong ones. In a situation in which one is making a real decision, there is usually a wide margin of error either way.

"There are times when you've got to have someone to push ahead with certainty, to say, 'come on, we can do it.' And you've got to protect such people from failure—say, to give them a certain immunity from the facts.

"And it's not quite like betting everything on a longshot. In a corporate environment, rarely do these 'longshots' result in total losses. But when they win, there are great gains that can be realized. Our problem is that people are timid enough already. If punishment for a failure like CARP were swift, sure, and drastic, you'd see fewer CARPs to be sure, but not many advances either. So when you find someone like Shelby with, say, a certain flair for getting risky projects underway you protect him, you move him where he's needed. He's too valuable to go down with the ship."

46

JUST IN CASE

With CATCHUP getting into full swing, just about everyone on The Company's staff was busy preparing presentations decribing the benefits to be had from the project they were proposing. Project proposals were Dr. Faust's bread and butter, and he did not take them lightly. This was one area in which he had turned art into science—and one of the axioms of his science was something he termed "contingency management." That is, he left nothing to chance, practicing endless dry runs of his presentations to insure that all problems (or "contingencies") had been anticipated, and that the proper responses had been concocted— just in case.

Thus it was that Dr. Faust one day invited Stanley to "react" to the presentation of his proposal for the "Subordinate Readiness Program for Professional Personnel." "You understand," he explained, "that I want you to be as critical and nit-picking as possible, so as to . . . ah . . . simulate the type of reaction we can expect from the management review committee."

"Right," said Stanley. "Fire away." He watched as the cover sheet was removed from the presentation easel, much as a painting by a leading artist might be unveiled for the first time. But what the . . .? Given the importance Faust placed on this sort of thing, and the amount of time he had spent on this particular one, Stanley was completely taken by surprise.

There, boldly sitting on the easel, was a crude, hand-lettered chart entitled: "SUBORDINATE READINESS PROGRAM—PROFESSIONAL PERSONELL." Obviously, Dr. Faust had done it all by himself. And it hadn't been just dashed off, either, but had been elaborately, painstakingly constructed. It bordered on illegibility, it was crimped up against the right-hand margin as though Faust had run out of room and then had to compress the second half to get it all on the board, and there were several blatantly misspelled words—"personell," "permanant," and others. But not, Stanley noticed, "mnemonic." Words like that unerringly were spelled correctly.

"Um, Dr. Faust, when you have your charts put in final shape by the graphics department, make sure to remind them to correct the spelling of 'personnel' and 'permanent,' " Stanley suggested diplomatically.

"Stanley," said Dr. Faust decisively, "these charts *are* in final shape, unless of course, you come up with something new."

"But they don't look very, er, professional," suggested Stanley. "Won't they make a poor impression?"

"Precisely!" Dr. Faust declared. "A poor impression, but . . . a proper one as charts."

"Huh?"

Dr. Faust paused to light his pipe. "Look at it this way. There will always be a skeptic in the group (probably a financial officer) who doesn't understand the—ah—necessity of the consultant's function. And inevitably this person will say, 'Faust, with the money you put into those charts I bet we could have declared a stockholders' dividend. What's all this going to cost, anyway?' Well, that is the sort of question one likes to avoid, as it only distracts from the matter at hand. So, one avoids having his charts look too—ah—professional. In point of fact," he added, "doing the charts up this way, by myself, cost The Company substantially more than it would have cost to send them to the graphics department, but . . . "

"Okay, I understand that feature," Stanley allowed, "but don't you think you've overdone it? I mean, look, if you can correctly spell 'mnemonic,' I know you can spell 'personnel' and 'permanent.' "

"Of course I can . . . but *he* can't."

"Can't *what*?"

"Can't spell 'mnemonic.' That's why one has to choose words like 'personnel'—he'll spot that one right away."

"Who is *he*?"

"Who else but Franklyn? He always feels honor-bound to put in his two-cents' worth, to find something wrong. He doesn't care what it is, as long as he can nail you on something. So, this way I get it over with right away, so that we can get down to business. The first chance that comes up, he'll say, 'Faust, they ought to send you doctors back to grade school for reeducation—personnel has two n's, not two l's.' I will be slightly embarrassed, naturally. Then he'll shut up. Otherwise, he would continually be interrupting the presentation."

Contingency management . . . , thought Stanley. Faust continued with the presentation. After a couple more charts Stanley said, "Could I interrupt?"

"Certainly," said Dr. Faust. "Did you find something amiss?"

"Well, I don't know," said Stanley, "but it seems to me that the feature of the program you just explained doesn't have any real application here—no value at all to The Company that I can see. In fact, it looks suspiciously academic."

"Interesting that you should see it in that light," said Dr. Faust. "Is there anyone in particular who you think might object to that feature of the program?"

"Why, Kerry Drake, of course, " said Stanley. "You know how he feels about . . . " As Stanley says these words, Faust's next line flashes though his mind even before Faust opens his mouth.

"Precisely! That will take care of Kerry. Oh, I won't give up that feature without a fight, of course. But I'll reluctantly agree to let it go, and Kerry will feel that he had cut his share of 'fat' out of the program."

Two more charts, and Faust is through with his presentation. He flips up the final page, and Stanley is surprised to find a new title page beneath it:

"SUBORDINATE READINESS PROGRAM—PROFESSIONAL PER-SONNEL: FINDINGS AND CONCLUSIONS."

"What's that?" asked Stanley.

"Don't pay any attention to that," said Dr. Faust. "I just did it up in advance. I won't actually use it for several months."

"But how can you have the findings and the conclusions already?"

"No problem," explained Dr. Faust. "I already know what I have to find." He noticed the suspicious look Stanley was giving him. "Don't worry, I'll do the study all right. But with subordinate readiness, as with so many things, in the limit it becomes a matter of judgment: How 'ready' is 'ready'? I can guarantee you that after we finish interviewing all our plant managers and executives, plus our top professional personnel, we'll find that they aren't 'ready,' and thus we will come up with the findings and conclusions here in the charts."

"You're sure this isn't some kind of cheating?" asked Stanley.

"The naive observer might come to such a conclusion," admitted Dr. Faust, "but, look, in all my experience in this field I have never once encountered a group of professional people that was at an acceptable level of 'readiness.' No large organization rates highly with respect to 'subordinate readiness,' and the higher in the corporate ranks one goes, the truer that is.

"But another thing you have to understand is that Marsh wants this particular program rather badly. I wouldn't be here if he didn't." Again Stanley was eyeing him suspiciously, so Faust went on, "Let me tell you about a distinguished colleague of mine. One time he was making a presentation to Marsh and his aides. It happened that Marsh really believed in that particular product, and my colleague was expressing doubts. Marsh finally said, 'I can't accept that!' 'But,' my colleague said, 'those are the facts.' Marsh told him, 'Well, I don't like those facts. Get me some new facts.' And, you know, Marsh turned out to be right. He had understood the market potential of that product, and wanted it badly enough that he made it go, in spite of my colleague's 'facts.' After all there are plenty of facts around, and one is free to select from them as he will.

"So, you should see that my role as consultant here is to help Marsh get done what he wants to get done. He knows that I'm already sympathetic to The Company's need for a Professional Subordinate Readiness Program. This way, he knows that he'll have my report to back him up . . . just in case."

47

TOP SECRET

"Need to know?!" bellowed Ben Franklyn. "For Chrissakes, we only 'need to know' because we can't meet *their own* goddammed specifications if we don't know what they are! You get back on the phone and tell 'em that I'm going to backcharge them five hundred dollars a day— starting this very goddammed minute—for every day I've got those guys sitting around on their tails waiting to find out what to do next!" Ben was never much of one to take obstacles to progress lightly, especially obstacles like security regulations, when they seemed to be completely irrelevant to the task at hand. He stabbed his finger accusingly at Stanley. "You go and tell that guy that in this business . . . "

But by that time Stanley was out of Ben's office and halfway down the hall to his own. There was no sense talking to the engineering officer at The Agency again, he figured, so he dialed the security officer this time. He was not optimistic, however, because during his brief military career he'd been cleared for "Top Secret" at Another Agency, and he knew a little about the security business. He knew, for instance, that security officers typically were not the brightest people around, and that they lived in the completely ordered world of their book of security regulations—and liked it.

And so his phone call to the security officer at The Agency held no surprises for him.

"Yes sir, that project is classified as Top Secret."

"No sir, it isn't *my* responsibility to say whether or not a project should be classified. That judgment is left to the engineering officer."

"Yes sir, it says here in two five six dash c that such information is available to those who establish a reasonable 'need to know' as described in S. R. two eight zero prvn five sec three." (Good grief, thought Stanley, he even pronounced the abbreviations!)

"No sir, it isn't my responsibility to say who has a reasonable need to know; that judgment is left to the engineering officer."

"Yes sir, glad to be of assistance."

Well, what else could you expect? mused Stanley. Wait 'til Ben hears this. But by that time Ben had simmered down, and when Stanley entered his office Ben was talking with Ted Shelby. "Sorry, Ben, no luck," said Stanley.

"Oh, it's okay, Stanley," said Ben. "I was just trying to save ourselves some trouble. Actually, we can figure it out from the other specs. It'll take a few days, but we can do it. But we could sure do a better job if I knew what they were going to use it for—what kinds of conditions, how far from basic supply sources, how much continuous operation and so forth. And you know, I'll bet that anybody who really wanted to find out that stuff could do it. You can bet that the Commies know everything about it that's worth knowing. Sometimes I get the feeling that the main point of all this security stuff is to keep our *own* side in the dark."

At that remark, Ted Shelby spoke up. "No, Ben," he said in a concerned tone of voice, "I think you've missed the overall systems strategy here. When I was in the intelligence corps it was stressed in the officer training program (Ted never failed to let information like that drop in his conversations) that, yes, The Enemy could probably get any single item of information they wanted, if they wanted it badly enough. But Security kept them from getting enough pieces to fit the Big Picture together. That's why every piece, no matter how trivial it might seem, has to be guarded in the same manner."

This was too much for Stanley. "Well, Ted," he said, "that may be what they told you, but I had some experience on guard duty in a secret military equipment depot, and from what I saw there, I'd say that Ben is closer to the truth.

"You see, during the war, I was a corporal assigned to guard duty in a top secret area at Another Agency—not very exciting, but better than getting shot at. Mostly, it was a depot full of stuff dreamed up by the technical warfare specialists at Another Agency. And you wouldn't *believe* some of the things they had us guarding. Rube Goldberg couldn't have come up with gear like they had in there! Just for example, there was this tall frame scaffold sitting on top of the body of an earth-moving rig. And there's this three or four ton weight that's supposed to be hoisted up to the top of this frame, about twenty feet in the air. The weight has a pointed rod underneath it, and the whole idea of the thing is to punch holes in enemy roads to plant charges in. You hoist the weight, let it go, and zonk! It punches the rod through the pavement. Then the demolition guys run up, stick the charge in, and it's done.

"Just one thing wrong with that gadget. Most roads are banked a little bit, and more often than not, about the time that four ton weight gets to the top of that twenty foot scaffold, the whole business falls over on its side. No wonder it was never used in combat. That thing would have spent most of the war like a beetle on its back.

"And there were a lot of other things in that top secret depot just like that. In fact, if there had been some way to get the enemy to put those 'secrets' to use, the war would have been over a lot sooner. I finally figured out that those machines were classified because Another Agency didn't want *our* side knowing what they'd been up to."

Ben Franklyn looked at Stanley with new respect. "You mean that the kind of security the project director at The Agency has in mind is his own job security? Har, har! That's pretty good. Come to think of it, there's a few things around here that I'd like to have gotten 'classified' myself."

At this point it was Ted Shelby who could stand it no longer. "Now just a minute," he said, excitedly. "The kind of thing you're talking about may have happened in a few isolated instances, but as a general rule . . . "

But nobody was listening. Ted spends a lot of his time trying to explain why it is necessary and proper for things to be the way they are; but meanwhile Stanley (and Ben Franklyn) pursues the more profitable course of trying to learn *why* things are the way they are. Ted, finding it necessary to fit everything into the framework of what he already believes, has a difficult time learning from experience, while Stanley in this case has observed and understood a fundamental fact—that all organizations have counterparts of security and intelligence. Companies are aware that competitors would like to possess their proprietary information, and therefore it must be restricted to responsible people only.

And who decides what information should be kept secret, and who should be allowed access to it? Why, just about everybody with people below them. Yes, you begin to see. By using the unquestionable reasons of "security" (Company or national), management has a useful and flexible device for hiding its gaffes and/or controlling the behavior of subordinates. Well, if you keep your eye on the tube or read the newspapers you know all this. And you must have noticed that the classified information would have done The Enemy very little good, although a fair amount of it has made some people on our own side look pretty bad.

48

MANAGEMENT BY OBJECTIVES (or) THE $500,000 MISUNDERSTANDING

"The thing to remember, gentlemen, and ladies," Ted Shelby intoned, "is that no matter how high up in The Company we are, we are all subordinates to *somebody*." Twenty-six superiors/subordinates murmured their agreement. Ted was addressing the Subordinate Readiness Session, level 5, on *Management By Objectives*.

"From this perspective," he went on, "it becomes crystal clear that superiors and subordinates up and down the line must have a clearly spelled out understanding of what is expected of each. I might add that this comes out loud and clear in our interviews with top management subordinates. Briefly stated, the objective of Management By Objectives is to eliminate totally all possibilities of misunderstanding between superiors and subordinates, and to assure that everyone has a crisp and hard-hitting set of objectives to measure himself against. We don't want the kind of situation at year's end where someone says, 'But I didn't know . . . .' No sir, no excuses. We got where we are today through tough, two-fisted management—fair, but tough. And that's the way we want to keep it. If you can't take the heat, get out of the kitchen, right?" This last remark earned him a round of applause.

"Now, I want each of you to have the opportunity to talk to a plant manager in person. I want each of you to get a hands-on feeling of how this program works . . . "

As a new management trainee, Lesley was assigned to interview Ben Franklyn, the Plant Manager at the old plant in Providence. Several days later she drove up there and was ushered into Ben Franklyn's office. "So you're the gal that Shelby sent to get some 'hands-on' experience with management by objectives?" Ben pronounced the words with exaggerated clarity, as he invariably did with words he found distasteful. And if it were a staff-generated program, you know already that he found it distasteful. "You would probably like to see my objectives as Plant Manager at Providence. I hope you've got a little time today, because they need some explanation.

"You know, the guys who write these things up, why, I don't believe they've ever been in a plant in their lives, except when Mr. Marsh makes one of his speeches here. These things are clear and—what's that word they use—'objective' (distaste again) to them only because they haven't got the first goddammed idea of what goes on in a manufacturing plant. Here, look at this."

Lesley pulls her chair over to Ben's big desk, and Ben opens up a file and spreads some papers and graphs out. "Now," says Ben, pulling out a sheet titled "Production Objectives," "these are more or less okay, even though I don't have any real control over them. Let's take this one: 'Scrap as percentage of finished product.' Know how I handled that one? Well, now I inspect all the raw material coming in twice as careful as I used to. That's because it isn't only what my boys do, a lot depends on the job they do in the foundry at Fayetteville. It used to be that I could play ball with those guys; if the stuff they sent wasn't completely lousy, I'd give it a try. But not now. Now I just send it back unless it's top grade. What else can I do? It's a waste of time and money, but I make my objective.

"Here's another one: 'Production man-hours as percentage of standard time.' Now, that one's easy enough to meet. Maybe you don't always get your production up, but you can look okay if you ..." Ben went on to describe his procedures for claiming downtime on machines and a lot of other things that Lesley didn't understand except that they didn't sound very productive. Next Ben pulled out a set of objectives labeled "Behavioral."

"I know you're going to find these perfectly clear, just like me—har," Ben started off. "Here, look at these ..." There followed major headings such as "Morale," "Subordinate Readiness," "Interpersonal Sensitivity," and the like. Ben took a sarcastic tone: " ... 'shall act to improve man-manager relationships at all levels of plant management.' And if you like that one, there's plenty more. Look, I can't even keep track of all my 'behavioral objectives,' let alone make sure I'm on target. And I don't think that the top management really cares about most of these anyway —at least not until somebody gets excited about something."

"But then why don't we use just the objectives that really count?" Lesley asked.

"Why?" said Ben. "Because what I've got here on my desk is the whole catalog of excuses our plant 'lawyers' have given in the past to explain why they didn't hit the target on the objectives that really count. But here, look at this. This is what I really wanted to show you. What's today, December 20, right? Okay, now here's my expenses as percentage of budget—108 percent. That's fine, they give us a leeway of 10 percent over. And take it from me, I busted my tail to hold it there. So, yesterday what comes down to me from New York? This!"

Ben is holding a sheet with a lot of figures on it; but Lesley never was much at accounting and looks mystified. "Let me tell you about this," says Ben. "If you read between the figures what it says is 'Mr. Franklyn, you now have five hundred thousand bucks of additional expense as of December nineteen. We regret that this may cause you to miss your expense objective.' "

Lesley doesn't need to say, "I don't get it," because it is written all over her face.

"This is the work of the big financial brains in New York," Ben explains. "They did some brand new forecasts of next year's business, and also found they had just received a big hunk of unanticipated cash income this year and a lot of other stuff I don't understand too well. But the result of it, that I understand all to well. They've written off some stuff early, reallocated some expenses here and there—mostly here—to make our 'tax picture' look better."

"But what could happen from that?" said Les. "Surely anybody can see that your missing the objective is simply a misunderstanding."

"Anybody that wants to see it that way will," said Ben. "And if anybody finds that it's convenient to forget it, they'll do that too. And sooner or later, *nobody* will remember how it happened. All that's in the books is that I missed the objective.

"It's the same with the rest of the objectives. You can't possibly meet them all, and they'll do what they've always done anyhow—find some way to give you the boot if they don't like something you've done. Only now it looks better—'no misunderstandings,' 'clear objective criteria,' (here he did a surprisingly good imitation of Ted Shelby). Ted says there's a lot of meat here, but I say that meat's baloney!"

What Ben means is that "management by objectives" sounds good if you're on the end that's evaluating it, not on the end that's trying to do it. What if the objectives don't hold still? What if the people up above perpetrate a "misunderstanding" or two on you? And, even barring unforeseen problems, how good you look may have more to do with how well you juggle your budget estimates than how well you actually manage.

The real value of such measures is to provide an objective definition of failure after the fact. At some later date you "realize" that objectives three, six, and eight are really important ones, not one, two, and five. It is a very convenient "management tool."

Incidentally, Ben Franklyn lasted only six months longer at the Providence plant. It seems that, in addition to failing to meet his "expense objective," he came up short on several of the more important "behavioral objectives"—and incidentally, took an unpopular position on the necessity of Subordinate Readiness training.

49

AS I RECALL

"I still say drawing a straight flush is impossible. Only an idiot would expect—"

"Better watch your language, Kerry," Ted cut in, "maybe one of the Doc's recommendations will include a new head of Automation Engineering."

Typically, the pre-meeting banter centered on last night's poker, its winners and losers. Dr. Faust (winner) felt little need to justify his game to Kerry Drake (big loser). And in truth, in his role as consultant the good doctor tries to avoid liberating too much of his companions' loose cash. For he is well aware that the big game lies elsewhere.

Finally Ted brought the meeting to order. "Gentlemen, as you know we have been extremely fortunate to have had the services of Dr. Faust full time with us in our first phase of the CATCHUP program. I know of no one better suited by experience and training to carry out this important mission."

The meeting had been called to deliver the results of CATCHUP— Phase I. Kerry, Ted, Ben Franklyn, some staff people from New York, and several top management people from manufacturing were present. The importance of the project was underscored as well by the presence of one of Mr. Marsh's "handlers." And Stanley was there too, having spent the past year putting together a detailed development program.

"I am sure you are aware of our charge here," Ted continued. And now he read from a document. "The CATCHUP task force is charged with the responsibility for examining *all* phases of our Company manufacturing activities with the end in view of devising a comprehensive master plan to bring The Company abreast of recent explosive changes in the manufacturing environment." The words, of course, were Ted's own.

As Chairman of the Task Force, Ted would report on the results today, as would Faust. And as for Dr. Faust, being Chairman of The Department at The University, he had been accorded responsibility for developing a detailed master plan for both the technical and "people" components of the program, and for developing the data to back it up. Accepting this challenge had required a year's leave from The University (for which The Company had shown its appreciation in a most tangible way).

"So, before we get to the results, let me bring you all up to date on what we have been doing. Dr. Faust and I have visited every one of The Company's manufacturing locations this year, and personally interviewed both top management and groups of our top technical people." (A man is known by the company he keeps, thought Stanley.) "In addition . . . "

Stanley's attention wanders. He's heard this all before, many, many times. It is embellished and improved each time, naturally, but the basic itinerary is the same. The fact remains, however, that just about *all* that Faust has done during the year past has been to visit and talk. And it seems to Stanley that Phase I calls for a great deal more than that. Certainly a year's effort ought to produce something tangible, something concrete. But if it has, I haven't seen it, Stanley is thinking.

"So that's about it to date, gentlemen," Ted has finished his recapitulation. "Now let's take a look at some of our findings. Dr. Faust?"

"Ahem, yes. I know that you people have a great deal to think about, so I will not bore you with the details of our findings. These will be in a later report. (Always a later report, thought Stanley.) So let me go over the highlights, the key findings of this phase of CATCHUP.

"Number One. We have a clear and pressing problem of obsolescence, both in equipment *and* in people. As our plant manager at Portland put it . . . "

Nice one, thinks Stanley, can't lose on that. And best of all, nobody's fault in particular, so no one is going to fight you on that. Nice one. As Faust went on Stanley had a growing sense of déja vu, of revisiting the past. Sure enough, there were those surveys of Other Companies (a consultant's role is to bring in the bigger picture). Sure, all those points—the "Findings"—are right from Dr. Faust's original proposal. What do you know. The Company *did* have these problems after all.

As Dr. Faust went along ticking off the "focal issues for action" and documenting them with highlights from the data, Stanley had the distinct and uneasy feeling that CATCHUP—Phase I is about where it had started one year ago, at least for Faust's part. As for Stanley's own involvement, it is now clear to him that his detailed plan for the Subordinate Readiness Program stands by itself as perhaps the one real accomplishment of Phase I.

"Thank you, Dr. Faust. So much for our data base." Ted went on in his crisp/confident tone. "I think you can see that we have been exceptionally fortunate to have Dr. Faust involved in the mission of this task force. Certainly his credentials are unique, and he's proven himself once again to be the hard-hitting, no-nonsense type of person you want when the chips are down." Beaming, "Nice work, Doc."

Stanley notes at this juncture that while polite approval is being expressed about the table, enthusiasm is lacking. But not for long.

"Now, where do we go from here? As I recall . . . " Ted began by recounting the goals of Phase I. *The* major goal had been to define the goals of the program, for only then could satisfactory solutions be found.

Oh? thinks Stanley, that's new.

"We have been acutely aware of the manufacturing challenges in today's marketplace—methodswise and peoplewise. There are the modern management methodologies: information systems, cybernation, automation. And there are the contributions of the behavioral people. As we saw it a year ago, I recall . . . ."

Ted went on now setting forth, point by point, the goals of Phase I. And as he did so he neatly reconstructed the original purposes to bring them quite nearly into line with what Dr. Faust had delivered, including credit for the conceptual development of Stanley's Subordinate Readiness Program. Bewildered, and becoming increasingly angry, Stanley wonders what in the world is going on. Why is Ted doing this? Can't he see that Faust produced little that entire year, except perhaps a hole in the budget? Why doesn't Ted show him in his real light, as having dropped the ball? True, the Phase I position paper was a bit vague in outlining specific goals, yet Ted had in the early meeting spelled out a strategy that was quite different from what he had said today. Why was Ted (to put it charitably) "rewriting history" here today?

Why indeed? Had Stanley been around a bit longer, though, he would have seen the truth immediately. As it is, it will dawn on him pretty soon.

Why was Dr. Faust there at all? *Answer:* Because Ted Shelby had brought him in.

And why was that? *Answer:* Because Dr. Faust was the best answer to the question—What are we doing to push ahead on CATCHUP? ("We've got the best there is—Faust from The University on it, full time. He took a leave from The Department just to do this.")

But still, why pretend that Faust has accomplished things that he hasn't . . . and, closer to home, why give him credit for doing things that Stanley had done?

Perhaps you already have the answer yourself. Ted Shelby is defining the situation and rearranging the credits because *he* is responsible for

Faust and what he achieves. In cases like this The Company is not judging Faust, but Ted Shelby. Thus it well behooves Ted to make Faust look good. He is short-changing Stanley, that's true; but he's not hurting him, because no one outside of the Task Force knows or cares about Stanley. He has little to gain from his contribution and is now losing little by not being properly credited. He is still just another face in the corporate crowd.

Ted, on the other hand, stands to lose plenty if Faust comes off as a highly visible, and expensive, flop. So Ted borrows a little bit against the future. For all Ted knows, he'll be out of this position in six months or a year (and in fact he was), so skate fast when the ice is thin . . . .

So this is his strategy: Reconstruct the goals of the past and borrow from the future; announce to all involved that you've had a smashing success achieving your goals (which do indeed seem to be well matched by the achievements), and hope for the best.

For the Stanleys of the world, the message is: Be patient and learn. You will get your turn.

And as for Faust—he's trading on his reputation, and the action is brisk. He'll write this one up in glowing prose for his academic resume, and the time is near when Another Company will need that experience. He's come out looking good as far as The Company is concerned, because somebody had a strong vested interest in precisely that outcome.

But you say, what of Ted and his relationship with Dr. Faust? Once burned twice shy, eh? No more business there.

Sorry, wrong again. Give Ted some credit. He knew quite well what he was, and was not getting. Faust is no better nor worse than any consultant. (An expert, as Ben used to say, is just an ordinary guy fifty miles from home.) But Dr. Faust gives Ted what Ted needs most, expert legitimacy in the eyes of his superiors and hence the authority to say what must be done. True, Ted had to do some quick reshuffling at the end, but after all, that's all in the management game.

50

THE ROPES TO KNOW (VI)

While certainty in the behavioral and social sciences is certainly elusive, one of the well demonstrated verities in the domain of psychology is the perceptual set. Once you've perceived a situation or an object in a certain way, in a certain context, chances are that you keep seeing it that way in later situations. To illustrate the principle, psychologists have devised a number of clever devices and experiments. We have those reversible figure-ground illustrations—is it a young woman or an old hag? And once having seen the illustration in a particular way, say, as figure on ground, we find it very difficult to break the *perceptual set* and see the equally likely ground-figure arrangement.

The principle can be demonstrated experimentally in various ways. One familiar experiment is the water jug problem, the one in which you're given a five-gallon, a one-gallon, and a one-quart container and asked to come up with exactly three and one-half gallons in the fewest steps. The solution to the problem requires a sequence of pouring from one to the other, adding and subtracting liquid, and finally winding up with the required three and one-half gallons in the five-gallon jug. In the classic version of the experiment, you are given three or four problems using about the same sequence of steps. Typically, people solve each of these more quickly than the first because they soon get the hang of it.

Now, the last problem in the sequence has a fairly obvious and much more direct solution than the first ones. But most people overlook it and keep on using the method they picked up in the preceding problems. Why? Because they have gotten in a rut. They see the new problem in the old way, and it interferes with their ability to see it in other ways just as your initial perception of the figure-ground problem prevents you from seeing it the other way.

What has this got to do with organizations? Well, it illustrates the principle that once you have defined a situation for others in a certain way they continue to see it in that way. Which brings us to the importance of *situation management*. Don't sit around and wait for others to organize the figure and ground for themselves. They may not see it as you'd want. So here we have a key lesson of career management: understanding how to define the situation for others.

Let's put this in context. Let's go back and pull together what we have done so far. In our first section we introduced you to organizations and to the ways in which you learn how things take place—some fundamental lessons in socialization. In the second and third sections we used this background to illustrate the art of presentation of self. This was our first lesson in career management, a demonstration of the art and principles of *impression management* and of how role expectations influence perceptions.

Moving on, we then introduced you to organizational game situations. Our intent here was to help you predict likely outcomes of typical situations and to be able to anticipate traps—unexpected consequences from presumably successful strategies.

Now, with these lessons in hand we have moved on to *situation management*. Once again we have had to call on only a relatively few principles. The first of these is simply good management. Don't leave the outcome to chance. Or (to put it somewhat differently) learn to be a midwife for your desired outcome.

The second principle is one we have just elaborated—the principle of perceptual set. Establish the context in which your efforts will be evaluated. Your task is to make sure that others in The Company see the correct figure against the appropriate ground. In our illustrative sequences we see this taking place in different temporal contexts: before the situation develops, as the situation develops, and after the situation has developed.

In *Stitch in Time* we saw situation management at its best. Kerry let the headquarters people know that the work was done and trusted to it that when they actually saw the new site they would perceive it in the proper way. In *Success Story* we had a somewhat different and more complex problem. It won't do simply to thrust Cooley Bell into top management when all others in The Company are required to demonstrate competence. Yet you can't afford to leave his getting there to chance either. And so we count on the fact that the faithful of The Company are used to seeing announcements of executive promotions replete with past accomplishments. Well, so here's another. And who knows . . . ? Finally, in *The Rating Game* Ben is setting up a figure-ground experiment of his own. He has carefully constructed the ground against which he wishes his figure to be perceived. And that ground is one of a competent person who somehow has been overlooked in the earlier balloting.

Situation management gets a little trickier when you haven't had the chance to rig things in advance and the situation must be managed "on the fly" as it were. In *Just in Case* we have a mixed case. Faust doesn't know exactly what will happen during his presentation so he's leaving room for contingencies. His hope is that in drawing attention elsewhere, to misspellings and the like, he will draw attention away from the important issues. This sort of distraction is, incidentally, the basis of the craft of the illusionist and the ventriloquist.

Both *The Pearl* and *The Most Valuable Player* (one story really) require defining outcomes as they take place. The written word is an aid here. Ted does two things. First, as trouble develops he defines the project as being really two projects, one for which he will be responsible and the other for which his successor will be responsible. Then he creates the impression that his part had been done just fine, and—whoosh—off to firmer ice.

We are left with the final and most difficult situation of all, redefining the situation after the fact. As we have said, this is a good situation to stay out of, but, then, sometimes it's unavoidable. In *Top Secret* we saw how the military handles the problem (and other government agencies as well), just hide the outcome of your work. After all, who can challenge "national security"? Unfortunately, in other organizations it is not usually so simple. That was the lesson of *Management By Objectives*. Facts and objectives *can* change after the fact and *can* have uncomfortable consequences. Yet we did see that accomplished figure skater, Edward W. Shelby IV, performing in *As I Recall*. Nice work, Ted—not easy, of course, but effective.

In closing, a final admonition: Bear in mind that situation management is much less complex for the innovator, the shaker, the mover. The "front end" of the action is simpler to manage since few constraints have as yet developed. Remember, your job is to "set the parameters." Use a broad sweep of imagination, get things underway, and move on.

PART VII

THE POWER OF
LOWER PARTICIPANTS

Introduction To Part VII

While in the past decades it has become unfashionable for university students (and professors) to participate in the "military experience," still there are some for whom memories of the company Clerk-Typist and First Sergeant are vivid. Yes, these two are classic "lower participants" in the military organization, just as Bonnie and Jimmie Szekely are lower participants of The Company. Why be interested in such people? Because they wield a great deal of power in organizations, that's why, and because the existence of this power is mostly overlooked.

Well then, who are they? Generally you can identify them by these characteristics:

— They hold dead-end jobs or jobs with no planned steps upward through the organization.
— The jobs provide fewer material *and* nonmaterial rewards than those of upper participants.
— Their activities are less meaningful because they generally are not "in the know" concerning the broader context of their work.

These characteristics add up to one important fact: The organization offers very little to its lower participants and so it has little to take away. Hence, lower participants are difficult to control.

An example? Yes. The secretary or stenographer is an exemplary lower participant. Quite typically, the secretary is a working wife, perhaps waiting to have a family when a little more secure economically. Analyze the situation. Put yourself in her place.

— There are lots of jobs in your city that are no worse than yours.
— The possibility of promotion to a better job is very remote, which is okay anyway since you don't want the hassle of a demanding job.
— Most of the things you do don't mean a damn thing to you, and you don't know where they came from or where they are going.
— In short, the job is boring.

So there you have it. The four basic motivating tools of management are missing: pay, promotion, and interesting work. Oh yes, four. Well, they could fire you, but that's hard to do, and you wouldn't care anyway. In sum, there is nothing that management can or will do that serves as an incentive to compliance. And this means that you, secretary, as a lower participant, can be quite difficult to control if you wish to be. Oh, there are things you must do. You've got to get to work on time, for example. But short of not doing the job at all, it's pretty much up to you what you will or will not do, and when you will or won't do it.

By way of contrast, crawl under the skin of Edward Wilson Shelby IV. Yours is a good job, but your experience is all with The Company. Might be a little difficult to find another job as good "on the outside," especially since you lack solid credentials of technical expertise. Then, you want the next promotion so bad you can taste it. And you can see the next steps beyond that one, too. You also are getting to the position where you can see how the big picture fits together. Power is heady stuff, isn't it?

Well, Kerry doesn't have to ask *you* twice, does he? Doesn't make too much difference *how* he asks either, does it? But he had better treat Bonnie right, eh?

Now back to our "classic" lower participants, the clerk-typist and the first sergeant. Anyone who has lived with these two will agree that indeed they wield power far beyond the measure of their official status in the military organization. How so? Let's look at the reasons one at a time.[1]

The first is lack of interest or apathy on the part of higher order participants. Officers, the people in command, don't want to fool around with details. So the clerk-typist makes up duty rosters (assignments to undesirable tasks) and consequently can omit or substitute names of the unfortunates appearing on the roster. Suffice it to say other favors can be obtained in "trade." Similarly, first sergeants carry out many functions that "the book" requires of officers.

A second source of power is "bureaupathic" compliance with the myriad rules of bureaucracy. This, of course, is the classic strategy used by the top sergeant to thwart that commissioned officer who attempts to command "by the book." Incidentally, such attempts are generally the result of the officer's realization that his sergeant actually *does* run things. So he'll say "Sorry, Szekely, but we go by the book in this outfit." Well, now. This will last a week or two at best, when, inundated by paper and pestered beyond endurance, the officer will say, "Uh, Sergeant Szekely, why don't we just handle this—ah, informally?"

Finally, expertise related to critical or problematic organizational functions is the third major source of power. This factor is most crucial when such expertise is not formally codified and its existence is unsuspected.

Yes? You would like that explained? Surely. For consistency, let's continue with our military participant, though there are better examples in industry and government. As has been said already, it is nearly impossible in the military to get things done as regulations contend they should be done. Consequently, through years of experience and informal instruction, a good first sergeant knows how to get what is needed from the Commissary, the Motor Pool, the Headquarters Company. These things are not written down, nor will they ever be. Keeping these products of hard-won experience to himself guarantees our First Sergeant a continuing source of power. And this, of course, is one reason why superiors continually plead with subordinates to set down all procedures in writing.

All right, then. We have described who these lower participants are, have pointed out that they occupy positions with relatively few rewards, and have shown that their power stems from several different sources, not the least of which is that upper participants don't want to be bothered with carrying out these duties. Still, you say, what if the superiors *do* care, for example, the officer who wants the sergeant to do things his way? You think the case is overstated a little. After all, the organization still has ultimate control. And yes, you know of a top executive who maintains, "fear is the greatest motivator"—so, just fire them or threaten to fire them and that's that.

Oh no, friend, that is most definitely *not* that. First of all, there are lots of people you can't fire because union and civil service regulations say you can't. That is why those union and civil service regulations were made in the first place. But even so, firing is really a last resort. It's bad style and it's ineffective—and it's pretty tough to pull off in instances other than flat out nonperformance of duties.

Still, in all fairness to you we should deal with the point you've raised. How *do* lower participants get away with such cavalier treatment of superior's interests? Basically, this nonvulnerability has two aspects—

— a lack of upward aspiration or opportunity for upward movement in the organization
— a position of unique and necessary expertise
— or a happy combination of both.

Let's take the first. You should be convinced by now that the organizations rely far more on the manipulation of rewards to gain compliance than they do on threats of such ultimate penalties as firing, and that the Shelbys of this world are far easier to handle than Bonnies in this regard. But in addition to those for whom the organization cannot provide additional rewards, there are those who don't desire anything more, or don't desire it at the personal price they would have to pay. A common example is the salesman with a good income, in a sales territory he knows and likes, who doesn't want a promotion. He's doing well for himself and the organization, but he doesn't follow the rules quite the way you'd like. Well, you've got to be careful how you handle these people because they're protected by the normative system.

The *what?* The normative system; that is, those unwritten standards and expectations which people in The Company implicitly agree upon as being right and proper treatment. These standards and expectations are quite pervasive. And the normative system says that you don't punish someone who's doing his job successfully just because you don't like him or the way he works. That's bad style too, and *your* management won't put up with that. Well then, you can't stomp him and you can't withhold something he wants, so what do you do? That's what we're talking about.

The second source of nonvulnerability is obvious—the uniqueness of necessary skills. The key element here is the way in which the lower participant protects his knowledge; the accountant who keeps vital sections of "the books" in his head, the executive secretary whose filing system is a vast, complex, and incomprehensible wasteland to all but herself. Examples are legion. Add to this the requirement that the function be a vital cog in the day-to-day operation of the organization, and you can see easily that more problems result from replacing the troublesome lower participant than in putting up with him or her.

One final word before we move on. As you read the following chapters, note that a subtle transition has been made from the last chapters—a transition from exemplary stories about games *you* play to stories about games that are played *on* you. Naturally, this is assuming that surely, in your own mind at least, you are no longer thinking of yourself as a lower participant. So remember, you're reading this from a different perspective. You are not thinking of yourself as a lower participant but as one finding ways to control lower participants. Good luck!

51

COFFEE BREAK

"Can you imagine the nerve? Honestly, some people in this Company really need a lesson in manners. Who does he think he is?"

This last question stuck firmly in Ted's mind as Bonnie described her encounter in a Corporate Headquarters elevator. Bonnie, for her part was irate, the picture of virtuous outrage.

"And without so much as an 'excuse me,' mind you, he *pushes* himself into our crowded elevator and spills half the coffee. (Well, almost half.) So I told him he ought to be more careful."

Ted's interest indeed is starting to grow. Bonnie had just come back from "outside" with a carton loaded with coffee. Company policy (in *this* building, Mr. *Marsh's* policy) frowns on going out for coffee. Looks bad. So a coffee cart comes through once a day in the morning, presumably to wake you up, and that's it. But that's *not* it for the coffee-addicted faithful of The Company. They need an afternoon kick as well. So in keeping with the spirit, if not the letter, of Company policy, Ted has Bonnie go out for afternoon coffee for his section.

"So then he starts giving me this lecture, all about profits and the stockholders. *Honestly!* Where do I think The Company would be if we all took the afternoon off? The nerve!"

Ted is growing visibly apprehensive.

"Well, I wasn't going to take any more of that so I told him. I said they get tired in the afternoon, and this helps them work better. And this way they don't have to go out themselves. We do it all the time. Everyone does.

"So then he asks me where I work. Can you *imagine?*"

Ted blanched visibly, "You didn't tell him, did you?" But he knew the answer.

"Of *course,* I did. And then he got off the elevator on the 28th floor."

"Oh, my God." Bonnie had never seen Ted more agitated. "Bonnie, do you—do you, ah, have you ever seen Mr. Marsh? Do you know what he looks like? You don't? Would you describe this person to me?"

The next day Ted was on tenterhooks all day. What should he do? A personal note to Mr. Marsh? No, that wasn't it. But what? The following day Ted was even more sure the hammer would fall (why hadn't it fallen already?).

Then, that afternoon an unprecedented event took place. The coffee wagon! For the second time that day! Accompanying the wagon was a sheaf of announcements—(take one).

It has come to my attention that scheduling a second coffee run in the afternoon may be necessary. In keeping with Company policy you are expected as usual to remain at your desks during this period.

M. M. Marsh

Ted could hardly believe it. How could Bonnie bring off in a few minutes something that the personnel specialists had been trying to do for a year?

The answer? Probably because as a lower participant Bonnie's directness and honesty are evident, and because clearly she has nothing personal to gain from the outcome. (Also, she has nothing to lose by speaking out on a matter of such trivial importance as this.) While Ted Shelby is chary of "rocking the boat," Bonnie (correctly) saw no harm that could befall her for voicing an honest, innocent opinion (although, if she'd known it was Mr. Marsh himself she might not have been *quite* so forthright).

52

HASTE MAKES WASTE

Braang! The phone slammed down in an obvious display of evil temper and spleen.

"I can't believe it. I just *cannot* believe it. Three weeks! Three weeks and Data Analysis still doesn't have that job for me. You know how long it takes to do that on the computer?"

Stanley nodded appreciatively, although in fact he had no idea how long or what job.

"Two point three seconds, that's how long. Two thousand three hundred milliseconds, and they can't get it done in three weeks. Three weeks!"

At this point Stanley cut in hoping to avoid further rendering of temporal equivalents.

"I know it seems a long time to wait, Lesley, but The Computer Department is busy, and that job of yours probably has a pretty low priority. And you've got to remember it takes more time to set up a job than to run it."

"Hell, that's just it. I'd do it myself and get it done faster—but they won't let me."

"Of course they won't. If everybody like you were let loose running around in the Computer Room things would be so fouled up that nothing would get done."

"Say, you sound like you're on his side. Listen, what I want to know is, does this guy work for The Company or not? If he does, then why doesn't somebody shape him up or get rid of him?"

"Lesley, you don't have it as bad as you think. Let me tell you a story about how bad it really can be."

Stanley wandered back in memory to his student days when he had accompanied the redoubtable Dr. Faust on a visit to The Agency. Actually, The Agency was one of a number of government agencies involved in the highly unpopular venture of giving money away. Why *un*popular, you ask? Simply because you never can make friends by giving things away. Your constituents have only complaints: they should have gotten more than they did; this one should have received but that one not; or the money didn't arrive on time . . . .

But this is digression. The Agency was a large agency and gave away lots of money to lots of people. And the process was the usual one for such agencies; that is, on regular schedule checks were sent out through the mail to the Agency's "customers." Now, this business of giving money away is very political, and, as we've said, the customers of The Agency are frequently unhappy and complain to people in The Government— who consequently make life miserable for the people who run The Agency.

But back to the point. Stanley recalls vividly the despair and sullen resentment expressed to Dr. Faust during his visit to improve the "administrative efficiency" of The Agency.

"Is it your customary practice here to tally these forms off by hand from the carbon copy?" Faust's tone was slightly incredulous as he queried the section chief of Vital Statistics and Control.

"Yes, it is our practice," came the sullen reply.

"I—ah—I mean, wouldn't it seem, ah—more direct to compile these statistics by machine processing methods?"

"It would," this time not so much as glancing at Faust.

"Ah, well, I hate to ask the obvious question, I'm sure that . . . "

Faust was cut off sharply.

"You're going to say that you're sure there's a good reason why we do it this way aren't you? Well, there isn't."

Faust cleared his throat, paused, thought better of it, and started to fill his pipe. Always good in an emergency, thought Stanley.

"Ah, thank you for your time, sir. Would it be all right if we stop back again and talk a bit?"

"If you want to."

As Faust and Stanley passed down the hall to the elevator they caught a brief conversation.

"Got that report for me yet?"

"Not yet."

"Any idea when? We've got to have those numbers. It's been two months."

"Sorry, you'll have to ask Kenny. Two weeks, two months, two years—who knows?"

"But can't you *do* something? Tell Sypher it's important. We can't move until we've got that stuff."

The other speaker uttered a very strange choking sound and just walked away.

"Well," said Dr. Faust, "now I think we are making some progress." Their appointment with the Director for Administration was revealing, for Faust now had some pointed questions. "I get the feeling that your group is completely overburdened by paperwork." Dr. Faust began, "Now, my guess is that you know this as well as I, and that you also know what to do about it, but for some reason you can't."

"Yes, you are quite right, Dr. Faust. Obviously, the answer to our paperwork problem is machine processing. But, in actuality, you know, it takes more time to do it that way than the way we do it now.

"You see, our problem is that all our machine capacity is taken up getting these payment checks out. I've talked this over with Kenny Sypher, our Chief of Computation, and he says that there is just no give in the system."

"But might you not run an extra shift?"

"We run three shifts right now."

Now Faust is incredulous.

"On that machine, *three* shifts, and you're running to *capacity!*"

"That's what Kenny tells me. You know, Dr. Faust, you really have no idea what a time-consuming job it is getting those checks out. You ought to go down and talk to Sypher!"

"Ah, I probably shall. But first, couldn't you rent time on another machine. Wouldn't that solve your problem?"

"No, I've tried that. First, I have no money in my budget for that, and besides, since we have our own machine, regulations won't allow it. Next, I have no positions in my organization outside of Sypher's shop for people to do that kind of work, so I'm right back where I started. No, I'm afraid this problem is just something I've got to live with."

Later, Stanley and Faust did visit Kenny Sypher and learned a great deal. Not from Kenny. His discourse on the "details of his operation" was an exercise in total obfuscation. But they did learn that Kenny's key personnel were "his boys." Brought up from the ranks, totally secure and totally loyal, knowing key parts but only *parts* of the total operation. No one talked to anyone in Machine Operations unless and until cleared by Kenny Sypher.

"Well, what is your diagnosis, Stanley my boy?" Dr. Faust seemed incongruously jovial as he leaned back to light his pipe. Obviously he was enjoying something.

"I'd say this Sypher is the fly in the ointment, Dr. Faust. Listen, I don't care how big the job is, with that machine he's just *got* to have time to help out. He's either incompetent or unwilling or, probably, he's both.

"But still, I can't figure out why he's not willing to help out, why he drags his feet so much. Some of those people we talked to waited three months for piddling little jobs that could easily be squeezed in within a day or two."

"And what effect do you suppose that would have?" Dr. Faust was leading Stanley ahead.

"Well, certainly things would get done faster and better."

"And . . . ?"

"And what?"

"Ah, how would others react?"

"Well, they'd — yes, I guess they would. They'd say, let's get Sypher to do this. Yeah. And they'd also dream up new things to do. No problem, Sypher can run it off for us this afternoon."

"Precisely."

Stanley is now racing ahead in the excitement of discovery.

"So he puts them to the test. If they really need something, they'll keep after it. If not, forget it. After all, haste makes waste. He figures most of the things people ask for are just matters of convenience anyway, no harm done. And it makes his job a lot easier."

"Well, you do understand then."

"I do, and yet I don't. I guess I forgot the reason why we're here in the first place. A lot of things *don't* get done around here, and we know that Sypher is the reason. Now that can't be lost on the Director either. Why doesn't she get rid of him."

Again, strangely, Faust was smiling.

"Indeed, why not?"

"Oh, I know he can't be fired—regulations. But remove him?"

"How would The Agency get its job done without him?" posed Dr. Faust. "Remember, his—ah, boys are intensely loyal—owe their jobs to Mr. Sypher. None of them knows the entire operation. In fact, key parts exist only in one place, Sypher's head."

"I guess I do see. So if we dump Sypher the whole operation grinds to a halt for a few weeks or a month and . . . "

"And, the tempest breaks loose when the money is not delivered," Faust interjected, "and the one who is to blame is the Director . . . "

"Who *can* be fired," Stanley completed. "Well, let's see. We can't set up a parallel operation, no way to justify that because you've already got one, and you would have to admit you were doing a lousy job of management. You can't get to his boys, because really you've got nothing to give them and they're under Kenny's thumb anyway.

"But look, why doesn't the Director lay it on the line. Kenny can't just ignore her, or directly disobey an order."

"Yes," said Faust, "in a formal sense she certainly does have the authority to do that. But look at the game, think about the payoff matrix. The Director can order this 'extra' work to be done or not. Kenny can choose to do it or not. But he can also influence the outcomes. He prepares a memorandum in answer to The Director's order. This memorandum cites the order and points to the fact that Machine Operations is currently so close to capacity that in event of unforeseen machine breakdown the checks to The Agency's—ah, customers, may be delayed as much as two weeks, perhaps more. Of course, there would be more to that memorandum, but you can fill in the details for yourself."

"Okay. And I think I see something else, too. The Director can't be sure but she's got to suspect that the chance of 'unforeseeable' machine breakdown gets pretty high if she pushes that order. So Sypher's in the catbird seat there."

"Quite right. The Director's maximum loss comes under the condition of ordering the extra work, and being a minimaxer, she will avoid that condition."

"But one thing still bothers me. Doesn't Sypher know that he can be caught if someone, say an outside expert, is called in to report on what goes on? Why doesn't that keep him honest?"

"I never said the man was not honest, Stanley, nor do we know that he has actually done anything. It is simply that the possibility exists. As for your outside expert—how much did we learn about Machine Operations in our tour?"

"Well, not too much, but we didn't have much time."

"Ah, time. It *would* take time to learn the operation and then to verify what had happened, wouldn't it? And you could not call this expert until after the disaster had occurred, could you? By then where do you think The Director would be? Relieved of her duties, of course. But wouldn't she be cleared eventually? Possibly, possibly not. For in a very real sense, she is responsible for the political turmoil resulting from the incident, so reappointment is unlikely."

"All right, you've got me. I guess there *is* nothing that can be done. But honestly, you've been acting as though you're enjoying this. I'd think you'd be pretty unhappy about it."

"Perhaps, Stanley, perhaps I should be. Yet I've always found pleasure in viewing the work of a consummate artist."

FIGURES DON'T LIE . . . ?

Often, when I'm called upon to make a point by way of illustration, I reflect on Stanley's experience in the construction business. The examples seem to be particularly vivid. I suppose this is because Stanley was new to The Company then, and consequently everything seemed a bit larger than life to him. Take the matter of cost estimation, for example. Because he was so new to it, Stanley perceived accurately some things to which most of us would have paid no attention.

". . . And the machine base will be set true and level to plus or minus one-eighth of an inch and dry packed with sand-cement grout not to exceed one-half an inch in thickness."

Stanley had just finished the construction specifications for the new addition to Ben Franklyn's expandrium mill building. Ben had told him that these specifications were extremely important because they would be the basis for contract bidding.

"You can't trust these bastards," growled Ben (presumably referring to the antecedents of *all* contractors). "If you haven't got 'em pinned down right to the letter they always call it 'extra work' and you pay through the nose for it."

Before Stanley could ask the obvious question—if it's so important why am *I* doing it?—Ben had handed him three older sets of specs and told him simply to copy appropriate paragraphs and make the necessary substitutions for place and date. As in so many other things, Stanley had learned, no job is ever done from scratch. What appear to outsiders to be monumental efforts commonly are but the results of the most recent exercise in accretion and substitution on the part of some organizational nonentity. So it goes.

As usual, Ted Shelby had been assigned from the corporate staff to coordinate the construction work. Not that Ted knew a great deal about construction (that was not required). Rather, it was an "opportunity," Ted's chance to be exposed to yet another phase of The Company's operations. And again as usual, Ted never let lack of knowledge stand in the way of his managerial efforts.

After the bids came in Stanley was going over them with Ted. He skimmed through several, then observed, "Doesn't it strike you as kind of funny, Ted, that these bids are so different from one another? I mean, look, here's one for seven hundred and fifty thou, and then here's another for a million five! You get the idea that these guys are really shooting from the hip on these bids, that they really haven't got any idea of what this job will cost."

"No, you're wrong there, Stanley. These fellows have precise methods of estimation. When I was an officer in the Corps of Engineers . . . "

Not *again,* thought Stanley. Ted had spent six months active duty in the reserves, and you'd think he was another, well, whoever.

". . . we had *precise* methods of estimating cost and time factors for all elements of the work. No, I'm afraid you're wrong, Stanley. You should see the records these outfits keep, what every job costs, broken down by manpower, machine time, you name it. No, I think you will find the variation comes from two sources: efficiency and motivation. Some, naturally, are better businessmen than others; their costs are lower. But mainly, some want the job more than others do. Your high bidder there, the one with double the costs, he just doesn't want this job so he will make sure that he doesn't get it with that high bid. They always bid, of course, because they may want the next job."

"Okay, maybe that does make some sense, but look at this." Stanley waved his hand at the cost breakdowns for the various subsections of the work. Different contractors were obviously in wild disagreement with one another. "How do you account for that?"

"Oh . . . those differences just reflect different accounting procedures, I'm sure. Oh, listen, I've got to get down to see Ben Franklyn. I'll give you the full rundown when there's more time."

Sure you will, thought Stan. Skate fast when you're on thin ice. Ted always had an answer even when he didn't know what the hell he was talking about.

As the mill job got underway, Stanley learned quite a lot about the cost estimation business. The first thing he learned was that he was pretty good at it. He had a simple formula. First, he would make an educated guess about the number of man-hours he thought it ought to take to do the job, then he would multiply by two. Worked pretty well. And in the process of doing this he also learned something else; he learned that although the hours were recorded *correctly,* they were *not* recorded *accurately.*

You don't understand? Well, maybe we should let Woodrow Sawyer, the construction foreman, explain it as he did to Stanley. He and Stan had become pretty good friends, and late one afternoon, involved in his cost estimation exercise, Stanley asked Woody if he could see the day's time sheet.

"Checkin' up on us again are you?" asked Sawyer with mock suspicion.

"Oh, you know I'm not, Woody, I wouldn't know what to check if I was . . . Now let's see, the way I figure it . . . ahh, six men times eighteen hours, then multiply by two and . . . hey, wait a minute, this isn't right! You've got three men over by Bay Twelve all day and you *know* nothing's even started over there. I mean, don't get me wrong, I'm really *not* checking on you, you know that's not my job, but . . . but I mean, how come?"

Stanley was obviously a little flustered, as though he'd found something he really was not supposed to know. But Sawyer put his big bear paw around Stanley's shoulder in a comforting way.

"Don't worry, no problem. Just a little internal accounting. We're an honest outfit; you know that, and I know that, else you'd never have seen that time sheet. Those men put in those hours today, didn't they?"

Stanley nodded yes.

"It's just that they didn't put 'em in like it says here, right?"

Again, yes.

"Well, you see I got this problem. The guys in the office who bid this job think that the work in Bay Twelve should cost about twice what this here will. But I happen to know that it's more likely to be just the other way around. So—so I make it come out right. No problem. Don't worry, kid."

And with that Woody was gone, cursing out the crane operator who had just nearly dismembered one of his men.

Next day in the office Stanley was debating the wisdom of confronting Ted with his new insights on cost estimation when Dr. Faust dropped by to inquire after his sometime protege. Stan quickly rattled off his new discovery and asked the opinion of the master.

"Yes, it does seem that you have observed a modest instance of an ubiquitous fact." Faust paused to light his pipe, a sure signal that an instructional dialogue was at hand. "Now, let's suppose that you, Stanley, were the one commissioned to work up the bid price. How do you think you would go about it?"

Remembering his experience with the specifications Stanley replied without hesitation. "I suppose I'd look up our records on how much jobs like that had cost in the past, and I'd make the bid about the same. Maybe a little higher than average just to be safe."

"But what if you couldn't find another job like it? What if this were the first of its kind?"

"In that case I suppose I'd ask . . . or maybe I'd use some kind of factors . . . or I suppose I'd just have to make some kind of educated guess. Wouldn't I?"

"No matter," said Faust, "you have grasped the main point. What appears to be the most reliable way to make a bid is on the basis of past experience, and where that is lacking there is much guesswork involved."

"Excuse me, Dr. Faust, but it seems that we're off the track. What I was getting to is that this 'past experience' is phony. And you're trying to tell me that it's the best way."

"You," commanded Faust with the stem of his pipe, "*must* learn to listen. I did not say *best* nor did I say *is*. I did say *most reliable* and *appears to be*."

"Sorry," Stanley murmured contritely.

"Now think a bit. Since this past experience is, ah . . . as you say 'phony' (Faust pronounced the word as if it were a bit unclean) why then do we find that, (a) foremen do nothing to correct it, and (b) management never uncovers it?"

"Oh, the second part I can understand all right. How could they? I suppose if we were talking about some real small job they could. But these big contractors don't bother with the small stuff. And out here (Stanley swept his arm panoramically) where men are moving from job to job all day, why, who can tell?"

"Precisely. Then you can understand management's problem, but you cannot fathom why the *foremen* act in this way. Yes, I suppose it is difficult to comprehend. We shall need several principles. The first is our old friend, the minimax, and the second is what I shall call coincidence versus accuracy. Now, you do understand that each contractor has an historical record of estimated and actual costs for each type of job; that is, the bids and their actual costs. As the job progresses the foreman sees that bids and costs do not agree. So he has a choice. He can go for accuracy or for coincidence. If he chooses the former—"

"He's got some explaining to do, no matter what," interjected Stanley. "But if he goes for coincidence, for agreement with the estimates right down the line, well, he's a good manager. Sure I can see that, but that's no big deal. And where does your minimax come in?"

"Yes indeed, where? You are making an assumption, Stanley, the assumption that the contractor will be satisfied with the job done by his foreman. But what if he is not. What if costs seem a little excessive, if the job is unprofitable. Then what do the strategies imply?"

"Okay. I do see. If the foreman goes for accuracy then a lot of his numbers don't look anything like the estimates. Obviously bad management, right? And since, historically, estimates and costs agree pretty good . . . "

"Pretty *well*," supplied Faust.

"Since they agree, why he's going to have a hard time convincing management that in the past the cost figures have always been phonied up. So the foreman's maximum loss is where he records his costs accurately and later comes out on the short side on profit, which is bound to happen sometimes."

"Of course."

"But if he's pretty much in line with experience, well, it's not good, . . . but it happens to anyone now and again."

"Precisely," Dr. Faust added the oral QED to the logic.

"And uncertainty is the important element here. One cannot know the overall outcome until it is too late to change the cost allocation, so why take a chance? And perhaps it *would* be possible to convince management, but perhaps not. Again, why take the chance? It is simply a question of good career management."

"Just one last question. Don't any of the guys who are doing these things get into management? And if they do, why don't they put a stop to it?"

"Why yes they do, and they do stop it, or they try to for a while. But you know what it is like to try to verify those records, it is next to impossible. And after all, in the final analysis the system works, and with human nature being what it is . . . "

What Dr. Faust left unsaid is that it is management's greatest folly to believe that organizational members called upon to supply information that can directly affect their own organizational well-being will be neutral with regard to the content of that information. And in spheres of endeavor as diverse at the military, the church, the government, the charities, and industry, influential managers ponder pages of statistics that are tributes to little else than the creative imagination of human kind.

54

FAIR DAY'S WORK

"Excuse me . . . uh, sorry . . . ah, say is that seat taken? It is?" So began another hour of that test of flesh and spirit called commuting. Stanley now knew that assignment to New York was a mixed blessing. Among other things, cattle on the way to their final reward rode better than did the average suburbanite headed for The City.

"Oh, hi, Ted. Say, mind if I take that seat?"

Ted was especially glad to see Stanley this morning because he was involved once again in a new program and wanted to talk about it.

"Well," he was soon saying, "the upshot of Dr. Faust's study—and you'll find this hard to accept, I know—is that we are operating at only sixty-five to seventy percent of industry standard.

"So *measurement* is the key. You know Mr. Marsh, Sr. always went on the assumption that Company people, *because* they are Company people, give you one hundred percent." Ted went on to explain that there were some ways of giving one hundred percent that were better than others. And that his new program was aimed at worker education, aimed at helping them understand this. Procedures Improvement Program—PIP—it would be called, and its slogan—"work smarter not harder." Measurement was for feedback and individual improvement, not for policing, he emphasized.

"You see, the problem has always been one of determining what constitutes a fair day's work. We simply want to make sure that we're getting a fair day's work for a fair day's pay. These scientific work measurement procedures will do that for us."

"Uh, how do you figure the fair day's pay?"

"*Well*, that's what we pay." Ted's look portrayed disbelief that such a question could arise in The Company, so Stanley let it drop and proceeded on a new tack.

"How do you think the guys in the mill are going to like this? I mean, my guess is that they're not going to see it the same way you do."

"We've thought of that, and that's why the educational aspect of this thing is so important. Remember, we are working on *Procedures Improvement*—Work Smarter not Harder." Ted relished the words. "This is *their* program and *their* company."

A week or so later Stanley was back in Pawtucket, digging out some data on the modified expandrium line. Strange, while it had been some years, it seemed as though he had never left . . . so much so that without giving it a thought he stopped over to see Ginny Szekely in the packing department. For eighteen years Ginny had been doing about the same thing—packing expandrium fittings for shipment. So well practiced was she that she could do the job perfectly without paying the slightest attention. This, of course, left her free to socialize and observe the life of The Company as it took place about her.

Today, however, she was breaking in a new packer. It was instructive. "No, not that way. Look, honey, if you hold it that way, well, then you have to twist your arm when you pack this corner, see. This way it's easier."

"But that's the way Claude Gilliam (methods engineer) said we had to do it."

"Sure he did, honey. But he's never had to do it eight hours a day like me. You just pay attention to what I say."

"But what if he comes around and says I should pack the other way?"

"Oh, that's easy. When he's here you do it his way. Anyway, after a couple weeks you won't see him again."

"Slow down, you'll wear yourself out. No one's going to expect you to do eighty pieces for a week anyway."

"But Mr. Gilliam said ninety."

"Sure he did. Let *him* do it. Look, here's how to pace yourself. It's the way I was taught, and it works. You know the *Battle Hymn of the Republic* (Ginny hummed a few bars). Well, just work to that, hum it to yourself, use the way I showed you, and you'll be doing eighty next week."

"But what if they make me do ninety?"

"They can't. Y'know, you start making mistakes when you go that fast. No, eighty is right. I always say, a fair day's work for a fair day's pay."

55

PLAYER PIANO

"I won't do it! I *will not* do it; for you, Mr. Marsh, for anyone. Yes, that's final!" Ben, as though shot from a cannon, almost knocked Stanley down as he bolted from the office. Then, without so much as a hello (Ben probably didn't even realize Stanley had been away from Pawtucket for over a year), "Can you believe it? *Can* you *believe* it? That dumb bastard (Ted) is going to try to come in here and hold his stopwatch on our guys." Stanley wished Ben would let go of his arm.

"His old man (Shelby III) would've had more sense. At least he knows what the inside of a mill looks like. These guys will crucify him—and *me* in the process."

Then, suddenly, "Say, how'ya doing, Stanley? Nice to see you back." And with that he was off down the hall.

Now, Ben wasn't the only one concerned. Down on the mill floor, talking to his old friends, Stanley found that word of the new program was out.

"Seems like they don't trust us," Jimmie Szekely was saying. "But you know, we've always given The Company a fair shake. And for his part, Ben's been fair with us. We don't need nobody coming in here to hold a stopwatch on us. Look, you know, if I've been working on this line for—oh hell—ten—twelve years, well I'd have to be pretty dumb not to know how to do the job, wouldn't I?"

Ted's very thought, mused Stanley.

Jimmie continued, "Ben leaves things on the line pretty much up to us. Hey, here, see this piece. That's scrap. But look . . . ." Jimmie went on to show Stanley a way he'd worked out to salvage those hundred dollar expandrium castings. "Takes a little longer but you gotta figure The Company comes out ahead.

"Lemme tell you what we do if those pinheads come in here with the stopwatch." Jimmie opened the fusebox and yanked out a wire. The line stopped.

"Y'see, somehow, I don't know why, when we run these type A castings that overloads the line and the breaker goes out. First time it happened I got the mill engineer over here and he don't know what to do, so I just jump the breaker. You're not supposed to, but this line will take it." And with a chuckle, "Uh, whatya think I'm going to do when the watchbird's watching me? You bet, down time. A free coffee break."

"But Jimmie," Stanley asked, "isn't that going to make it more difficult for you to make your quota?"

"Yeah, I know what you mean. That worried me too." Then, looking kind of sideways at Stanley and pointing upstairs, "Say, you're not with *them* on this are you?"

"C'mon, Jimmie, you know me better than that. I don't even *know* any of those time study guys."

"Well, I thought so but . . . . Anyway, Joe over there came here from Another Company, and he says there's all kind of ways to beat the system. Like if the line goes down from overload here. I can't help *that,* can I? So they, what'd he call it—they, uh, yeah, they 'adjust your base.' He says that means you can get to one hundred percent when you're even making less pieces. Then there's scrap. You get your base adjusted if you got bad stock to work with. You get time to replace tools that burn out." And with a grin, "Y'know, if you try to run the line too fast they just seem to burn out left and right."

They didn't, of course, thought Stanley. But setting those tools was an art known better to no one than Jimmie Szekely. And Jimmie never had, and never would, tell the Industrial Engineers what he knew about that line. Every now and again they would try out something new on the line. Mostly it didn't work, but Jimmie dutifully did what he was told. No more, no less. For their part the IEs didn't care much about that line anyway. They got what they wanted from it and it wasn't a very interesting process, so . . . .

For his part, Jimmie had a firm idea of what was fair for The Company, and what was fair for Jimmie; you might say it was his own unwritten, unspoken contract with The Company.

"Uh, Jimmie, now don't get me wrong, but what if these stopwatch guys really do have a better way of running the line? Wouldn't you be better off?"

Once again Jimmie gave Stanley a suspicious look. "How? They going to pay me more? They going to give me time off? Look, you know what really bugs me about this, it's these guys out there checkin' on me. Makes it seem that I'm not doing my job, that you can't trust me. Fact is, I do more for them than they think. I don't have to save those pieces from scrap that I showed you. But I figured out how to do that and, well, it puts some interest in the job and saves them money too. But they don't care about that. They just want to make sure you do it their way."

Later that day Stanley thought back to his talk with Jimmie. Was Jimmie right? No and yes. It all depended on whose point of view you took. For Jimmie it seemed to be a matter of pride and a struggle to keep from being turned into just another machine. And from the engineer's point of view it was simply a question of return on investment. Jimmie Szekely was being paid to run the line as effectively as possible. So if they came up with a better way, what was the problem?

Typically, the more Stanley thought about it the less certain he was of his conclusion. But one point did seem clear, you were mistaken to idealize the motives of either Jimmie *or* The Company. And with that conclusion Stanley decided to drop the whole matter.

But Ben Franklyn did not have such a direct solution open to him. Ben understood well the trouble that was brewing; that was one advantage of having come from the ranks. Any system that man can devise man can beat. And here Jimmie Szekely and the rest of the "lower participants" on the mill floor distinctly had the upper hand.

They understood Ted's slogan—"work smarter not harder"—far better that did Ted. Hell, they invented it! Ben knew very well that if it came to a showdown the mill hands had it, and the engineers didn't. Oh, the staff guys would show numbers telling you that percent of quota (adjusted) had gone from seventy or eighty to ninety plus. But what those numbers wouldn't reflect would be the real gains or losses in productivity that resulted and the strain (unadjusted) in the relationship between Ben and his mill hands.

So anyone within hearing distance (say a block or two) of the Pawtucket plant manager's office can tell you Ben's decision.

"I told you last week and I'm telling you again for the last time; *no,* I will *not* do it! *Yes,* I am prepared to tell Mr. Marsh that personally. Yes, you *will* have to fire me first!" And anyone who knew Ben knew as well that he meant it.

56

POINT OF NO RETURN

"Can you beat that?" Lesley was mumbling to herself. She turned and, tossing the just crumpled paper ball at the wastepaper basket, exulted, "two!"

"Can you beat what, Les?" Stanley, passing through the Corporate Communications Department, had his interest piqued.

"Oh, hi, Stan. Nothing really. Besides, you know we're not supposed to talk about Company announcements until they're announced."

Stanley, now genuinely interested, had to engage in a little information bartering before Lesley would fill him in.

"So I've been working on the announcement of this Franklyn guy's promotion for about a week. That (pointing at the successful basket) was the eighth try. For some reason they wanted it just right. And *now* they tell me forget it. Seems he's not going to get the job after all."

"What job, Les?"

"Oh, Corporate Director for Manufacturing. But why would they go through all the trouble of preparing an announcement if they weren't sure they were going to give it to him, Stan?"

That question stumped Stanley as well, so, you guessed it, the next time he ran into Dr. Faust he requested another reading of the Corporate tea leaves.

"So that surprises you does it?" mused Faust, "Well, it should not. You still have the same problem, I'm afraid."

Silence. Faust knocked out his pipe and reamed it over the massive ashtray on his desk. Stanley waited. Then.

"You are overfond of making assumptions. Otherwise, the facts are clear enough. So let us proceed first with the facts. What do you know about Ben and Pawtucket that seems related to this?"

"Uh, let's see, well, The Company's going to install the PIP program there."

"Assumption," Faust barked accusingly.

"The Company is *trying* to install the PIP program at Pawtucket," Stanley corrected. Faust nodded.

"And Ben says 'over my dead body'—ah—I mean, he actually says 'not while I'm plant manager.' "

"Go on."

"But that's just what I don't get. Why are they thinking of promoting him when he's making all kinds of trouble for them?"

"The *facts*, please," with an exaggerated air of patience.

"Uh, let's see. Ben's been at Pawtucket twenty-six years now. Well, it's his home. And he's doing a good job. I've heard people say that lots of times."

"Correct."

"Okay, so they decide to promote him because he has done a good job, but now he fouls the whole thing up and they change their minds."

"Assumption. False conclusion. Assumption." And then with a mock sigh of despair, "I can see that you are not as—ah—organizationally mature as I had thought. But these things take time.

"Assumption one: that they, whoever that may be, decided to promote Ben because he is doing a good job. False conclusion: that Ben—er—'fouled up' his chances by his rejection of PIP. Assumption: that 'they' withdrew the promotion. Obviously you fail to understand. Let me give you a little help. Do you think Ben would like the Corporate life here?"

"Oh, Lord no! He'd . . . ."

"Yes, of course, and so?"

"So he never would have taken that promotion in the first place. Then why? . . ." Stanley mulled over the facts momentarily, then, "So someone was twisting his arm. Figure they give him something he can't resist, get him out of Pawtucket, then Zap! PIP. But whoever it was didn't know Ben very well."

"Curiously enough, that seems to be the case."

"But he really has to take it doesn't he? I mean, if push comes to shove can't they just say, 'It's this or out!' "

"Fire him? Much too crude, and really impossible. And no one in The Company *has* to take a promotion. Of course, it is highly unusual not to; after all, moving ahead is the reason most are here. But fire him? Marsh wouldn't hear of it. How would it look? You said it yourself, Pawtucket is one of our most productive facilities. And many people in this Company are personally loyal to Ben."

"Well, if all this is true, then what I can't see is why they just don't leave him alone, let him do it his way?"

"No, no you do *not* understand. Mr. Marsh *does* want this program very badly, just as badly as his plant managers do *not* want it. Now they will fall in line, partly because they do want that next promotion and partly because they have been told that *all* plants are participating. Yes, you see the problem. Now, my guess is that Marsh has given his Vice-President for Production direct responsibility for the success of PIP, so it's really *his* problem. For what is he going to tell Marsh? 'I can't get Franklyn to fall in line.' Oh no. He knows the answer to that, they all do. Marsh says, 'That's *your* problem. If you can't handle it, I'll get someone in here who can.' You've got to realize that Mr. Marsh probably values Ben more than this vice-president. He can always get another vice-president but effective plant managers are a rare commodity."

Stanley frowned. "You make it sound as though Ben can get away with anything he wants to."

"It may sound that way, but that is not what I said, of course. Ben is in a strong position primarily because there is nothing The Company can give him that he does not already have. He's well off financially, he wants to stay in Pawtucket, and he thinks plant manager is a more important job than President. So your usual—ah, motivational tools do not apply. But he's only resistant, not *immune*. He's in an unstable position now, and he will have to give on something. My guess would be that he will take some modified version of PIP with the objectionable features removed. In return I think he will have to make some promises about productivity increases that may be difficult to keep. I don't know. This thing is far from being over." With that Dr. Faust seemed to tire of the discussion, looked at his watch, and abruptly walked off.

Now, the lesson of this story concerns upper participants who have in common some of the sources of power of lower participants. In this case there is nothing they want that The Company can give them and consequently threaten to withhold. This is a key reason why the management of The Company devotes so much time to planning managerial mobility. Occasionally, though, you do run across a Ben Franklyn or his counterparts in other functions. And usually this is pointed out as being bad for The Company. "Prevents younger people from getting experience in that position," it is said. True. But what is also true and what is *not* said is that these Ben Franklyns are, in a way of speaking, past the "point of no return." They have the power of *both* upper and lower participants, and they often have difficulty in putting things in the "proper perspective."

57

THE ROPES TO KNOW (VII)

Did you enjoy our exemplary tales? Possibly they have made you feel the weight of dealing with troublesome lower participants. But to move on, let's see now, where to start? Yes. The word "power" in the title *Power of Lower Participants*. Not much has been said about that, and when you think about it, power is a difficult concept to pin down. So a little digression will be necessary to illustrate the concepts of power, authority, and persuasion—ways of getting lower participants to do what you want them to do.[2]

For the sake of illustration, let's think of an imaginary dimension along which to classify ways of getting people in organizations to do things. And let's say at one end of this dimension is raw coercion—the ability to force someone to do something regardless of their wishes—and at the other end is persuasion—relying completely on the ability to convince the subordinate to do something because the outcome will be pleasant or otherwise desirable. Now let's take a moment to examine these two ends of the dimension before taking up the question of what is meant by *authority*. If at the outset you'll accept that this analysis of power won't stand up to intensive academic scrutiny, and that all that is wanted is to make some useful distinctions, then *power* can be defined generally as the ability to make things happen or keep them from happening regardless of the wishes or interests of those against whom power is being invoked. For example, "Szekely, you'll do as I say or you're fired."

Power can be exercised specifically and directly as from superior to subordinate, or it can be exercised in diffuse indirect ways, as when the executive secretary makes it impossible for certain people to get needed information from the files.

Pure persuasion, at the other end of the spectrum, requires that subordinates be convinced that this is a desirable action in its own right. It assumes that the person to be persuaded is free from threat and is giving active consideration to the merits of the action, pro and con.

Now somewhere between these two extremes is the relationship described as authority. The key element of authority is the willing acceptance of the compliance relationship by the subordinate, the willing suspension of critical judgment in acting on the authoritative request. For example, when Mr. Marsh asks Ted Shelby to work up a memo for him of the new Subordinate Readiness Program, it never enters Shelby's head to say no. It doesn't enter his head to ask himself whether or not he should do this. Nor does it enter his head to rehearse for himself the consequences of not doing it; that is, to consider that Mr. Marsh might use his power to make Shelby do it if he so chose. That is what is meant by the willing suspension of critical judgment as being the essence of the authority relationship.

Another concept will also be useful in understanding authority. It is what Chester Barnard, in his classic *Functions of the Executive* termed "zone of indifference." Basically, zone of indifference refers to the range of authoritative requests through which the subordinate is willing to suspend critical judgment, hence, to which he is indifferent. Requests falling outside this zone of indifference will receive critical consideration from the subordinate and consequently cannot be considered part of the authority relationship. Put another way, such requests will require the use either of persuasion or power or both to gain compliance.

Examples, you say? "Bonnie, will you type this letter for me?" Coming from Ted Shelby this is an authoritative request. Both Ted and Bonnie know that this request is well within the bureaucratic definitions of their rights and responsibilities, and so it falls within Bonnie's zone of indifference. Oh, of course, Bonnie might say something like, "Mr. Shelby, is it all right if I finish this first?" But this is just a request for additional information and does not imply consideration as to whether to do it at all. Such consideration could occur only if the authority relationship had completely broken down.

But how about, "Bonnie, run down to the Deli and get me a pastrami sandwich." That one falls outside their mutually accepted definition of Bonnie's responsibilities, and she might or might not decide to do it. Even more to the point, Ted might drop by with a thick wad of scribbled notes and say to Bonnie "I'll need these by Wednesday," which happens to be tomorrow. Now, if their relationship is informal, Bonnie may point out that it can't be done and that they should try to work out a way or a time in which it can. But if the relationship is not informal, Bonnie will say nothing and simply make up her mind not to do it. Oh, tomorrow there will be reasons why it couldn't be finished on time. But the real reason will be that Bonnie has decided that it is too much to do in that period and that she is not going to do it. And in this manner an alert secretary will eventually instruct her boss indirectly as to what is, and what is not a proper workload.

Now then, this power of lower participants has two basic aspects—

— the ability to ignore many authoritative requests; that is, the ability to maintain a narrow zone of indifference; and
— the ability to exercise diffuse power; that is, the ability to bring about desired organizational outcomes in addition to those involving the authority relationship.

Since the characteristics and sources of power of lower participants have already been set down in the Introduction, let's go back now to the examples and extract some generalizations.

First, in *Coffee Break,* the only real point is that lower participants can interact with superiors in ways that Ted Shelbys and Kerry Drakes and even Stanleys cannot. This is because lower participants as individuals have no real influence (or so it is thought) on the important affairs of The Company, and consequently in matters of policy are above suspicion of self-serving or competing interests. This is why Bonnie's outburst was successful in getting the afternoon coffee break.

Next, in *Haste Makes Waste* there is the issue of nonvulnerability. In fact, Kenny Sypher has just about everything going for him in this regard. But is he a lower participant? Probably not by the classic definition, though his terminal position in a Governmental agency has most of these characteristics.

Figures Don't Lie conveys a number of messages. But the story really is about Woody Sawyer, the construction foreman. True, not much is said about him, but Woody is a typical foreman. He's come up from the ranks, and he isn't going any further. He's like the First Sergeant, of the management but not in it. Consequently, he runs things his own way, following the path of least resistance and generating information that's taken seriously only upstairs. Once again, the actual task of timekeeping seems trivial enough to be carried out by lower participants (once the overall design of systems and categories has been devised)—an example of abdication of responsibility as a source of power.

The concluding three chapters are really one and are reflections on the folly of expecting people to behave as machines. It is, of course the futile wish and hope of the management that ways can be arranged to make lower participants as predictable and orderly as the machines they tend. The resulting socio-technical system might then function with the machinelike efficiency so dear to the heart of the industrial engineer. *Fair Day's Work* serves to introduce this theme and make a simple point: that lower participants and management are equally interested in a fair day's work, but use different standards. The somewhat obscure title *Player Piano* is adopted in reference to Kurt Vonnegut's classic story about the dehumanization of men by machines made by men. But here we see the other side, the power of lower participants to resist the mechanization of their efforts—power stemming from their particular expert knowledge and experience.

Finally, in *Point of No Return* is illustrated that needing nothing the organization can offer—a key source of power of lower participants—can be applied conceptually to the strategic position of certain upper participants as well. The result in this case is that Ben has a relatively narrow zone of indifference *and* the nonvulnerability to accompany it.

So there you have it, the general principles that show how lower participants exercise power independently of the management and ignore authoritative requests generally. Now, from your new stance—that of bringing about organizational outcomes—your position would be that of most managers: understand who and what these lower participants are, and try to keep them from getting out of hand. But when you must deal with *upper* participants who have the characteristics of lower participants, real problems develop. They are, after all, the people who must implement your decisions. For this reason we move now to our final set of illustrations—illustrations of how to deal with noncompliance, or at least how to recognize certain strategies for doing so.

ENDNOTES

1. These characteristics are described in David Mechanic, "Sources of Power of Lower Participants in Complex Organizations," *Administrative Science Quarterly* 7 (1962): 349-64.
2. This argument is adapted from Herbert A. Simon, *Administrative Behavior.* (New York: Free Press; 1965) chapter 7.

PART VIII

COOLING OUT THE MARK

Introduction to Part VIII

On the occasion when capricious mischance falls your way, the homespun philosopher is likely to tell you that yes, life is full of little disappointments. Unfortunately, life also is full of bigger disappointments. And it is interesting how people cope with these. For if you stop to think about it, a great deal of time is spent defining and redefining disappointing events in ways that make them seem acceptable.

Consider the following situation. The scene is a singles bar in a relatively fashionable section of town. And there's Ted—yes, Ted Shelby. In fact, Ted is a semiregular here. At a nearby table there are two men and an attractive woman. The men are talking quite earnestly. Pieces of their conversation can be heard. "A sure thing," "No, he won't take small amounts. He doesn't want to fool with it."

Ted, standing at the bar, notices the woman. In due course, Ted makes her acquaintance and learns that the two men are her brother and his friend. The two men are talking in earnest. Their problem seems to be that they don't have enough money to do something or other important. Ted isn't really listening to them, but he can't help picking up part of the conversation. Presently, the brother's friend leans over and asks the woman a question. She replies so that Ted can hear, "No, not that much, but I wish I did. A chance like this comes once in a lifetime."

More to develop his conversation with the woman than anything else, Ted asks what is going on. She tells him that she really can't talk about it but that they have this opportunity to double or triple their money, a sure thing. But like most of these things, it takes money, and they just don't have it. Turns out that they need about $5,000 but they only have $2,000.

Now Ted gets a little more interested. "What's the deal?" he says. With this the woman turns to her brother and tells him that Ted wants to know more. "Is it okay if I bring him in on it?" But the brother is uncertain. After all, she doesn't know Ted very well, to say the least, and we don't want to blow this one. An opportunity like this comes by once in a lifetime. "No, you better not tell him." The men go on talking in earnest and shortly leave. Ted asks the woman to dinner, she agrees, and that is the end of the evening.

The next evening, Ted returns. After all, he's a semiregular. And the trio is there as well. This is not unusual in a place like this with a steady clientele. But now the two men are really agitated. It turns out that tomorrow is the last day to cash in on the "opportunity." So they relent. Presumably they know Ted a little better now so maybe it's okay to let him in. However, the other one, not the brother, is reluctant. He cannot see why they should let a stranger in on this. However, the brother persuades him. If Ginny says he's okay then you can trust this guy.

The scheme revealed is this. They've got a tip on one of the big numbers games in town, and they know how this one is rigged. They just happened to chance on it through a friend who owed them a favor and took this way to make it up. But it's a secret. They can't let it out. The problem is that this is a big game, and the operator doesn't take less than $5,000. It's for high rollers.

"Oh," says Ted, and he visibly backs off. At this point the friend says, forget it, don't waste your time on him. For her part the young woman looks very disappointed and a bit disapproving. "No, wait a minute," says Ted, summoning his courage. "I just think it's unusual, that's all."

"Okay, then, listen. Tomorrow is the time. We've scraped up two thousand but that's all we can get our hands on right now. Next week would be another thing, but right now we need another three thousand to make the five thousand it takes to play. And, of course, it's got to be cash. But listen, man, we stand to make fifteen thou. You get nine plus your three back and we get six."

Ted looks hesitant. "Well, I see, but look—don't be offended—but how do I know I can trust you?"

At this Ginny starts to make an angry statement about what kind of friend is this, but her brother quickly interrupts.

"Don't get your neck up; Ted's right. How can he know? Shows he's got some sense. Listen, I'll tell you what. When we leave here you take our money. Two big ones. Hold it until I meet you tomorrow afternoon and you bring your three. That'll show trust. We'll go over together and place the bet, then meet here tomorrow night and divvy up." And that's just what Ted does.

Now, of course, you know the rest of the story. Ted will never see the brother or the woman again. But the other man does show up. Ostensibly he also is a victim. As they wait that evening, he conveys to Ted his own growing realization that he's been taken and so also has Ted. But more than that, as Ted suggests possible action they might take to reclaim their loss, the "cooler," for that's his role in this con game, provides Ted with all the reasons why the different actions Ted suggests will be ineffective.

"Go to the operator? Are you nuts? Admit we were working a rigged setup? Not me! You go if you want to, but at least I've got my scalp."

"Well, hell, then let's go to the police," says Ted. "Maybe we won't get our money back but at least we'll have some satisfaction."

"Uh, maybe that's not such a good idea. You know, playing the numbers is illegal in this city. And I've got to think about my job. An arrest wouldn't look very good on my record, it would be kind of tough to explain. I tell you though, you go if you want to, that's up to you."

Well, now, Ted has a job to think about too, doesn't he? And The Company isn't the kind of outfit to take moral turpitude lightly either. Finally, the cooler plants the philosophical frame of mind in Ted by way of adopting this attitude himself. Well, he says, at least we're in this together. Let's have a drink. After all, if both of them could be suckered into such a scheme then maybe neither is that foolish. And so ends the story. Perhaps it has not been quite fair to defame Ted in this incident, yet things like this do happen.

Erving Goffman in his stimulating essay, "On Cooling the Mark Out," suggests that the methodology of the con game provides an interesting analogy to other social adaptations to failure. The "mark" is set up by the "operators" of the game who arrange a "play" to relieve the mark of his cash. The play has typical phases through which the mark is taken—phases that later define the situation for the mark. After the "blow-off" or "sting" in which the play is revealed and the mark's money disappears, the mark is highly motivated to do something to gain recompense. Hence, the need for the "cooler": the need to cool the mark out in order to "define the situation for the mark in a way that makes it easy for him to accept the inevitable and quietly go home."

Interesting, but what does this have to do with organizational careers, you say? Indeed, there may be some rascality among management people but precious little downright illegality.

But bear with me a minute. The point is that a great deal more than the mark's cash is involved. The crucial loss is that of his self-respect, his commitment to the fact that he is a competent individual. And it is this loss of respect, this self-doubt, that generates an enduring motivation to undo the "play." In consequence, the basic function of the cooler in the play is to provide a new definition of the situation that restores everything but the lost cash.

Oh yes, organizations. A major problem organizations face is that of controlling the consequences of the disappointment experienced by individuals who do not receive expected promotions or, more poignantly, are removed from positions of influence by reason of suspected incompetence. The problem presents itself to the organizations as one of managing definitions of the situation, of redefining failure in status-preserving ways.

Why bother, you say? Well, for several reasons. First, you must remember that few of us in organizations are in the happy circumstance of being so secure that he can afford to be known as one who has handled a delicate situation poorly. There is at least one executive (inherited through family ties) of whom others in management used to say "For Chrissake, don't let X handle this in his usual ham-handed way." Consequently, if the mark puts up a squawk, it is difficult to tell exactly where the final judgment may come to rest. No, a little dispassionate analysis of the payoff matrix suggests that the coolout is the minimax solution.

Then again, it may be that the mark will simply turn sour. That is, he will cease to be the bearer of attitudes and motivations appropriate to his position in The Company. And after all, one bad apple . . . .

Finally, it may be that even without the trappings of a coolout, the mark neither squawks nor turns sour but simply goes about his business as usual. Well fine, you say, then that's that. Oh no, my friend, that most definitely is not that. For the lesson is not lost on each of the myriad other prospective marks in the pay of The Company. Each one thinks to himself, "There but for the grace of God go I." A lack of attention to the cooling out process, or otherwise insensitive treatment of the mark, can easily produce parallel consequences in others anticipating their turn. So beware.

Well, enough of this sermonizing. Let's return to Stanley, Ted, Dr. Faust, and The Company to get a firsthand glimpse at the play.

58

MORE BANG
FOR THE BUCK

Stanley was doing his best to get some sleep on the "redeye special" from New York to Los Angeles, but he'd always experienced a certain uneasiness with air travel (if God had wanted man to fly he'd have given him wings), and consequently he occupied the hours in a kind of somnolent reverie. Why in hell were these research laboratories always located so far from Company Headquarters? For even when they got to L.A. there would be another three to four hours of travel by car. Oh yes, they; Stanley and Faust were making this trip together on a mission for the CATCHUP program. But more about that later.

Stanley had been to the The Company's Research Laboratory before, and it was indeed a beautiful spot. But then, there were beautiful spots near New York also. Stanley then dozed off for what seemed like a minute, to be wakened several hours later by the groan of the hydraulic gear as the pilot lowered the flaps on his big jet. But Stanley's thought train was right where it had been. Yes, in fact he did know some of the reasons The Company gave for the location of this research laboratory. He had asked in preparation for this assignment. The Company wants to be, and is, number one in industrial research. But basic research is a delicate and time-consuming process, and basic researchers are delicate and time-consuming people. Or so it was thought. So one reason for the remote location was to relieve the researchers from the continual piddling inquiries by Company management as to their contribution to the profit structure of The Company. Indelicate questions like that were assumed generally (and quite rightly) to upset delicate researchers. Consequently, because of the time, distance, and the difference in lunch hours, there were effectively only three or four hours of the day for telephone communication. The difficulty of travel made personal visits unattractive. Well, maybe the remote location was necessary.

Next day Dr. Faust and Stanley arrived at the Research Laboratory a little later than usual. They were there at the request of Ted Shelby, who had recently been assigned as Personnel Manager. This, of course, was simply another way station along the road of Ted's personal development as a Company executive. It really didn't matter that Ted knew nothing personally about research. He didn't have to. After all, this was a "managerial experience," wasn't it?

Which is not to say that Ted was incompetent. Ted knew how to do certain things exceedingly well. Among these was the ability to "sniff noses and tails" as he called it, by way of getting the lay of the land in a new situation. And it was because some of the noses and tails didn't smell quite right that Faust and Stanley were here—Faust as consultant and Stanley as support from the CATCHUP project.

"Something's wrong; something just isn't right out here," Ted was telling them. "I can't put my finger on it but we just have too many people moving through here. After all, we've moved this operation out here because in our judgment this would be the proper climate for research. But just in the last six months, why, I think I've separated or transferred at least five or six scientists—no, make that seven; we just processed Giles Selig yesterday.

"You see what I mean? *Seven* in six months. I don't know what Kerry's thinking about, but then, these technical people don't make good managers anyway. I think we've got a chance to bring this place around." Ted now was falling into his crisp/urgent tone. "Yes, I think it's up to us. I think CATCHUP can make a real contribution here. You see, what concerns me is that these people should be unhappy about leaving here, and yet, they don't seem to be. That's not right. Even the ones leaving The Company for The University talk about this being 'a good experience.' " Ted underlined the words by emphasis.

With that Ted suggested that Stanley and Dr. Faust spend some time interviewing scientists and their management, Stanley the rank and file scientists, and Faust the more sensitive management assignments.

So it was that Stanley and Dr. Faust spent an interesting two days listening to the complaints, fears, and successes of an array of doctors of chemistry, physics, mathematics, and engineering. On the third day they got together to exchange notes. Faust was already there when Stanley entered their temporary office. He was obviously quite relaxed, puffing slowly on his something-less-than-aromatic pipe. "Well?" he said.

"It's tough to know where to begin. Each one of these people is different in so many ways that it's hard for me to say what I found. But there is something; there *is* something funny here. First of all, I did talk to a couple of guys who seemed to be completely happy. They both seemed to be doing exactly what they wanted to do and doing pretty good at it."

"Well," interjected Faust. (He just couldn't help himself.)

"Uh, doing pretty well at it. In fact, one of them thinks he's going to get a Nobel Prize for his work. But the others, well, I guess you could say there were two types. Or maybe there's three. Anyway, the rest of them don't seem to be very happy.

"See, there's this one guy I just talked to who's really got the red-ass—"

"The *what?*" Faust looked as though he'd been touched by something unclean. But Stanley, now into his tale, went right ahead.

"He's really burning. Thinks The Company has screwed him over (again the look of distaste from Faust) and wants to leave. Says he was promised all sorts of things that he never got. He wants to get back to basic research at The University. But he's the only one like that.

"The others, well, the others I just don't know how to describe. They're unhappy all right, but they seem to be more unhappy with themselves than with The Company. It's like they look around them and see some people doing big things and winning Nobel Prizes and they ask, But what have *I* done? They're making pretty big money, and they seem to have gotten used to it, but it's funny, you know; they seem to feel they owe The Company something. That they haven't really carried out their part of the bargain."

"Ah, yes, yes, that seems to fit." Faust wasn't listening to Stanley any more but rather puffing his pipe slowly and staring at the ceiling. "Yes, that fits. Interesting."

Faust would say no more to Stanley other than that it seemed time to talk with Kerry Drake, Manager of the research function in the laboratory.

Again, in their meeting with Drake, Faust was unaccustomedly silent. About all he did was to outline the basic function and mission of project CATCHUP and the concerns of Ted Shelby. Of course, Drake knew most of this since it is customary to clear these things with management before proceeding. But beyond that Faust said nothing but to ask Stanley to fill in Kerry on this conclusions. Indeed, when Stanley had finished, Faust turned to Drake and asked for his reactions to what Stanley had just said. It seemed that Faust was not going to commit himself before he had seen all the cards.

"So that's what you see, do you?" said Kerry. "Well, I can't say I disagree with you. Yes, our scientists have a certain self-image of what they are, and you (pointing to Faust) and the rest of The University people are responsible for that. When you people in the big-time universities finish with them they think they're going to be . . . or they think they want to be . . . Nobel Prize winners. And I guess if they didn't think so we probably wouldn't want them here.

"But hardly any of these people are going to succeed—partly because success in this kind of work has a strong element of chance and partly because very few, if any, of us are Nobel calibre to begin with. Well, what that means is failure by our standards. But we don't want to put it that way. So, in fact, very few here are asked directly to leave. We want them to come to that conclusion for themselves. Now, some just don't find what they want in The Company, and we give them a year or two to go to The University or even to Another Company if they wish. But you've seen it, most want to stay with us. They've gotten used to a good salary, and the benefits, and they've even gotten used to The Company. They have friends here. And you know, Stanley, you're right. They even feel a little guilty for having pulled down a good salary for a few years and given The Company nothing in return. Yes, they feel they owe The Company something. So we arrange to transfer them to a more applied kind of work at one of our other locations."

"But that doesn't make sense," Stanley blurted out. "Why does The Company want to keep failures?"

Kerry looked at Stanley but left it for Faust to say, "Did Kerry say they were failures? I don't think he did. I thought I heard him say they were failures by the standards of the laboratory, and that is quite a different thing."

"Exactly," agreed Kerry. "That's exactly the point. These are very talented people, make no mistake about it. But they've tried to do something that very few of us can do. We know that, but they don't. But what if we tried to tell them that in the beginning? Naturally they wouldn't listen. What if we said, 'look, don't fool around with basic research, take a job at our plant in Pawtucket. There's lots of really important things you can do for us there.' Well, you can see, we'd never get any of them that way. And so we wait. We wait until they find out for themselves they aren't made from the stuff of Nobel winners. Yes, we let them get a taste of failure. They they'll come to us and say, 'Isn't there something I can do in The Company that will be a little more useful that what I'm doing now?' And so we say, 'Why yes, there's this job in applied science at Pawtucket.' Now, really, we need good people out there too, but you take your typical graduates of one of your big Eastern technical universities—we'd never have got *those* people there in the first place. In this way we do. So you see how it works."

Once again Stanley was puzzled. "Okay, now I understand that, but then why are *we* out here? Why don't you just explain that to Ted and let it go at that?"

"No, don't do that," said Kerry with a hint of anxiety in his voice. "Look, Ted won't be here all that long, and by the time he's ready to leave he'll probably have figured it out for himself. But right now I don't know what he'd do if he understood the system. I want Ted to do his job, counseling our people on other job opportunities. If he knew what was going on he wouldn't be half so effective."

With that the meeting was over. All that remained to conclude a successful trip was the meeting with Ted to present the recommendations. Now Stanley understood why Faust had been so noncommittal; he had understood the situation from the beginning. *His* problem was to satisfy Ted without upsetting the whole applecart. And in the end that wasn't so difficult either.

Dr. Faust skillfully steered Ted to the conclusion that things were about as they should be, that because The Company had such high (high, but realistically high) standards for its reseachers there would be failures, it was unavoidable if excellence were to be maintained. And just as Ted was beginning to get a bit uneasy, the "solution" was delivered. Yes, a "training package."

". . . And it would be appropriate for this to come out under your name, of course, with myself listed as consultant. Here . . . ."

With that Faust produced the first few draft pages of *Personnel Management in High Stress Environments*. Ted beamed.

Now, what we have just witnessed is an exemplary "play" by the con artists of The Company. The Company wants its Research Laboratory, make no mistake about that. But even more, The Company wants its applied research scientists working in its production plants; "more bang for the buck" as they say. The "mark" is the scientist and the "sting" comes at the point of realization that he hasn't got the stuff of genius. Ted, in this case, is cast in the play as the "cooler," offering alternative attractive roles to the mark; providing a new definition of the situation that satisfies both the operators and the mark.

59

INCREDIBLE

It's not that Ted and Ben don't like one another personally (although, as a matter of fact, they don't); it's just more the way it is with cats and dogs. God intended them to do very different kinds of things. And as age old experience with normal, healthy cats and dogs has shown, when placed in the same room the fur will fly.

And so it was that a certain amount of fur littered the conference table in room S-211, Corporate Headquarters, where Ted, Ben, his staff, and the staff people from New York plus one of Marsh's handlers were discussing the latest program to help Ben run his plant. The topic of discussion, if we may call it that, was Ted's newest wrinkle on subordinate readiness—his GOALSETTER program—GOAL SETting Through Exchanged Roles. Ben, for his part, was getting more impatient. Of course, Ben had been born impatient. But there were production problems at Pawtucket. The big, new rolling mill was down, and nobody could figure out why. So Ben was in no mood for subordinate readiness.

"Ben, we realize that the decision on this is entirely up to you. But it's a two-way street. With every other plant in The Company (not quite true) really starting to get some mileage out of modern behavioral technology, I don't understand why it is that we always have to drag you into the twentieth century .. ." Ted had slightly transgressed the bounds of his usual decorum with that, but for a change, he wasn't acting. He had a big stake in this program, and Ben as usual had turned out to be his main stumbling block. But then, Ben never noticed things like this anyway. Ted went on.

"I don't know why you're unwilling to accept the facts we have about Goal Setting Through Exchanged Roles." Ted's tone was urgent/agitated. "Our trial run at Paducah showed that subordinates set goals twenty percent higher in the role exchange situation. Now that's good enough for us, and it's good enough for Mr. Marsh." There was just a hint of hopeful uncertainty in that last statement.

Now it was Ben's turn. "Listen. I'm the first one to admit that I don't know a damn thing about your behavioral technology, if that's what you call it. And it's not likely I ever will. But I *do* know something about getting a product out the door. And what I know is that I'm goddamned well not going to get a product out the door with all my managers and half my millhands sitting around and getting confused about who's boss so they can decide what they ought to get done next year. I can tell you what they'll get done that way—not a damned thing. And what's more, I'll tell you who sets the goals. Me. That's just the way it is, and that's the way it's going to be."

"Now just a minute, Ben. That's a distortion of what our program is all about." One of Ted's staff men was talking. "We're not trying to confuse anyone. Quite the opposite. It's a healthy thing for the men to step into their manager's role and vice versa. It helps them see their problems more clearly. That's why we observe the phenomenon of increased goal expectation and saliency." (The staff man was a psychologist.)

Now again it was Ted's turn. "I hate to say this, Ben, but it seems to me that you're deliberately distorting the character of this program just to find reasons for not doing it. But it's up to you. As we said earlier, if you just don't want the program—if that's your reason, that you just don't want it—then say so. We can't force it on you. But I have to say that I think you're being unreasonable."

"Unreasonable!" Ben's color now matched the volume of the last exclamation. But then slowly, and most unusually, Ben slipped into a thoughtful calm. It must have been an enormous effort of willpower for him, but those who know the old Ben Franklyn could sense that it was a calm similar to that in the eye of a hurricane.

Ben started to speak slowly and deliberately. A crease of humor showed about his eye and just a hint of irony in his speech.

"Unreasonable. I guess you all know that I spent a lot of time in this Company as a millhand before the old man (Marsh Sr.) made me a foreman. And you know I've been mill Foreman, mill Superintendent, and now Plant Manager. I've had to learn everything the hard way. And maybe I don't talk quite right and maybe I'm a little rough at times, and maybe that's why first they sent me to middle management school and then, since I've been Plant Manager, they've sent me to executive school.

"Now maybe that didn't make much difference but, you know, I did learn one thing: as I said, I came up as a millhand, and back then when I heard something that was horseshit, I used to say horseshit! Now at executive school they told me that that didn't sound so good, that instead of saying 'horseshit' I should say 'incredible.' Well, Ted, what you've just suggested to me—well, it's incredible."

With that the meeting dissolved in laughter and little further business was transacted.

What? You say that you enjoyed the story but you don't see what it's got to do with our topic. Okay. It's such a good story it had to go somewhere, and it just seemed to fit here. But seriously, there is an element of "cooling out" here. Ben, in a dramatic way, has put subordinate readiness into perspective. In a sense, he's cooled out Ted by reminding him of his subordinate staff role in an indirect fashion and by putting possible protest more on a personal ground than a material one. And after all, that's one of the main functions of cooling out—to make protest unlikely.

60

THE LIFE OF STAFF

Up toward the front of the seminar room were the usual paraphernalia required for a presentation. There were the flipchart easel,
flipcharts, the pointer, the little portable microphone that dangled from
a cord, and, of course, the water jug. Up above a sign read WELCOME
ABOARD, and a little beneath that it said, "Orientation Seminar—New
Technical Personnel."

Toward the rear of the seminar room sat the new technical personnel.
The general understanding was that they were here to learn something
about The Company's general personnel policies and in particular about
a scheme called the "dual ladder of management opportunity."

Ted, exuding an unusually crisp and hard-hitting appearance, strode
into the room, and the general murmur diminished appropriately. Ted
was fresh back from a tour of duty as Personnel Manager of the Research
Laboratory and had fittingly fresh insights into the process of research
management. He was here at the Portland plant to deliver personally
the orientation seminar for newly recruited engineers. Now you must
understand that The Company has literally hordes of these technical
people, all college graduates and all expecting some day to become plant
managers at the very least. But people in The Company know that this
is not going to happen; there's no way it could. Consequently, the
invention of the dual ladder of management opportunity. The *what*, you
say? Let's listen to Ted.

"Welcome aboard. I'm sure you know that you are the most carefully selected crew of young technical people in the country today. (Murmur of approval, yes they did.) We've hired top-notch technical people like yourselves because The Company knows that without you we can't remain Number One. And we know something else. We know that we've got to reward superior performance by recognition of that performance. I want you all to know right here and now that everyone of you is management material, and if you do your job, as we think you will, you're going to be in management in the next five or six years. (Another murmur of approval.)

"Now in most companies that might be a problem because in most companies management means supervision, it means that you've got to stop doing what we hired you to do in the first place—technical innovation." Ted paused for a minute to let that turnabout sink in. Then, with a dramatic sweep of his hand he rolled back the first flipchart and armed himself with the pointer.

"We want to make sure that our 'individual contributors' don't get saddled with the supervisory drudgery that usually goes with management. That is why we've developed the dual ladder of management opportunity. And I'll tell you this, we're really proud of our thinking here." With this he pointed to a diagram on the first flipchart that looked something like a two-pronged tuning fork with some little boxes below and more little boxes above in parallel arrangement on the two forks. Then, pointing to the little boxes on the bottom, "Here we have our usual premanagement positions, our entry grade, our engineer, and our associate engineer positions. As you can see, these distinguish levels of achievement. We expect every successful engineer to be promoted to the associate grade when he has achieved the necessary experience.

"Now, for those with distinguished ability, we have three additional levels of management opportunity. Note that I said 'levels.' Let's take a look at this side first. Here we have three levels of professional achievement for our *supervisory* management while over *here* we have three equivalent levels of professional achievement for our *staff* management." The assembled newcomers greeted this with murmurs of interest and puzzlement.

"So you can see we have arranged it so that you don't have to go into supervisory administration to get management recognition. Our strong technical people, our individual contributors, keep their specialties. After all, that's where they make their real contribution to The Company. So we're talking about professional recognition. We are all managers but the work is different.

"Here, let me read some job descriptions. Let's take the top positions here and see what's really expected of our top professionals." Ted went on to read the descriptions for division engineer (supervisory management) and that of engineer consultant (staff management). As might be expected of most job descriptions, they were somewhat inflated. The position of division engineer stressed demonstrated capacity to direct the efforts of others and experience in previous supervisory positions, while that of engineer consultant stressed background and technical achievement, "Ph.D. or equivalent with ten years of experience, a level of demonstrated technical achievement rarely observed in others." Finally, with the formal part of the presentation over Ted was prepared to field questions. There were questions on salary. Answer: yes they were equal, well, in most instances they were. Questions on what happened if you wanted to move on a parallel between staff and supervisory management. Answer: yes, that happens. You might get tired of supervision, or you might be pressed into service as a supervisor for a particular project.

Through all this Stanley had been sitting in the rear of the room taking notes to capture the questions asked in order to be able to give Ted feedback. He had also been able to record some enthusiastic remarks from the younger seminarians.

A little later Ted and Stanley were sitting in the Portland Personnel Manager's office when his secretary announced that there was a Calvin Kulas to see him. It seems that Kulas had some complaint or other about a promotion he was to receive, a complaint his manager felt needed to be resolved by Personnel. As it turned out he had just been told by his manager that next month he would be promoted to first level staff manager and that he was very unhappy about this turn of events. After a brief discussion with the Personnel Manager, they returned to the office.

"Ted, I'd like you to meet Cal Kulas, one of our engineers. He's got some questions about our dual management system. Would you mind if we took a little of your time? I've told him that we don't want to get into his personal complaint, but I think he'd get a better understanding of how our system works from the expert."

Notwithstanding these instructions, Cal did get into his personal problem. He didn't want to be promoted to staff manager. He wanted to stay on the premanagement ladder until he could get a real promotion to manager. (His words.) He told them that he felt once you have been moved over to the staff side that you were "branded," that your chances of getting into management weren't nearly as good. With that Ted began.

"Cal, I don't think you're looking at this in the right way, you *are* in management—staff management, not supervisory management.

But Cal was not to be easily put off. "Don't tell me that. Managers have something to manage. That's why they call them managers. And you can't be in management if you're not a manager. And you can't be a manager if there's no position to come up for promotion. It's as simple as that. That's why I don't want to be promoted until there's a management position open, because if I take this promotion then maybe they won't think of me when the next *management* position opens up." Ted was sorely tempted to explain again the difference between management and supervision. It was so obvious. Why did this Kulas person persist in misunderstanding?

At this point the Personnel Manager cut in. "I don't understand why you insist on saying that promotion to staff management is being branded a failure. I think those were your words, Cal."

"Oh you don't? I'll tell you why. Look at this." Cal produced a little notebook with some statistics in it. "There's supposed to be movement back and forth, right? Well, here's the only two guys who went from manager to staff (Kulas persisted in his wrong-headed usage of the words). One of 'em I don't know, but the other I do, and I'll bet you that one is like the other. I mean, I know why Drew Bolt went the other way. He couldn't manage his way out of a paper bag. So they canned him."

Now it was Ted, eager to explain and interpret.

"Why that's bound to happen, Cal. We make mistakes in predicting supervisory ability, certainly we do. So we want to be able to return the man to more suitable work. But to say he was, as you say, 'canned,' why, that misunderstands the logic of the whole process. The point is that we have an arrangement here that provides, ah, *flexibility* to make the best match between a man and his work."

Kulas was not satisfied. "Yeah, flexibility. I suppose that's why *every* one of our Engineer Consultants used to be a manager until he . . . ." Ted was not prepared to listen to any more.

"That's not right. You just don't have the facts. Why right here at Portland you've got one of our true technical geniuses in The Company. Gregor Mendel."

"Oh yes, I *do* know that, but he doesn't count. Look, nobody ever *sees* him. I think he's nuts. He works from nine at night until three or four in the morning. How many guys like that can you use, anyway?"

With this the Personnel Manager felt it necessary to intercede. "Really, Cal, I think we're getting off the track and too much into personalities. You came here with a personnel matter didn't you?"

"Well, I did and I didn't. I guess what I wanted to do mainly was to explain to you that this dual management system you talk about is a lot of baloney, at least the way it's run here. We ought to do it right or forget it.

"Yeah, and another thing, you say that the 'staff opportunity' is equal to that of the manager. But look what happened to Drew Bolt when they unmanagered him. They took his office away!"

Ted looked concerned, "Did you? Now that would not be right."

"Of course not." Now it was the Personnel Manager's turn to get a little hot. "We simply did what is always done. Since Bolt didn't have supervisory responsibilities any longer he didn't need the space and furniture for group meetings. We simply changed his office from the standard A-7 to the standard A-3 layout."

"You sure did." Cal's tone was one of derision. "And I suppose he doesn't need that lousy carpet either. Go on, tell me that it helps to keep the noise down during those group meetings."

It was just a few days later when Stanley ran into Dr. Faust on the occasion of one of his consulting forays into New York. Stanley, eager to share his new insights, pieced together the past few days' experience for Faust. Finally, he summed up his conclusion that the dual opportunity idea simply could not work. The Company ought to do away with the whole thing, stop the sham.

"Well, let me see. I'm not sure that this dual management opportunity system is so bad as you say. Let's go over your logic.

"Now to begin with, tell me why you think The Company's got this—ah, arrangement in the first place."

"Oh, that's easy. I think it's pretty much like they say. You've hired those people to be technical guys, not managers—I mean supervisors."

"Yes, that is what you mean. Now think a minute Stanley. Why all the fuss? Why bother at all with this dual opportunity business? Why not just pay those people what they are worth and let it go at that?"

Stanley looked puzzled. The answer was either too obvious or too obscure. He couldn't see it.

"But that was the problem in the first place. Wasn't it?'

Faust said nothing.

"Well, wasn't it? I mean, it's because all these people went to college, and when you go to college you ought to be in management, and . . . ."

"And?"

"And—uh, and, and yeah! You've got your mom and your Aunt Doris and everybody asking how you're making out on the job and did you know that Jimmie Szekely next door who never went to college is store manager of something or other—and what do you tell them? You'd like to think you're getting somewhere but it looks like you're not. Sure, you ought to be in management by now."

"Yes. Now why is it that one is not in management?"

"But, I just told you, Dr. Faust. The Company needs these people in technical work."

"Oh yes, The Company does, though apparently not all of them. But for the sake of idle speculation, let us say that The Company did promote all into, ah—'supervisory' management."

"You *couldn't* do that. Why . . . . Sure. I mean, I know there wouldn't be room for all those chiefs with no Indians . . . but that's the problem, isn't it! They all come into The Company expecting to be chiefs, and if they don't make it, why they're failures. And because The Company's got so many of 'em in the first place, why, there's going to be a lot of failures—a lot of unhappy, high-priced gripers who spend more time thinking about how they've been screwed than in doing their job."

So Stanley finally understood that the dual opportunity structure wasn't a failure at all. It was true, of course, that the opportunities weren't always equal, and that the staff management side was a convenient dumping ground for unsatisfactory supervisory management types, and that it's logically impossible to be a manager with nothing to manage. But it *was* a most satisfactory cooling out device. The Company—wittingly—and Ted—quite unwittingly (he bought it completely, for others of course) had redefined a situation of failure as success and had gone to great lengths to elaborate the logic of that success. And faced with the choice of defining himself a failure (under the old system) or a success (in staff management under the new system), the mark chooses the coolout. It works, all right. It's just that some are more equal than others.

61

THE THREEFOLD WAY

And here we are nearly at the end of our story. So let's move ahead a few years and take a look at the finale of two distinguished careers.

Despite Dr. Faust's ominous predictions about the situation at Pawtucket, Ben weathered the storm and was subsequently made Plant Manager of the big new manufacturing plant at Portsmouth. Why? Because Marsh trusted Ben, believed in his loyalty to The Company, and felt that the technical hot shots at Portsmouth needed a bit of toning down by way of a large dose of practical experience. Ben was that large dose of practical experience. But subsequently things hadn't gone so well at Portsmouth. No, it wasn't Ben's fault. He did what he was supposed to. But innovation is always accompanied by trouble. And then, Ben was still the bull o' the woods, and that didn't help smooth things over. He still was convinced that there was only one way to run an expandrium mill, and he had difficulty getting out of that role into the role of Plant Manager of a modern, automated plant. So go back for the minute and read again the introductory story (p. xvii) to recall what happened.

What really happened, of course, was that Marsh's handlers and the technical executives in New York persuaded Mr. Marsh that Ben had to go. And in the end it took a personal trip from Mr. Marsh himself and a direct order that Ben take the new corporate job of Safety Director. It also turned out that Ben downright refused to move to New York to take the job. He hated the place. So, as Ted would put it, The Company exhibited "unusual flexibility" and came up with some good reasons why the Corporate Directorship for Safety should be set up at Portsmouth. ("Portsmouth represents the manufacturing future of The Company, and we want our Director for Safety to be right there getting hands-on experience with safety problems." Not that Portsmouth is *unsafe,* of course.)

So in one sense Ben had been cooled out, but in another he hadn't. Ben knew what had happened to him, and he made no attempt to deny it. But then, for a millhand he hadn't done too badly, and The Company had been good to him. No, the coolout was for students of The Company bulletin board.

Now, in some ways Ben's story is unusual, though in others it isn't. So let's try a more typical problem. Take a look at what Kerry Drake has been doing out at the Research Laboratory. And here's a secret: The Company isn't happy about it. Now, the stories that follow are going to depart a bit from usual practice. The problem will be set up for you as The Company sees it, and then the story will finish with three alternative scenarios. In that way you'll be able to see the coolers of The Company at work and get a better understanding of the realm of the possible in the art of the play.

Actually it's not quite correct to say that Kerry Drake was a problem for The Company. Kerry was one of the original engineers in the modern history of The Company and had a long, successful, and distinguished career first as an inventor and then as a technical manager. And actually, it's a little misleading to speak of Kerry as a technical manager. He never had much interest in supervision, but rather exercised leadership through example. Kerry led his technical people with helpful ideas and with a sharp sense of where new developments in the field were going.

Sounds pretty good, you say? How does someone like that get in trouble? He gets in trouble when The Company changes and he does not. When The Company was small Kerry would invent something or cause it to be invented, and it was usually good. Then The Company would market it. That strategy worked out pretty well when The Company was small, and in no little measure was responsible for the fact that The Company no longer was small.

And with that growth came the development of new functions and new specialties. For example, Ted Shelby was now Corporate Director for Financial Plans and Controls. New products were planned by a marketing organization peopled by specialists who had only a glimmering of knowledge as to how the product might be designed. But that was the game today, long-term planning, market development, recovery of capital investment, and planned obsolescence. All this, of course, meant that product development wasn't nearly the fun it once was. And it was this fact that Kerry Drake in steadfast waywardness simply refused to accept.

Stories about Kerry's "misunderstandings" with executives were legion. Yes, Kerry was greatly admired by less resourceful counterparts throughout The Company. There were stories about executives making that time-consuming trip from New York to the West Coast, having a no-nonsense, this-is-it confrontation with Kerry, then getting back as far as Chicago before realizing that once again they'd been had. One apocryphal tale even had it that the executive, upon reaching Chicago, had turned around and gone back for another session. All to no avail. Kerry was master also of the art of long-distance passive resistance. Directives from New York would state that work on such and such a project would terminate and would commence immediately on such and such a project desired by Corporate management. Dutifully the paperwork would be put through, and it would look for a time as though the skirmish had been won. But those close to the Laboratory could tell you that while the project numbers and project descriptions were now different, you would find the same people working on virtually the same problem under that different title and project number.

Wait a minute, you say. Aren't you stretching it a little? No one can get away with just plain insubordination.

Well, now, that isn't exactly what was said. Kerry never flatly refused to do what he was asked. As a matter of fact he always very carefully complied with exactly what was asked. It's just that, well, who's to say what the final shape of a product design will look like, and who's to say that something quite different won't emerge along the line, something which may be better than the thing that management was looking for? Oh, yes, and sooner or later the Corporate executives will get the thing they wanted (usually later).

And so it wasn't that Kerry was not doing an *acceptable* job. He was. But Kerry was a burr under the executive saddle and had aroused the universal suspicion that perhaps a manager who was more flexible in his thinking, more sympathetic with modern planning techniques, would be considerably more productive from the standpoint of return on investment.

So, you say, that's the point. Who's running The Company, anyway? Dump Drake and bring on someone who is, as you say, more "flexible."

Wait a minute. You sound as though you haven't learned very much from our stories. And that's a little disappointing. Look, you can't just dump someone who's responsible at least in part for making The Company what it is today. That is, you've got to dump him in the right spot. Kerry's got a lot of friends in The Company, many of them people The Company needs badly, and they will find what happens to Kerry very instructive. He's been productive in spite of Company wishes, and there have been occasions when he's been right and The Company wrong. You can't forget that either. All this adds up to the fact that he's got to be carefully cooled out. So there's the crux of the problem. Kerry likes that Research Laboratory, he's independently wealthy, and there's just not much that The Company can give him that he hasn't got. Well—almost nothing.

NEW YORK

People at the plant locations held New York in a kind of awe. Oh, it wasn't that they thought New York was always right; they knew that wasn't so. New York asked for some pretty stupid things now and again. But the people in New York all had fancy titles, had an awful lot to say about what goes on in The Company, and quite obviously were the cream of the crop. Not many people ever made it to New York, or so it was thought.

Now Stanley had spent a little time in New York himself, which in itself provided him with a faint aura of success. But what Stanley had seen there didn't square very well with the generally accepted image prevailing in the provinces. Far from being an Olympus peopled by beings with more than human abilities, the people in New York were a pretty common lot. Oh yes, Mr. Marsh was there and some of the others, but then how many executives were there? Twenty, thirty, forty? And there were a hell of a lot more than forty people in that New York office. Maybe ten times forty. Stanley honestly had never thought about how many people you can get in a twenty story office building. Well, of course, they weren't all executives, but a lot of them were. Corporate Directors of this, that, and the other thing. Vice-Presidents, Assistant Vice-Presidents, Assistants to Vice-Presidents, and a mystifying abundance of senior thises and thats. Where did they come from? What did they do? Yes, they all were doing something. That much could be seen. So in one of his tours there, he compiled an informal occupational history of the denizens of 711 Gotham Avenue. And that history, he has since found out, was typical of what was happening now to Kerry Drake.

The Vice-President for Research and Development was speaking. '. . . And we think you're the man for the job, Kerry. It's still wide open you know. You can shape it pretty much the way you want to. But we've got to have someone who can pull our development picture together and give us a planned approach to new technical applications." The position being offered was that of Corporate Director for New Technical Applications. As Kerry had been told it was a new position, created presumably out of the recognition that to remain in the forefront of modern technology, The Company needed it. The Vice-President had been very persuasive. It would be a sizable promotion with increased benefits and a good hike in salary. Only trouble was that Kerry didn't want it.

Kerry had been around long enough to know what was going on. He didn't have to take the promotion, and they weren't going to fire him. He also knew that they'd like to get a new Laboratory Manager, but then, that would change. The new line of expandrium applications they were working on would change all that.

"John, I'm very flattered that you've thought of me first for this job. But really, I think my work out here comes first. Listen, I know of three or four young people around The Company who can do that job better than I. And it would really be a good opportunity for them. Take . . . ."

With that Kerry rattled off a few names of people he thought might like a job like that for a few years. But no one was fooling Kerry. The Company didn't want that job done nearly as much as they wanted Kerry to do it. And that is the way a lot of those New York positions came into being. It's a good coolout for most. But then, Kerry wasn't interested in that play. So move on to the next attempt. Parenthetically, it's a funny thing how those positions created for special purposes somehow become permanent needs.

EDUCATION

"And in today's age of rapidly exploding technology we can't afford to let ourselves become obsolete. What this means, gentlemen and ladies, is that every ten years or so we owe it to ourselves and The Company to get a technical retread. Oh, it's expensive all right, but not nearly as expensive as not doing it." Ted, using his best concerned/sincere tone, was outlining his latest innovation, the MAnagement TEchnical Sabbatical program—MATES. The basic notion was that at least every ten years all middle and executive managers would be required to spend six months at an outstanding university program in their specialty, chosen by The Company. It could be in finance, marketing, engineering, or any specialty. The basic purpose would be to "come abreast of the latest technical thinking in business." As usual, Ted was quite pleased with the MATES program, seeing in it one answer to the continual challenge of being Number One.

The challenge, however, was presented to Kerry Drake in a somewhat different way. "Now hold on, Kerry, I am *not* trying to say that. It's just that, well, none of us has the time anymore to keep up with all of the developments in our field. You can't hold down a full time management job in The Company and keep up with everything else. You just can't. Hell, I'd snap this up in a minute myself if they'd offered it to me."

What was being offered was not just six months but a year at full pay at The University. Kerry would have the chance to take some courses in the latest technological applications and also have the chance to give some seminars himself. And if that wasn't enough, he was also programmed for some short stays at European and Japanese universities specializing in Kerry's field. It was very tempting.

"I don't know, John, I just don't know. Let me think about it a little bit. At least I want to go home and sleep on it."

"Certainly, of course. There's no rush, take a week if you want. But we do want you to do this, and we'll have to start making arrangements soon in order to be ready by the fall."

It was that night, thinking about what "the arrangements" might be, that kept Kerry from getting much sleep. This was to be a full year, not just six months. And no, you couldn't run a laboratory for a full year without a manager. Maybe you could do it for six months but not a year, and, of course, if you brought in someone else to run the Laboratory for a year—well then you just couldn't let him go when Kerry comes back, could you? Oh, no. You'd say, "You know we never really intended it to work out this way, Kerry, but young so-and-so here, he's really into this new project, and we just can't afford to interrupt leadership on this thing. Tell you what, now that you've got a fresh look at the latest technologies we could really use you in New York as Director for New Technical Applications . . . ."

And so as the next day dawned, a sleepless but resolute Kerry prepared for his meeting with the Vice-President.

"John, this has been one of the toughest decisions of my life, but I feel that I just can't take your offer. I probably would at any other time, but right now we're in the middle of developing this new line of applications. I don't think we can risk a change in leadership at this point."

DISTINGUISHED SCIENTIST

Not too many years age Mr. Marsh became quite concerned about what was happening to the technical people who in such great measure were responsible for The Company's success in the market place. He knew (and he was right) that there were a number of these people who, if they had never again lifted a finger on behalf of The Company, would have more than earned their salary until retirement. Well then, shouldn't there be a way to recognize this and in doing so perhaps even tap the well once again?

So it was that the Distinguished Company Scientist program was born.

Now the immaculate conception of the program didn't prevent some of its appointments from being conceived in original sin. The operators in The Company knew a useful play when they saw one. And so a number—well, it would be more honest to say a few—of these Distinguished Company Scientists were distinguished more by their record of accomplishment than by their current popularity with the corporate powers that be.

So, having lost the game twice to date, our Vice-President for Research and Development has studied his game films assiduously and is preparing his final assault on Kerry's stronghold. First, he requires a stream of progress reports. Then he institutes a new technical progress accounting system requiring in-depth monthly reports directly from the Laboratory Manager. Then a new appointment. A young financial planning type is assigned to a new position of Laboratory Manager of Plans and Controls. His assignment requires that he work directly with the Laboratory Manager to secure complete financial accountability and "demonstrate optimum resource allocation to program effort." Oh yes, and he reports directly to New York, not to Kerry.

You guessed it. This is the kind of harassment that Kerry can't stand. So pretty soon he calls for a meeting with his Vice-President. "John, you're making a shambles of this Laboratory. We are so tied up getting the *approval* to do something that we never get the chance to do it."

"Sorry, but you might as well get used to it, Kerry. This is the wave of the future. You need to know that we are taking a hard look at all our research and advanced technology efforts to see whether they've got the kind of payoff that warrants the investment. The old days are gone forever." And then as though an afterthought and somewhat wistfully, "I guess I'd have to say that the only ones who can have the kind of technical freedom we used to have in the old days are the fellows lucky enough to qualify for one of our Distinguished Company Scientist appointments." Then quickly, "But that's neither here nor there.

"No, as a Laboratory Manager you are going to have a lot more controls on you now. Look, while I'm here we might as well go over a few of the new monthly report forms." John thumped a big briefcase on the desk and withdrew a sheaf of forms that must have been an inch thick.

Kerry blanched visibly. "Wait a minute, I got you out here to talk about cutting out some of this nonsense and what do you do, bring me more? Looks like enough to stuff a paper elephant."

"Kerry, that's just not in the cards, and you didn't think I came all the way out here just to listen to you bitch about it—did you? Here, let's look at this first one. The Technical Personnel Resources Allocation report. Now this one is relatively simple. All it requires is that you identify the type of effort and average hourly project allocation by type, and *document* it satisfactorily. Now then here . . . ."

Kerry didn't sleep much that night. John did. Kerry's thoughts kept turning on the old days in the warehouse at Pawtucket. Things were so much simpler. Fact is, nobody even asked them what they were doing. So long as a good product idea or two was delivered every year nobody asked any questions. Why couldn't it be that way now?

Yes, and by now you've guessed it. John let the situation ripen for a month or so, and then one day Kerry got a letter informing him that he was one of three nominees for a position of Distinguished Company

Scientist. Did he want to be considered? So Kerry thought it over, and well, there was nothing to lose by just being considered. Other details of the program were attached to the letter. It seemed that each Distinguished Company Scientist in addition to a handsome stipend (they actually called it a stipend) would be provided with physical plant and personnel resources of his choosing (limited, of course). The only requirement was that the work of the scientist be somehow related to a potential market area of interest to The Company. And of course, that was almost anything. A lifelong license to play in the technical sandbox!

So that was how Kerry Drake became the eleventh Distinguished Company Scientist, a move he regretted occasionally whenever he thought The Company was doing something egregiously wrong-headed with The Laboratory—but he never regretted it for long.

62

THE ROPES TO KNOW (VIII)

Have you noticed? This chapter portrays exclusively people like yourselves or like those you hope to become; people in professional and executive positions in organizations. This is no accident, because professionals and executives have a much greater commitment to an image of themselves as high-status organizational participants—and hence they have more to lose. They also have greater expectations about future high status roles.

Compare this to the position of Jimmie Szekely. Jimmie doesn't want to lose his job, but then another job at the same pay somewhere else will be just as good. The job itself means not nearly as much to him as the money attached to it. And after all, this is the point to be made in the analogy to the coolout: it's not so much the money as it is the loss of self-respect. For hell hath no fury like an executive scorned.

Why does the necessity for coolout arise? Well, organizations must manage the process of upward movement for at least two reasons: first, the desire to move upward in management can be used as a "gentle incentive" to work hard and behave well. But there is room for just so many bosses, so "opportunities" must be conserved. Second, there is the necessity of offering desirable, but organizationally impossible roles in the process of recruiting professionals. Either way, somewhere along the line the need will arise for a consolation prize.

Consider the first of these functions. Probably no one in an organization gives more for less than the upward aspirant "junior executive."
Organizations don't *need* to give much because the junior executive has
his eye trained on the pot of gold at the end of the rainbow. But sooner or
later, inevitably for almost everyone, the vision fades and something
new, something palpable is needed. The situation is similar with
professional staff people. Of course, the fact that such upward aspirants
are paid less than might otherwise be required for their services has as
much to do with the selection process as it does with simple economics.
After all, this is a good way of testing the commitment of future
executives.

In time the sting comes in two ways: (1) in the form of a critical event
signalling an end to the hope of entry into the executive ranks, or (2) by
way of removal from a critical position along the path upward—an event
Kerry Drake used to refer to as a "transmotion." We gave an example of
Sting 1 in our story *The Life of Staff*. Cal's promotion into the staff
management side was a crucial event from his point of view. But in fact
Sting 1 can be marked by a nonevent (though not as dramatically). In
most organizations you know pretty well where you have to be at what
age to keep on moving up. Failure of promotion at the proper time can be
such a nonevent, sometimes accompanied by a cooling transmotion.
Sting 2—removal from a critical position on the upward ladder—hasn't
really been illustrated only because neither Ben Franklyn nor Kerry
Drake had an appetite for further promotion. And that is what made
their cooling-out so difficult.

Now let's talk about that second, related, but different situation
involving the loss of a valued role and the consequent coolout. The
necessity for recruiting professionals with highly idealized and unrealistic role aspirations requires that organizations hold forth hope of roles
that they know are impossible to provide. They count on the initial
experience to persuade the professional to adapt himself to what the
organization can offer. Put another way, organizations provide naive
professionals with the opportunity to see that their model of the
profession is unrealistic, and through guided organizational experience
they try to persuade the professional to assume a role that he had valued
less at the outset. This is the theme of *More Bang for the Buck*. And the
problem certainly is not unique to professional scientists. The profession of medicine, for example, handles the coolout in later stages of
medical school and internship, where doctors learn to accept substitute
values. The problem is handled not so well in the priesthood or in social
work where there is no managed coolout aimed at defining alternative
values. In general, the problem is greatest where there is the greatest
individual investment and hardship during the preprofessional training period, for sustained early motivation will require a highly

idealized, perhaps altruistic occupational myth. The sting is the realization that no such roles are available.

Simply stated, the function of the coolout is to provide the mark with a satisfactory (to him) explanation of what has happened. Goffman states, "For the mark, cooling represents a process of adjustment to an impossible situation—a situation arising from having defined himself in a way which the social facts come to contradict. The mark must therefore be supplied with a new set of apologies for himself, a new framework in which to see himself and judge himself."[1]

Goffman discusses several general solutions to the coolout problem. Some of these have been touched upon in the stories.

1. Offering a status which differs from the one lost or failed at but providing at least something to become. This, recall, is the theme of *The Threefold Way.*
2. The valued role may be retained, but the mark is asked to fulfill it in a different, "safer" context. One example of this might be a sales manager moved from a crucial office to one in which lesser skill is required. The example from *More Bang for the Buck* could be used, in which scientists retain their function, but carry it out in a different context.
3. Being kicked upstairs. One company retired an occasional obsolete plant manager within the local community through the simple device of naming him to the new post of "Resident Vice-President."
4. Providing a second chance to succeed at the failed role. A device effective for cooling individuals, though doing little to salve organizational apprehensions, is that of offering a second chance at the failed role. Individuals who may be motivated to protest are given the option of trying again. In most cases, of course, the individual does *not* try again, and the major function of the offer is to suppress protest. The success of this procedure organizationally requires the mark to drop out of the organization.
5. Blowing up. Allowing the mark to express otherwise unacceptable feelings or behavior is a direct way of providing relief. Other organizational members in this situation are freed from injunctions against listening to traitorous and possibly seditious suggestions by the mark, for it is recognized implicitly that this is a ritual coolout. However, this method fails to provide the needed alternative role.
6. Bribery. Finally, there is the form of bribery that allows the mark to pretend he has taken the initiative in the loss of role or status. Once again this requires the cooperation of other organizational participants in the play to maintain plausible dramaturgy.

So there you have it, ways which you will all recognize as common means for cooling out the mark. Now, despite the fact that these prescriptions are couched in terms of strategies for dealing with individuals, they are also strategies for dealing with *classes* of people. Said another way, while the coolout is an individual transaction between the mark and the operators of the confidence game, the analogy can be applied directly to transactions between say, professionals and The Company. (*More Bang for the Buck* and *The Life of Staff*.) In fact, the "participative coolout" is a widely used organizational strategy. The play here is to offer the mark a sharing of "decision-making power" in return for agreement to pursue goals specified by the management and, in general, to behave well. The participative coolout generally has been necessitated by the realization of Jimmie Szekely and his millhands that they are regarded as little more than extensions of the machines they operate, that they have lost their essential humanity. The coolout of participation is the illusion to being offered a higher status, demi-managerial role with "power to decide."

Yet a question remains to be answered. You find yourself asking, why the need for this pretense? What can be the organizational motivation for procedures that seem a bit, let's say, reprehensible?

In examining this question, first we must recognize that organizations, as such, don't have motives. Individuals within organizations do. Individual people make decisions about other individuals or classes of individuals. But members of organizations do share a consensus about appropriate actions (called norms), and nothing requires that the origins or reasons for these norms be known. Quite directly this implies that members of organizations may not themselves be aware of the supra-individual organizational functions of their actions or decisions.

And what could that mean? Well, for example, take another look at the Research Laboratory scientists in *More Bang for the Buck*. Ted's understanding of the situation probably is typical. The way Ted looks at it, The Company recruits the best scientists it can for the Research Laboratory. The Company spares no effort to hang on to those who succeed, and for those who don't they do their best to find alternative placements. This is only proper, since many don't make it, through no particular fault of their own. Note that this explanation advances altruistic motives for The Company's finding these alternative placements. The problem is that this explanation neglects consideration of what The Company would do to recruit first-rate applied research scientists if this setup didn't exist, and it neglects, as well, the fact that overall, recruitment is likely a more central function to the day-to-day activities of The Company than is the production of basic research.

Put another way, there is little doubt that in most cases the process of cooling out is pursued in The Company with other than the implied altruistic motives: that is, without reference to what is thought best for the individual in such cases. And what is thought best for the individual is mostly prescribed by the normative system—by implicit consensus as to what is right. The fact that these actions can be looked upon as cooling out the mark bears testimony not so much to cynical calculation as to the collective historical organizational wisdom of The Company.

ENDNOTE

1. Erving Goffman, "On Cooling the Mark Out: Some Aspects of Adaptation to Failure," *Psychiatry,* 15 (1952) p. 456. The list is adapted from Goffman, pp. 457-458.

MANAGING CAREERS—
THE ROPES TO KNOW

A restatement of original intentions by the authors is a good way to start a conclusion. Our aim throughout these pages has been to provide you with a set of ideas and illustrations to help you understand what is going on about you in organizations. Through this understanding, we think it likely that you will be able to foresee better the outcome of any situation as it develops. We hope, as well, that you've noticed by now that none of our explanations involves analysis of the personal motives of the actors. Oh, to be sure we've tried to provide you with the kind of information about people that you're likely to get in the everyday course of organizational events. You know something about Ted Shelby's motives simply by watching him. And the same thing is true of Ben Franklyn and Kerry. But what we're trying to point out is that our description and analysis inevitably involve the characteristics of the *situation* or the organizational *role* of the individual rather than the attribution of particular motives to individual actors.

So we feel it necessary to point out that we do recognize that different individuals have their own idiosyncratic motives and goals, and that they won't always do what our principles predict they will. From time to time you probably found yourself saying, "I know of someone in just that situation who did just the opposite." Well, that's right. But what we're saying is that most of the time organizational psychoanalysis is a chancey business, and, furthermore, in most situations you won't even know the actors involved very well. So when the time comes to bet on an outcome (and sometimes you will have to), the best bet is to go with probabilities. And that's what we are talking about, probabilities.

Another thing. Several people who have reviewed Stanley's adventures in The Company have asked, "How is it that large organizations can do the 'silly' things you say and still be successful?" Perhaps this question occurred to you, too.

Now in a way, since this is not a text about organizational design, this is not a question that concerned us. But, since you've asked, there are two answers at least. The first is the most straightforward: Many do not survive. Thomas J. Watson, Jr., then Chairman of the Board of IBM, wrote in 1962,

> Of the top twenty-five industrial corporations in the United States in 1900, only two remain in the select company today. One retains its original identity; the other is a merger of seven corporations on that original list. Two of those twenty-five failed. Three others merged and dropped behind. The remaining twelve have continued in business, but each has fallen substantially in its standing.

> Figures like these help to remind us that corporations are expendable and that success—at best—is an impermanent achievement which can always slip out of hand.

A few pages later Watson had the following to say,

> I believe the real difference between success and failure in a corporation [is] how well the organization brings out the great energies and talents of its people . . . despite the many rivalries and differences which may exist among them.[1]

In the years since Watson made those comments new clouds have appeared on the corporate horizon. Foreign competitors are beating us at our own game—product excellence. Our corporate "can't do" guys blame environmental restrictions, obsolete plant and equipment, and the like, and run to Washington for tax write-offs, loans, and other sorts of federal largesse.

But observers of the industrial scene aren't so sure that these are the problems. They cite the very kinds of behavior portrayed in these pages: the sacrifice of long-term organizational outcomes to short-term career benefits, the ascendancy of corporate staff financial and legal types at the expense of product people—the Shelbys eclipsing the Kerry Drakes.

So that is one answer.

The second answer is equally direct: Despite the problems we have portrayed, large organizations, when competing with small organizations, have advantages that accrue to economies of scale. When competing with other large organizations they are on an equal footing of disability. Consequently, the organizational problems that are apparent in the illustrations we have used for purposes of helping you understand organizational behavior are not necessarily fatal to large organizations. But they are inherent in size.

We have tried to show through illustration that organizations are really complicated socio-technical systems involving economic, technical, social, and individual components. So perhaps our message is: Not all things are possible. Rationality, understanding, and good intentions don't always produce the desired result. This book is intended to help you understand why this is so. When you get right down to it we have been trying to convey an understanding of three basic organizational processes: interpreting symbols, creating the context for decisions, and managing relations between superiors and subordinates. So here they are, one more time.

INTERPRETING SYMBOLS

Our concern has been to help you interpret individual and organizational actions for what they are, rather than what they appear to be. And this involves not so much looking for hidden agendas as it does learning the symbolism of acts and rituals, of rites of passage marking the move from one organizational status to another. Our concern is helping you learn how to express yourself properly, symbolically; or conversely, to understand what others are expressing to you. For instance, in one of our early stories Stanley brought on the wrath of Ben Franklyn by failing to use expandrium insulation. The fact of the matter is that expandrium may not be a better insulating material than that which Stanley used, but the act is symbolic. That's what made the issue so important. Finally, we've tried to convey some of the symbolism in the relationship between superiors and subordinates—the privileges of the men's hut as we've put it.

For in all things—in speech, dress, and manner—symbolism is important. This is our essential lesson. We think it important not so much for the fact you will want to tailor your presentation of self (though you may), but rather to help you understand what others are signalling. Every word and act of Ted Shelby, his appearance and manner, his crisp/urgent tone, all convey one message: "I'm management. If it can be done, I'll do it. Just ask." Ben Franklyn's impression is one that says, "There's only one thing that counts here and that's getting the product out the door. Everything else takes care of itself if we do our job—so don't bother me." Out on the brown, grassy slopes of the California hillsides the sneakered, scruffy, bearded scientist at The

Company Research Laboratory conveys a different message. "Look," he says "I may happen to work for The Company right now, but that means nothing to me. My work is far too important to bother with your silly games. And I don't have to work here either, you know. I'm different from the rest of you."

Finally, we tried to illustrate why the simple fact of being a female or minority in a male and white organization is not simple in its consequences. Once again we have people trying to make sense of their observations; we see that actions, situations, and expectations all have symbolic content. For if there are no female or minority executives in this company there must be a reason, not so? And if this better-than average-company hires better-than-average people like me, why then, it cannot be this company's fault, can it? And thus it becomes the presence of the lonely female or minority executive that requires explanation, not the absence.

So what we have tried to do in parts I, II and III is to alert you to the importance of these symbols, rituals, and nonverbal clues. You've seen as well that the real communication is often at odds with the ostensible meaning. But you'll have to take it from here. You'll have to do a lot of learning on your own. Our examples serve only to point the way.

CREATING THE CONTEXT FOR DECISIONS

Our second major concern is with the nature of the decision process. To paraphrase, great decisions are *made,* not born. For it seems to us that emphasis on making *the* correct decision is misplaced. In fact, it seems a bit naive even to believe in the existence of such a thing as *the decision,* existing at a given point in time. Decisions are better reckoned as a process starting with an initial awareness of the need for some action and carrying through to the point of final evaluation and, if need be, reconstruction of the situation. The decision then exists in a historical framework perhaps little resembling the actual process whereby the final outcome was brought about. Said a bit differently, decisions are made collectively and by accretion, often anointed after the fact. All the important features of a decision are contained in the process leading up to it and the effort following it, as well as in the strategic characteristics of the major actors involved. And so, to say it again, the great respect accorded key decision makers who strive mightily to come up with "optimum" decisions seems silly. The real heroes are the Ben Franklyns whose task it is to make whatever decisions there are come out right. So let's look once again at the key facets of the decision process: anticipating direct outcomes of decision situations and avoiding no-win contexts; understanding systems effects and making them work for, not against you; ensuring the payoff through proper preparation of the context. We take these in turn.

Anticipating Direct Outcomes

Now what we said in the text was that these outcomes can be regarded as reasonably predictable in the light of a few concepts, two major ones being the payoff matrix and the minimax. We were quick to point out, of course, that we are using game theory in a heuristic sense, rather than in literal application. The reaction of individuals or groups in organizations is predictable in principle; that is our point: decisions can be anticipated with high probability in certain situations. Now it follows from this that appeals to reason are not likely to produce the desired effects when the outcome you wish to bring about yields an unfavorable result in your opponent's payoff matrix. Watchdog behavior is a premiere example. Watchdogs, naturally enough, are 99.9 percent minimaxers. So even in situations where it is clear to you that the action which you hope to bring about is in the best long-range interests of The Company, if it's in the worst short-range interests of the watchdog, forget it. He's going to say no. He has to. So don't try to convince Watchdog on rational grounds. He's not listening. Either forget about it or bypass him—or don't ask. Remember this useful epigram: It's easier to get forgiveness than permission. Know also that organizations are full of watchdogs.

Understanding Systems Effects

The second point we tried to make in analyzing the decision process was about the systems effects of decisions—though we didn't put it quite that way. Our illustrations were intended to show that the unintended remote consequences of planned strategies often are unfavorable because the decisionmaker failed to take the entire organizational system into account. What we mean is this: The decisionmaker gathers his facts and, in a manner of speaking, sits down and says, "If I do A, then I ought to bring about B, and B is what I want." But how often does our decisionmaker go on and play out the chessboard? How often does he ask what further consequences will accrue—C, C', C" at least, and then . . . ? For B will lead to several unmanaged Cs and so on.

You see the point. Even the chess grandmaster can't carry this kind of thing too far, but perhaps just one step further will reveal the problem. And so we tried to illustrate what happens if you become the only technical expert in the plant. What happens if your financial system says that all dollars turn into pumpkins July 1 and then you start all over again? The "A leads to B sequence" looks okay—but we've shown that the B leads to C, C', C"; and that sequence leads to grief. And that is about all for that message. Just be alert. Avoid overadaptation in a changing organizational environment and think through at least some of the remote consequences of your strategies. Best of all, try to use our lessons to make sure that favorable outcomes will be attributed to you while at the same time avoiding possible unfavorable outcomes through use of the twin axioms of diffused and deferred responsibility. Beyond that you are on your own.

Ensuring The Payoff

Finally, our dissection of the decision process concludes on a more active level; we consider the things that can be done to make those unavoidable decisions come out right, to ensure that the game matrix has the proper payoffs and that the remote consequences are favorable. Or, in a more passive stance, at least to see when others are engaged in doing so. We are talking about casting a decision in the proper context so as to assure its correctness. As we have shown by example, this can be arranged before, during, or after the events that constitute the decision sequence. Once again, by way of illustration, we have tried to urge you to see that this means more than simply making your best case and letting others evaluate the outcome. Oh no, it means arranging things so that the outcome will be perceived as favorable, no matter what. And it's surprising how easy this becomes for the skilled practitioner of organizational arts. Remember what Kerry Drake did in *Stitch in Time*. Set the favorable context and rest assured that the probability is that that context will constitute at least half the reality perceived by others. And what if it doesn't? Well, as Kerry explained, there's little chance of that and even so, the worst thing that could happen to him would be what was bound to happen in any event had he not tried. Likewise we saw Cooley Bell's carefully managed ascent into executive management. Why take chances? Why leave room for the occasional carping dissident who might think Cooley Bell got where he was *only* as heir apparent?

These, of course, are examples of the context being prearranged. Careful work is justly rewarded. But what about when that can't be done, when you've failed to anticipate intervening events in the decision process that haven't gone your way? Well, since the outcomes can no longer be changed to agree with the goals, an equally effective, though somewhat riskier strategy is to redefine the goals. Yes, the trick now is to make the original goals agree with observed outcomes. And it's usually easier than you'd think. This is because goals almost always evolve over the course of action. Objectives are initially stated rather obscurely, partly because of sloppy habits of mind in the inexperienced, and canniness in the experienced. So you may wish to draw in the bull's-eye after your arrow hits.

And there it is for decisions. Once again, we want to help you recognize these things going on about you. You may want to use our lessons actively, or more likely, perhaps you may just want to recognize things for what they are. Your aim as always should be to avoid being caught in a game not of your own choosing.

MANAGING RELATIONSHIPS

Now we come to our third, and final lesson: being aware of, recognizing, and controlling the wayward impulses of subordinates. To prepare you for this task we have undertaken, first, to describe the sources of power of lower organizational participants; and then, to illustrate some organizational gambits for removing troublesome participants (lower *and* upper)—strategies for cooling-out the mark.

Sources Of Power

We have done our best to persuade you that control over subordinates is not the simple matter you casually may have assumed it to be. And really, we are doing little more here than invoking ancient wisdom that tells us not to strip a man of everything he has. For people with nothing to lose are *very* difficult to control. Looking at it from the point of view of the management (a comfortable perspective for us all), the trick is to arrange the situation so that at all times you have something to offer that can be withheld in instances of bad behavior. Otherwise you are in for trouble. And it is such a pity that so simple a principle so often is violated. It is violated not only for true lower participants of the organization, but for upper participants as well. And this, of course, endows these upper participants with the troublesome characteristics of lower participants. Consequently, we derive our general rule.

Also you must by now realize that lower participants wield considerable power. This is through a combination of those unlikely bedfellows, ambition and sloth. Ambition comes into play in this manner: aspirants to the executive suite understand that a mark of high status is attention to the big picture and a delegation of details to those of low status. Yes, broad brush strokes are the executive manner. It is true as well that the joy of seeing the grand plan is realized quickly, whereas the pleasure of achievement pales quickly as you face attending to the painstaking detail of bringing the plan to fruition. What the impatient and inexperienced forget, of course, is that great artists are masters of detail. Thus it is that sloth as well as ambition lead to the abdication of responsibility for detail. Yes, *this* is the major source of power of the lower participant.

What? You say you understand the message, but that you understood this much before. What you don't understand is why we should be so concerned about it. So subordinates have a little power? This simply is delegation of responsibility. That's what being an executive is all about, isn't it? That is the perspective you've urged us to take, isn't it? Well isn't it?

Sigh . . . no and yes. Delegation is fine *provided* that you have already assured what the outcome will be. For it is of utmost importance to keep in mind that different levels of the organization have different interpretations of organizational goals. Such goals are necessarily mixtures of local interpretations of organizational objectives and the personal goals of participants. Recall that Ben Franklyn's Vice-President wanted PIP because that was the objective set for him by Mr. Marsh in top executive management. The goal was for The Company as a whole to improve production through improved procedures *and* in a specified, uniform way. Ben Franklyn has the same general objective— he always has—but in an operationally different way for *his* plant. The dilemma for the organizational analyst is that both may be right. Franklyn says my plant is run best without PIP. His Vice-President says that The Company is run best with it, that PIP won't work *as a program* unless all do it. So Ben, doing what is best to meet the goal of high production in his plant, becomes a problem for his Vice-President, just as the Jimmie Szekelys (collectively) pose a problem for the plant engineers.

And *that* is something worth worrying about: the fact that different goals are pursued at different levels even though participants see them as the same goals. And with this multiplied manyfold throughout the various functions and levels of the organization, it becomes a lot to worry about. It's not a question of who is right and who is wrong; quite likely that is impossible to decide. Rather, it is a question of who has the *right* to decide. It is this kind of dilemma that accounts for many of our so-called communications problems.

What can be done? If you recall our recent discussion of authority, what can be done is to create the need to comply, to widen the zone of indifference of lower participants. In *Sunrise Service* we alluded to an historical solution to this problem—the imposition of a hut tax on native Africans thus providing a "gentle incentive to labor." In just this way, Ben's morning meetings created the incentive to comply. This zone of indifference, this willingness to comply with authoritative requests greatest in those classes of organizational citizens for whom the organization has most to offer and, consequently, most to withhold. A solid principle for application in individual cases. But more generally it is impossible willy-nilly to promote lower participants just to provide incentives that can be withdrawn conditional on bad behavior. There is a right wage for secretaries and millhands and technical people, and this is known to management. There is a well-defined upper bound on rewards necessary to preserve equity (and this also is known to the management). Similarly, there is the all-chiefs-no-Indians dilemma in consequence of which the numbers of professionals in supervisory management must be limited.

Recognizing The Coolout

These are the considerations that lead to the invention of organizational arrangements that can be used to supplement increased pay and promotion, the common incentives to compliance. And this is the second part of our final topic: how to recognize the organizational coolout. Most fundamentally, the coolout is the mechanism by which disgruntled members of organizations are persuaded to accept the fact that the organization has deprived them of a valued status or role. It is a way of assuring continued compliance and effort despite the loss of this valued status. We expect that with this principle you will be able to recognize many forms of the coolout in your own organization, so let's go over the major varieties: offering a substitute role; removing the role to a different, less crucial context; and the coolout by participation.

The first, and most common, is to create a *substitute role* with the illusion, though not the substance, of the more desirable, unobtainable role. This can be done both for a class of organizational participants—as in the case of parallel managerial hierarchies for professionals—or the role can be tailored individually for a particular circumstance. In each case the strategy is to find or to create a position in the organization having the generally desirable characteristics of the position withheld or withdrawn, but not having the troublesome characteristics of power.

A second approach, related to the first, is to allow the mark to retain the essential role but fulfill it in a *different context*. Sales managers are moved from an office crucial to The Company's success and allowed to continue in a less problematic one. Or, as in *More Bang for the Buck*, research scientists are moved to a more applied setting, less demanding of extraordinary creativity. Now an intriguing aspect of this technique is that, under certain circumstances, the coolout might be looked at as the game itself. Certainly this is the case for our scientists. And it is a time honored technique in the military. During World War II when the Army Air Force had great need of navigators, radio operators, bombardiers, and gunners to man the flying death traps called heavy bombers, a handy source of recruitment was the wash-out from pilot training. Isn't it just possible that people were recruited to pilot training at least as much as a source of personnel for these less glamorous roles as to provide the very best pilots? The coolout as the play.

A final major coolout strategy, the coolout by participation, is reserved primarily for true lower participants, although it works well at all levels. This is the strategy of offering to share some amount of power in return for compliance. The implicit bargain could be put into words thus: "Look, Jimmie, you seem to want to do things in your own way. And it seems to me that because of this you spend as much time working against me as you do with me. Now I don't have the time and energy to track down all your favorite tricks, so I'll tell you what; you agree to work toward my goals instead of yours, and I'll agree to let you do things your way. In fact, I'll even help you. Just remember, though, I'm the boss." And so it is with all forms of the coolout by participation. The incentive for compliance lies in the illusion that the status of the offered role is greater than the current role because it has some of the attributes of "management."

So there you have it. The summation of a lifetime's career wisdom— *The Ropes to Skip and the Ropes to Know*. To the beginner, perhaps, from his stance in the organization, the trip to the top may seem like an endless trek. But this need not be the case. After all, a career is a step at a time; many steps, many times. As Kerry Drake once remarked to Stanley in his early days with The Company: "It's not so hard, son. Just keep your head above water, and sooner or later you'll float to the top."

ENDNOTE

1. Thomas J. Watson, *A Business and Its Beliefs: The Ideas that Helped Build IBM.* (New York: McGraw-Hill, 1963) p. 3-5.

EPILOGUE

A minute ago we thought we were done. But a number of people who have worked with us on this text (as Dr. Faust would say, ah—our lower participants) have asked, "What *does* happen to Stanley?" All right, then, let's take a look at how things turn out for our people from The Company.

As you recall, Stanley had started out in engineering and then, for a quick promotion had gone to work for Ted in Personnel. However, as he learned more of The Company, it became evident to him that this move to Personnel was a mistake strategically. So he screwed up his courage and applied to the MBA program at The University. He was a bit surprised to be accepted.

Degree in hand, he now had to decide whether or not to return to The Company. In that process he discovered something about himself; he had developed a considerable loyalty to his Company friends and acquaintances, and to The Company itself! And so he returned to what he liked best—production.

Now the rest of Stanley's story shouldn't be surprising. In the early going he had developed a genuine respect for the people in The Company who "actually did the work." This sensitivity combined with a technical knack and his newly acquired managerial skills (plus some hard work) paved the way for his steady climb through the ranks of middle management. And oh yes, he'd also learned the ropes pretty well—at last—from his mentor Dr. Faust, from his buddies Kerry and Ben, and in a way even from Ted. So when we last heard he had just taken over Ben's former spot as Plant Manager at Pawtucket. His only worry is that someday the call may come to go to New York, for he can't imagine a job more important than Plant Manager. Still, who knows?

Lesley's career in The Company had begun very much as Stanley's. She also had come to The Company with a technical background and then had taken that quick promotion into Communications. But when she started to see that Communications might be a career deadend, she was able to call on a network of contacts who knew her intelligence and dedication. That was one difference between Personnel and Communications. At least in Communications you got to know some pretty important people first hand. So it was one of these people who helped her land a spot in the Company's prestigious new Systems Institute. Here she spent a year combining her skills in communications and technology with some "blue sky" concepts being developed in advanced communications systems.

From there, Lesley moved to staff assistant, branch manager and, at last hearing, to Corporate Director for Advanced Communications Systems. A very new and very exciting field. And as Lesley has moved up in The Company she seems to have lost what some people felt was a bit of a chip on her shoulder. Maybe the fact that she's very much in demand these days had something to do with that.

Kerry Drake. Let's see, when we left Kerry he'd just been cooled out of his director's job at the Research Laboratory and been confirmed a Company Distinguished Scientist. Well, you know, The Company really was right. Kerry didn't have what it takes to continue in the main stream of high-powered corporate research. He doesn't have the advanced technical training that's needed these days nor the motivation to work on other people's ideas. But he's still got that creative spark and the ability to generate enthusiasm in people around him. So he gathered about him a half dozen or so hand-picked technical castoffs and went into the developing field of medical technology. He's back to his old inventing ways now, and, as a matter of fact, he's built himself something of a national reputation for the things he's done. No, that is not in The Company's line of business, but that's OK, too. For he has brought national recognition to the research laboratory and helped to establish an image of altruism for The Company. And that image helps in recruiting new people too. All this for someone who, after all, has long since paid his way for The Company.

Ben. Well, Ben understandably was unhappy with the move to Portsmouth. But with typical Franklyn determination he decided that if this was his job he would do it the best he knew how. No matter that he would be retiring within three years. That was three years from now. But a surprising thing happened (maybe, knowing Ben, it isn't really surprising). Ben became completely absorbed in safety. And he was good at it, too. You see, his years as a millhand were not wasted. He knew production and its problems from all angles. And now, for the first time, he could look at safety as a human problem, where before it had been a management problem. It was a different matter when it was a question of a human being losing, or not losing, a hand or an eye. There was some personal satisfaction in that.

By the time retirement rolled around he had become so good at his work that he went into partnership with a Portsmouth safety consultant. It was an ideal setup. Not that he needed the money, but this was an opportunity to travel up and down the country touring different manufacturing plants, talking with management and the millhands. And he loved it. He worked only when he wanted to (all the time) and couldn't help wondering now and then why he hadn't gone into the safety business a long time ago.

Then there's Claude Gilliam. Oh, yes, for various reasons Claude had made up his mind to attend law school after several years with The Company. That was when Kerry Drake had his long talk with Claude, trying to convince him not to waste his time on law school, that he had a great future in technical management. Funny, neither could have predicted the final result of that session. For in the end Claude wound up specializing in patent law. Well, he's now The Company's Chief Patent Attorney, an important post in the high technology business.

Dr. Faust. We are sure that it will come as no surprise to you to learn that, over the years, Dr. Faust had become a man of independent means. When the truth of that situation struck him he promptly resigned his duties as Head of The Department at The University. Let someone else explain the fiscal exigencies of The University to visionary academic malcontents. And then, partly as an offshoot of his informal lectures to Stanley and other apprentices, he decided to write a book recounting his insights. No, not a technical book but a set of revelations, as it were. Aha! Just as you suspected, you say. Well, this caused a little trouble in The Company. Ted, among others, read it and became incensed at what he felt was an unsympathetic treatment of himself and his high-minded purpose. All to the good, thought Faust, for that was one less responsibility to worry about. In any event, this left him with considerably more time than he had ever had before to do the things he enjoyed doing.

Well, sooner or later we have to come to Ted. In our final pages Ted was moving along quite well. He had become Corporate Director for Financial Plans and Controls. This is not only a very strategic position but a very responsible one as well. Perhaps too responsible. In any event, Ted made the mistake of backing the wrong side in a "palace revolt." Certainly he should have known better than to back either side, but at the outset it looked like a quick step to the coveted Vice-Presidency, and *that* was just too much to resist. These mistakes are costly, of course, and as a consequence he had to do time in the corporate "penalty box." This was an assignment as Manager in the Saginaw sales office. But now, some years later, he's back to Corporate Director of Personnel. No, he'll never be President, and the chances are that he'll never be Vice-President. But he keeps thinking he will. And partly because of this, these days he does what he's told, no more and no less. Once bitten twice shy, as they say. And he's not ashamed to admit that The Company owns him body and soul. "If they tell me to eat Wheaties for breakfast, I'll eat Wheaties. If it's Corn Flakes, that's okay, too." So Ted is successful in his own way. He's got what he wants. He's a Company executive, he's got a good stock option, a pension plan, and a house on the hill. Yes, he's successful—but somehow . . . .

Wait, one more. Bonnie—Ms. Dell, that is. You know, it's odd how one thing can change a lifetime. One day when Bonnie was feeling particularly indifferent, the mail brought a brochure on sales opportunities in The Company. Of course, the brochure was actually sent to Ted in Personnel "to keep him informed." Now, Bonnie really didn't mind being a secretary, she just didn't know what else to do. She never had finished college and, well, there weren't many things for girls to do anyway. But this time, *this* time it was just one of those moments when everything comes together. Why not me? Why not indeed! So she applied, and waited, only to find out that a college degree was required. That *was* a disappointment. But then she learned that having worked for The Company as long as she had, The Company would help her finish her education. They wanted women in the sales force and especially people who already had experience with The Company. And so off she went.

You would never know her now. She finished first in her sales class, and new confidence has brought a new image. Next month she's to be promoted to Assistant Manager of the Portland office. She doesn't know it yet, of course.

════════ SELECTED READINGS

For those of you who might want some additional reading on the topics covered by our various chapters, here is a list of references keyed to the seven parts of our book. This list is not intended to be comprehensive; rather, it is a sampler of research and theory relevant to the points presented in the chapters.

PART I

These readings deal with various aspects of the socialization process, modern and primitive.

1. Howard S. Becker and Blanche Geer, "The Fate of Idealism in Medical School," *American Sociological Review* 23 (1958): 50-56.
2. Joseph Campbell, *The Masks of God: Primitive Mythology.* (New York: Viking, 1959). See chapter 2, "The Imprints of Experience."
3. Sanford M. Dornbusch, "The Military Academy as an Assimilating Institution," *Social Forces* 33 (1955): 316-21.
4. Rosabeth M. Kanter, "Commitment and Social Organization: A Study of Commitment Mechanisms in Utopian Communities," *American Sociological Review* 33 (1968): 499-517.
5. Edgar H. Schein, "The Individual, The Organization, and The Career: A Conceptual Scheme," *Journal of Applied Behavioral Science* 7 (1971): 401-26.
6. Victor A. Thompson, *Modern Organization,* New York: Knopf, 1961). See chapter 4, "Hierarchy."
7. Lionel Tiger, *Men in Groups,* (New York: Random House, 1969).
8. John VanMaanen, "Police Socialization: A Longitudinal Examination of Job Attitudes in an Urban Police Department," *Administrative Science Quarterly* 20 (1975): 207-28.

PART II

Here is a list that will give you the fundamentals of the social psychology of perception and a discussion of the art of impression management. Articles in the *Scientific American* are particularly good for the interested layman.

1. Ray L. Birdwhistell, *Kinesics and Context: Essays on Body Motion Communication.* (Philadelphia: University of Pennsylvania Press, 1970), part II: Isolating Behavior.
2. Robert Buckhout, "Eyewitness Testimony," *Scientific American* 231 (December, 1974): 23-31.
3. Erving Goffman, *The Presentation of Self in Everyday Life.* (New York: Doubleday, 1959).
4. Nathan Joseph and Nicholas Alex, "The Uniform: A Sociological Perspective," *American Journal of Sociology* 77 (1972): 719-30.
5. David Krech, Richard S. Crutchfield and Egerton L. Ballachy, *Individual in Society.* New York: McGraw-Hill, 1962). Chapter 2, "Cognition."
6. Newsline, "The Phony Doctor Fox," *Psychology Today* 7 (October, 1973): 19-20.
7. Constantin Stanislavski, *An Actor Prepares.* (New York: Theatre Arts Books, 1936).
8. _____, *Creating A Role.* (New York: Theatre Arts Books, 1961).
9. Victor A. Thompson, *Modern Organization,* chapter 7, "Dramaturgy."

PART III

These references are selected to cover some additional readings on the topics of sex and race structuring of organizations, together with an introduction to some of the fundamentals of attribution theory.

1. Joan Acker and Donald R. Van Houten, "Differential Recruitment and Control: The Sex Structuring of Organizations," *Administrative Science Quarterly* 19 (1974): 152-63.
2. John P. Fernandez, *Black Managers in White Corporations.* (New York: Wiley, 1975).
3. Betty L. Harragan, *Games Mother Never Taught You: Corporate Gamesmanship for Women.* (New York: Rawson Associates, 1977).
4. Rosabeth M. Kanter, *Men and Women of the Corporation.* (New York: Basic Books, 1977).
5. K. G. Shaver, *An Introduction to Attribution Processes.* (Cambridge, Mass.: Winthrop, 1975).
6. Lawrence S. Wrightsman, *Social Psychology* (2nd Ed). (Belmont, Calif.: Wadsworth, 1977). See especially chapter 14, "The Social Psychology of Sex Roles."

PART IV

The following readings are intended to provide a brief discussion of game theory and decision-making. The Ouchi and Maguire article is particularly relevant to the thesis of "Extra Effort."
1. Richard M. Cyert and James G. March, *A Behavioral Theory of the Firm.* (Englewood Cliffs: Prentice Hall, 1963). See chapter 6, "A Summary of Basic Concepts . . . "
2. Karl Deutsch and William Madow, "A Note on the Appearance of Wisdom in Large Bureaucratic Organizations," *Behavioral Science* 6 (1961): 72-78.
3. William G. Ouchi and Mary Ann Maguire, "Organizational Control: Two Functions," *Administrative Science Quarterly* 20 (1975): 559-69.
4. Anatol Rapoport, "Critiques of Game Theory," *Behavioral Science* 4 (1959): 49-66.
5. _____, "The Use and Misuse of Game Theory," *Scientific American* 207 (December, 1962): 108-18.

PART V

The remote or systems consequences of actions is the theme of Part V. Each of these readings in different ways relates to this topic.
1. Peter Blau, *Dynamics of Bureaucracy.* (Chicago: University of Chicago Press, 1955) chapters 2.4.
2. Edgar Dunn, Jr., *Economic and Social Development* (Baltimore: Johns Hopkins Press, 1971).
3. Fred Emery and Eric Trist, "The Causal Texture of Organizational Environments," *Human Relations* 18 (1965): 21-32.
4. Jay Forrester, *Urban Dynamics.* (Cambridge: MIT Press, 1969).
5. Steven Kerr, "On the Folly of Rewarding A, While Hoping for B," *Academy of Management Journal* 18 (1975): 769-83.
6. Richard J. Klimoski and William J. Strickland, "Assessment Centers—Valid or Merely Prescient," *Personnel Psychology* 30 (1977): 353-361.
7. Edward E. Lawler III and John G. Rhode, *Information and Control in Organizations.* (Pacific Palisades, Ca.: Goodyear, 1976). See especially chapter 6, "Dysfunctional Effects of Control Systems."
8. New York Times, "H.E.W. Study Finds Job Discontent is Hurting Nation," (December 22, 1972) p. 1.

PART VI

The concerns of this part can be framed in different ways. Perception is one concern, and the relationship between the evaluation of decisions and perception. But these themes can also be treated from the standpoint of the analysis of goals and goalsetting organizations. Hence, the following potpourri.

1. Richard Cyert and James March, *A Behavioral Theory of the Firm,* pp. 77-82, also chapter 6.
2. Daniel Guttman and Barry Willner, *The Shadow Government.* (New York: Pantheon, 1976). See especially chapter 1.
3. David Kretch, Richard Crutchfield and Egerton Ballachy, *Individual in Society.* See chapter 2, "Cognition."
4. Charles Perrow, "The Analysis of Goals in Complex Organizations," *American Sociological Review* 26 (1961): 854-66.
5. Leonard Sayles, *Managerial Behavior.* (New York: McGraw-Hill, 1964). See chapter 12, "The Manager and the Decision Process."
6. Herbert Simon, *Administrative Behavior.* (New York: Free Press; 1965), see chapter 4, "Rationality in Administration Behavior."
7. James Thompson and William McEwen, "Organizational Goals and Environment," *American Sociological Review* 23 (1958): 23-31.
8. Gaye Tuchman, "Objectivity, as Strategic Ritual: An Examination of Newsmen's Notions of Objectivity," *American Journal of Sociology* 77 (1972): 660-79.
9. Sheldon Zalkind and Timothy Costello, "Perception: Some Recent Research and Implications for Administration," *Administrative Science Quarterly* 7 (1962): 218-35.

PART VII

Understanding the sources of power of lower organizational participants requires as well some knowledge of group pressure to conformity and authority. Here are a few classic references in these topics.

1. Leon Festinger, Stanley Schachter, and Kurt Back, *Social Pressures in Informal Groups* (New York: Harper, 1950). See chapter 9, "A Theory of Group Structure and Group Standards."
2. Laura Gordon, "Bureaucratic Competence and Success in Dealing with Public Bureaucracies," *Social Problems* 23 (1975): 199-207.
3. David Mechanic, "Sources of Power of Lower Participants in Complex Organizations," *Administrative Science Quarterly* 7 (1962): 349-64.
4. Thomas Scheff, "Control Over Policy by Attendants in a Mental Hospital," *Journal of Health and Human Behavior* 2 (1961): 93-105.
5. Herbert Simon, *Administrative Behavior.* See chapter 7, "The Role of Authority."
6. William F. Whyte, *Money and Motivation,* (New York: Harper, 1955). See part I, "The Worker and His Work Group."

PART VIII

The management of failure is a topic whose importance seems to have been largely ignored in our success-oriented society. The Goldner article on demotion is particularly good.

1. Burton Clark, "The Cooling Out Function in Higher Education," *American Journal of Sociology* 65 (1960): 569-76.
2. Erving Goffman, "On Cooling the Mark Out: Some Aspects of Adaptation to Failure," *Psychiatry* 15 (1952): 451-63.
3. Fred Goldner, "Demotion in Industrial Management," *American Sociological Review* 30 (1965): 714-24.
4. Fred Goldner and Richard Ritti, "Professionalization as Career Immobility," *American Journal of Sociology* 72 (1967): 489-502.
5. William Gomberg, "The Trouble with Democratic Management," *Trans-Action* 3 (July/August 1966): 30ff.
6. Alfred Marrow, "Gomberg's 'Fantasy,'" *Trans-Action* 3 (Sept./Oct. 1966): 36ff.

INDEX

AFFIRMATIVE ACTION
Part III—Some Are More
Equal Than Others, 69-97
33. Praise/Criticism, 137

ASSESSMENT, EVALUATION AND TESTING
13. By Your Works Shall Ye
Be Known, 49
21. You Can't Be Too Careful, 83
22. My Brothers' Keeper, 86
38. Prophet Without Honor, 154
43. The Rating Game, 177
48. Management By
Objectives, 195
58. More Bang For
The Buck, 240
62. The Ropes to
Know (VIII), 262

ATTRIBUTION THEORY
10. Look Of A Winner, 39
15. Spacemen, 57
Introduction to Part III, 70
23. Scarlet Letter, 90
42. Success Story, 174
Managing Careers—The
Ropes to Know, 267

AUTHORITY
1. Rite of Passage, 5
6. Your Job, My Reputation, 21
7. Society of Equals, 24
12. The Sincerest Form of
Flattery, 46
Introduction to Part VII, 206
57. The Ropes To Know (VII), 230

CAREER PATHS
Career Advice Circa 1880, xiv
4. Ted's Boy, 15
14. Better The Devil You Know
..., 53
16. Like It Is, 61
27. Ghosting For Gain, 111
32. Cowboy, 134
37. Made To Measure, 150
38. Prophet Without Honor, 154
42. Success Story, 174
45. Most Valuable Player, 185
Part VIII—Cooling Out The
Mark, 235-266
Managing Careers—The Ropes
to Know, 267
Epilogue, 277

COMMUNICATION

7. Society of Equals, 24
8. The Men's Hut, 27
15. Spacemen, 57
27. Ghosting For Gain, 111
35. Don't Ask, 144
46. Just in Case, 188
47. Top Secret, 192
53. Figures Don't Lie . . . ?, 217

CONTROL SYSTEMS

26. Extra Effort, 108
28. Watchdogs, 115
37. Made To Measure, 150
47. Top Secret, 192
48. Management By
    Objectives, 195
53. Figures Don't Lie . . . ?, 217
55. Player Piano, 224
61. The Threefold Way, 254

DECISION-MAKING

Part IV—An Informal Theory
    of Games, 99-130
Part VI—Skate Fast Over
    Thin Ice, 167-204
Managing Careers—The
    Ropes To Know, 267

ENVIRONMENT

Foreword to the Second
    Edition, v
20. Bite of the Apple, 79
21. You Can't Be Too Careful, 82
22. My Brothers' Keeper, 86
36. Spend It, Burn It . . . , 147
39. Sic Transit, 158

GOALS AND GOAL FORMATION

30. Sunrise Service, 124
48. Management By
    Objectives, 195
49. As I Recall, 198
59. Incredible, 245
Managing Careers—The
    Ropes to Know, 267

GROUPS AND GROUP PROCESS

8. The Men's Hut, 27
14. Better The Devil You
    Know . . . , 53
20. Bite Of The Apple, 79
30. Sunrise Service, 124
43. The Rating Game, 177
59. Incredible, 245

IMPRESSION MANAGEMENT

Career Advice Circa 1930, xv
Part II—De Gustibus Non
    Disputandum Est, 35-68
18. "Hi Sweetie . . . ", 73
19. The Cat In The Hat, 76
42. Success Story, 174
43. The Rating Game, 177
48. Management By
    Objectives, 195
58. More Bang For The Buck, 240
Managing Careers—The
    Ropes To Know, 267

INCENTIVE SYSTEMS

28. Watchdogs, 115
34. Hellfire And Brimstone, 141
36. Spend It, Burn It . . . , 147
39. Sic Transit, 158
40. The Ropes To Know (IV), 206
60. The Life Of Staff, 248
61. The Threefold Way, 254
62. The Ropes to Know (VIII), 262

INTERPERSONAL RELATIONS

2. Hi, Call Me, 9
20. Bite Of The Apple, 79
23. Scarlet Letter, 90
51. Coffee Break, 210
59. Incredible, 245

LEADERSHIP

12. The Sincerest Form Of
    Flattery, 46
43. The Rating Game, 177
44. The Pearl, 181

LOYALTY
1. Rite of Passage, 5
3. Power Of Positive
   Thinking, 12
11. Friday Go To Meetin', 43
62. The Ropes to Know (VIII), 262

MEASUREMENT
5. Cleanliness Is Next To . . . ?, 18
22. My Brothers' Keeper, 86
37. Made To Measure, 150
43. The Rating Game, 177
48. Management By
    Objectives, 195
53. Figures Don't Lie . . . ?, 217

MOTIVATION
11. Friday Go To Meetin', 43
26. Extra Effort, 108
55. Player Piano, 224
56. Point Of No Return, 227
58. More Bang For The Buck, 240
61. The Threefold Way, 254
62. The Ropes to Know, (VIII), 262

NORMS
10. The Look Of A Winner, 39
24. The Ropes To Know (III), 94
    Introduction to Part VII, 206
54. Fair Day's Work, 222
55. Player Piano, 224
62. The Ropes to Know (VIII), 262

**ORGANIZATIONAL
DEVELOPMENT AND
CHANGE**
Foreword To The Second
   Edition, v
7. Society Of Equals, 24
34. Hellfire And
    Brimstone, 141
37. Made To Measure, 150
39. Sic Transit, 158
56. Point Of No Return, 227
59. Incredible, 245
60. The Life Of Staff, 248
61. The Threefold Way, 254
    Managing Careers—The
    Ropes To Know, 267

**ORGANIZATIONAL
STRUCTURE**
Prologue, xvii
7. Society Of Equals, 24
24. The Ropes To Know (III), 94
25. Hold That Line, 104
39. Sic Transit, 158
    Introduction to Part VII, 206
60. The Life Of Staff, 248

**PAYOFFS AND EXPECTED
VALUES**
Introduction to Part IV, 100
25. Hold That Line, 104
26. Extra Effort, 108
28. Watchdogs, 115
29. Back To The Drawing
    Board, 120
    Managing Careers—The
    Ropes To Know, 267

PERCEPTION
Introduction to Part II, 36
50. The Ropes To Know (VI), 202

POWER
11. Friday Go To Meetin', 43
    Introduction To Part III, 70
23. Scarlet Letter, 90
25. Hold That Line, 104
35. Don't Ask, 144
47. Top Secret, 192
    Part VII—The Power Of
    Lower Participants, 205-233
    Managing Careers—The
    Ropes To Know, 267

RISK TAKING
28. Watchdogs, 115
45. Most Valuable Player, 185
52. Haste Makes Waste, 212
53. Figures Don't Lie . . . ?, 217

ROLES
19. Cat In The Hat, 76
23. Scarlet Letter, 90
24. The Ropes To Know (III), 94
32. Cowboy, 134

SECOND-ORDER CONSEQUENCES
Introduction To Part V, 132
36. Spend It, Burn It . . . , 147
37. Made To Measure, 150
Managing Careers—The
Ropes To Know, 267

SELF-FULFILLING PROPHECY
Introduction to Part III, 70
22. My Brothers' Keeper, 86
Introduction To Part V, 132
38. Prophet Without Honor, 154

SITUATION MANAGEMENT
31. The Ropes To Know (IV), 127
Part VI—Skate Fast Over
Thin Ice, 167-204
Introduction to Part VIII, 236
62. The Ropes To Know (VIII), 262
Managing Careers—The
Ropes To Know, 267

SOCIALIZATION INTO THE ORGANIZATION
Part I—Enter The Men's
Hut, 1-33
20. Bite Of The Apple, 79
54. Fair Day's Work, 222
62. The Ropes to Know (VIII), 262

TRAINING
5. Cleanliness Is Next To . . . ?, 18
16. Like It Is, 61
54. Fair Day's Work, 222

UNANTICIPATED OUTCOMES
29. Back To The Drawing
Board, 120
Introduction To Part V, 132
33. Praise/Criticism, 137
35. Don't Ask, 144
37. Made To Measure, 150
40. The Ropes To Know (V), 163